Gierek's Poland

edited by
Adam Bromke
John W. Strong

Published in cooperation with
Canadian Slavonic Papers

The Praeger Special Studies program—
utilizing the most modern and efficient book
production techniques and a selective
worldwide distribution network—makes
available to the academic, government, and
business communities significant, timely
research in U.S. and international economic, social, and political development.

Gierek's Poland

PRAEGER SPECIAL STUDIES IN INTERNATIONAL POLITICS AND GOVERNMENT

Praeger Publishers   New York   Washington   London

Library of Congress Cataloging in Publication Data

Bromke, Adam.
    Gierek's Poland.

    (Praeger special studies in international
politics and government)
    Simultaneously published in the Canadian
Slavonic papers.
    Bibliography: p.
    1. Poland—Addresses, essays, lectures.
I. Strong, John W., 1930-   joint author.
II. Title.
DK443.B76   309.1'438'05   72-14208

PRAEGER PUBLISHERS
111 Fourth Avenue, New York, N.Y. 10003, U.S.A.
5, Cromwell Place, London SW7 2JL, England

Published in the United States of America in 1973
by Praeger Publishers, Inc.

Printed in the United States of America

ACKNOWLEDGMENTS

The editors would like to acknowledge with gratitude the help they received from the following people in the preparation of this volume: Mrs. Lydia Kasianchuk, editorial assistant of the *Canadian Slavonic Papers*; Miss Penny Morton, secretary of the *Canadian Slavonic Papers*; and to Mrs. Valerie Melnikoff for her translation service. They also wish to express their thanks to the Department of External Affairs of the Canadian Government for its interest and encouragement; to the Polish Embassy in Ottawa for its assistance; to the Institute of Soviet and East European Studies of Carleton University for its support; and to the Canada Council for its financial aid.

CONTENTS

Introduction

ARTICLES

Selected Documents

INTRODUCTION

This is in some respects a unique volume. Many books have been published in English on contemporary Poland. They have been written, however, either by authors in Poland or by those living in the West, and they have usually presented contrasting interpretations of the developments in that country. This volume is the first which was jointly prepared by Poles and outside observers of the Polish scene. The fact that this was possible, in itself testifies to the changed atmosphere of Poland in the 1970's, and indeed to the emergence of a new climate in East-West relations.

The publication in a single volume of the views of Polish and of Western authors does not mean, of course, that all the disagreements between the two sides have been eliminated. Many basic differences still remain. These stem not only from various geographical perspectives, but also from different ideological and political commitments. They are reflected in contrasting approaches, methodologies, and style. Yet, it is significant that the disagreements are not confined exclusively to those between the two sides, but also to those within each group. On occasion, the views of some writers from Poland are even closer to those from the West, and vice versa, than to those of other writers from their own side.

If there is any consensus among the authors, it is that Poland in the 1970's is a country undergoing a profound and rapid transformation. The outcome of these changes is not as yet clear. Some writers take a more optimistic view than others. None of them try to deny that the problems facing Poland are immense. The lesson of Poland's history, however, inspires hope. On many occasions in the past the Polish nation has been confronted with even greater difficulties than today and yet has managed to overcome them successfully.

Adam Bromke
John W. Strong
Ottawa, March 1973

Gierek's Poland

The Downfall of Gomułka

ZBIGNIEW A. PEŁCZYŃSKI

In Warsaw on 7 December 1970 Chancellor Willy Brandt signed the draft treaty concerning the bases of normalization of the mutual relations between the German Federal Republic and Poland. Although the treaty was yet to be ratified by the West German parliament and though it fell short of meeting in full the Polish demands *vis-à-vis* West Germany, it came pretty close to acceptance by that country of the Oder-Neisse line as Poland's western frontier. With the treaty the Polish Government scored an outstanding success, and a large share of the credit could be claimed by Władysław Gomułka. Not only had he been at that time (and since October 1956) the real political leader of the government, he had taken a deep personal interest in the solution of the Polish-German problem during his whole official career as the head of the ruling Polish Workers' (later: United Workers') Party. That early December day, when the treaty was signed, must have seemed to Gomułka a summit of his activity and influence in international relations and to have earned him forever the gratitude of his compatriots. Yet less than a fortnight later, on 20 December 1970, he was relieved of the post of First Secretary of his party and consigned to political oblivion. He left behind him a trail of wrecked buildings and bleeding bodies in four cities, country-wide economic chaos, and the Polish working class in an alienated and rebellious mood. Seldom has history played such a cruel trick on a statesman.

*   *   *

It is worth recalling the chronology of the major events of those critical December days before commenting on the spectacular reversal of Gomułka's fortunes.

December 1970

Wednesday 9th: Probable date of the Politbureau meeting at which wide-ranging increases in prices of consumer goods (partially offset by lowered prices of consumer durables) were decided.

Saturday 12th: The price changes given legal force by a Council of Ministers' decree. A Politbureau letter justifying the decision read out at meetings of Party activists throughout the country.

Sunday 13th: The official communiqué about the new prices published in the press, radio and television.

Monday 14th: The PUWP Central Committee meets in a plenary session in Warsaw to endorse the Polish-West German treaty and the price increases. A strike breaks out in a shipyard in Gdańsk, and working class demonstrators protesting against the increases clash with police in the streets. Public buildings are attacked and set on fire. Three members of the Politbureau (Kliszko, Loga-Sowiński and Kociołek), depart for Gdańsk, a fourth one (Foreign Minister Jędrychowski) flies to Moscow. Strikes and disturbances spread to Gdynia and follow similar pattern.

Tuesday 15th: The use of firearms by police and the employment of armed forces are decided on by Gomułka at an informal meeting of some of the Politbureau members and army leaders. Jaroszewicz arrives in Moscow for CEMA meeting.

Wednesday 16th: Army units with tanks sent to the two trouble spots clash with demonstrators. Disturbances spread to Elbląg.

Thursday 17th: Strikes and demonstrations break out in Szczecin. The Council of Ministers declares a state of emergency and formally authorizes the use of all necessary means to quell disorder. Its Chairman (Cyrankiewicz), in a television appearance, demands the return to work and the end of demonstrations, without offering any concessions to the workers.

Friday 18th: Gomułka is asked to summon a Politbureau meeting by a group of colleagues opposed to pure repression. In the ensuing argument he suffers a minor stroke, loses his eyesight and is taken to hospital. Talks begin about replacing him by Gierek. Probable telegram from Moscow that Soviet leaders are in favour of a peaceful solution of the crisis. Jaroszewicz returns from Moscow.

Saturday 19th:	The Politbureau meets under Cyrankiewicz's chairmanship and reveals deadlock on the leadership issue. After seven hours a majority agrees to ask Gomułka for his resignation, which is given in hospital.
Sunday 20th:	VII Plenary session of the PUWP Central Committee formally elects Gierek First Secretary and approves other changes in the Politbureau and Secretariat. Gierek appears on television, acknowledges the leadership's mistakes and promises a revision of economic and other policies. Strikes and disturbances die down and protests planned in other cities are called off.
Monday 21st:	Probable meeting of Gierek and Brezhnev, after which (on the 22nd) the Soviet Party leaders publicly welcome the changes in the Polish leadership.
Wednesday 23rd:	The Polish Parliament approves a number of important governmental changes. These include a new head of state (Cyrankiewicz) and a new Prime Minister (Jaroszewicz).

The official communiqué issued after the Central Committee meeting of 20 December merely contained the news of the changes in the Politbureau and Secretariat, and said nothing at all about their background. Gomułka's resignation was attributed to his "severe illness," and the Central Committee conveyed to Gomułka their "best wishes for a speedy return to health." When Gierek spoke to the country on radio and television in the evening of the same day he was a little more revealing. He blamed the events in Gdańsk, Gdynia, Elbląg and Szczecin at least in part on "badly thought out conceptions in economic policy" and on the faults of the political mechanism which produced them.

The iron rule of our economic policy and our policy in general must always be respect for reality, broad consultation with the working class and the intelligentsia, and the observance of principles of collegiality and democracy in the life of the Party and the functioning of supreme authorities.

The most recent events reminded us painfully of the fundamental truth that the Party must always maintain a close bond with the working class and the whole nation, and that it must not lose a common language with the working people.[1]

It was only at the subsequent plenary meeting of the PUWP Central Committee (6-7 February 1971) that the new leadership submitted a detailed assessment of the December events for discussion and approval of the Committee. The Politbureau report, together with the text of the speeches made during the session and written statements submitted at the end, is the fullest analysis of the circumstances of Gomułka's downfall by the men who participated in the events. While it does not explain everything and probably exaggerates certain features of the situation, it is a most valuable source of information and a great aid in arriving at a complete interpretation.[2]

* * *

The criticisms of Gomułka and his leadership expressed during the February session of the Central Committee can be grouped under three headings: (1) his mishandling of the unrest in the Baltic cities; (2) his responsibility for incorrect policies which had caused or contributed to the crisis; (3) his exercise of power and style of leadership in general, which were contrary to the correct Leninist principles.

(1) Although the news of the first disturbances reached Warsaw at about 1 p.m. on 14 December, when the Central Committee was still in session, the meeting was not even informed of the events, still less given a chance to discuss them, and for five days of the mounting crisis the Politbureau did not meet. From the beginning to the end Gomułka refused to concede any of the demonstrators' demands or to take any conciliatory steps. He denounced the disturbances as "counter-revolutionary" attacks on the Party and the state by anti-socialist elements. He totally ignored the dominant current of working class protest against a government decision that was highly unpopular and had not been properly explained — a protest that was justified even if its methods were not. The ruthless use of force undermined the authority, tarnished the image of the Party in the country at large, and opened a wide gap between the working class and its vanguard the Party and the nation and the people's state. As ferment was rife in other industrial centres, there was a danger of the disturbances becoming nation-wide and

---

[1] *Nowe Drogi* (January 1971), p. 7.

[2] The report of the Politbureau and the text of speeches and statements were published as a special issue of *Nowe Drogi* in May 1971. Although its circulation was restricted to Party members, copies have reached the West.

beyond control. Thus Gomułka's strong-arm policy carried a tremendous risk of general conflagration with "incalculable consequences," which was an unforgivable political gamble. The resignation of Gomułka and the election of a new Party Secretary was the only way to calm the situation on the Baltic and in the country, to back out of a political blind alley, and to begin the process of regaining the full confidence and support of the working class and the people.

(2) The faulty policies leading to the December crisis for which Gomułka was blamed at the February Central Committee meeting were both political and economic. The decision to raise prices which sparked off the strikes and demonstrations was only the immediate cause of the crisis. The fundamental cause was the stagnation in the standard of living of the population, and especially of its poorest strata. For years the standard of living and consumer needs received a very low priority.

According to the data of the Central Statistical Office real wages rose by 10 per cent during the period of the last five year plan, an average annual rise of less than 2 per cent. Similar increase in real wages took place during the whole period of the sixties. . . . There were even groups of employees where real wages fell. . . . Since the proportion of the cost of food in the cost of living rose relatively rapidly, its negative consequences were felt particularly by the families with lowest incomes. . . .

Particularly important was the uneven rise in earnings during the five years 1966-1970. During the first 3 years the rate of increase of the population's earnings was faster and on average amounted to 2.4 per cent annually, but in the years 1969 and 1970 it was brought to an almost complete halt.[3]

A similarly modest average rise was envisaged for the new Five Year Plan 1971-1975, and the so-called material incentive system of calculating earnings, which was to be introduced in the new plan, was widely believed to have the effect of freezing earnings during the period. Nor was only individual consumption neglected. Building plans for housing were cut and the shortage of accommodation was growing. Rail and urban transport, other communal and social services, and factory amenities were starved of necessary expenditure. The retail and service sectors of the economy were equally grossly neglected. All criticisms from the intelligentsia and signals of popular discontent were either ignored or provoked the angry retort from Gomułka that the country

---

[3] Politbureau report, *Nowe Drogi* (Special Issue), p. 67.

was already living "beyond its means" and there was no scope for improvement.

The resources withdrawn from consumption were devoted primarily to industrial investment. The ratio of capital accumulation to consumption in the national income was higher in Poland that in any other Communist country; at the same time the rate of growth in the economy as a whole was unsatisfactory and well below that of capitalist countries on the same level of development. The reason was the inability of Gomułka and his economic advisors to devise means of increasing productivity, which despite various expedients stagnated during the 1960's.

There was also a serious technological gap between Poland and other industrialized countries, (especially the Western capitalist ones), but Gomułka's ideas on how to close it were economically erroneous and socially disastrous.

Undoubtedly Comrade Gomułka was deeply conscious of the inadequate technical-economic progress of the country. . . . Many of the decisions taken in the last years, which must be deemed to be socially and economically erroneous (such as retail price reform, the system of economic incentives, restricting housing construction, etc.) originated against the background of this increasing conviction of inadequate technical-economic progress. . . . They were all subordinated to the one guiding idea — not to let the country lag behind the world's rate of progress. . . . This guiding idea that the problem of progress can be solved by increasing society's burden, and the policies following from it, were erroneous. . . . Our insufficient progress . . . is above all bound up with low economic efficiency. Low economic efficiency and small dynamism cannot be compensated by limiting consumption. The crux of our economic difficulties lies not in investing too little, but in making bad use of it. The restriction of consumption growth does not always assist economic progress and under certain conditions it can hinder it.[4]

Many faults of the economic mechanism were quoted in the report and the discussion, and attempted reforms were described as too frequent, too hasty, too narrow, and too primitive in conception. There was also a failure to capture popular imagination and inspire the population, especially young people, with a vision of a technological revolution within a socialist framework.

(3) Over and above all the individual policy mistakes, Gomułka was

---

[4] Professor Pajestka's statement, *Nowe Drogi* (Special Issue), p. 297.

accused in the Politbureau report and during its discussion of wielding authority contrary to the principles of collective leadership and internal Party democracy. His behaviour during the December events was said to illustrate a tendency towards "concentrating in his hands increasingly autocratic power." During the preceding five years the Politbureau met only "a few times per year and the Secretariat of the Central Committee met almost never." The proceedings of the Politbureau and the work of the Secretaries were dominated by the First Secretary whose decisions in fact always prevailed. "The possibilities of discussion and confrontations of positions diminished every year; as a result the unanimity of decisions in the Political Bureau of the Central Committee became increasingly formal and illusory."[5] Gomułka was also criticised for forming within the Politbureau an "inner leadership" of a few men who had freer access to him and who supported him whenever necessary. Only two of their members were explicitly named and singled out for severe censure: Kliszko and Jaszczuk. The former, who had been responsible for ideology and cadre policy within the Secretariat, was blamed for the ideological weakness of the Party, which showed itself during the student demonstrations in March 1968 and during the December events. He was accused of bias against many deserving candidates and favouritism towards others in the appointments to top state and Party offices which he controlled. He was also censured for interference, incompetence and intransigeance in December when in charge of operations in the Gdańsk area. As the Central Committee Secretary in charge of economic affairs under Gomułka, Jaszczuk was subjected to a veritable torrent of criticism and invective. He was described as the virtual economic dictator of the country, scornful of the views of colleagues, industrial managers and experts, full of half-baked "pseudo-scientific" ideas on every aspect of economic policy and administration, and particularly close to Gomułka whom he flattered, fed with distorted information and strongly influenced in economic matters. Both men defended themselves, Kliszko meekly and Jaszczuk vigorously, but in vain. They were officially censured by the Central Committee at the end of the February session and expelled from the body. The censure of Gomułka was by contrast relatively mild, and the mention of his "serious mistakes" was balanced by an acknowledgement of his "former services for the Party and the country." In view of his illness and absence

---

[5] Politbureau report, *Nowe Drogi* (Special Issue), pp. 52, 53.

from the Central Committee meeting his membership in it was only suspended.

So much for the official analysis of the December events and their background. In a time-honoured way in Communist politics the new Party leadership felt they had to find a scapegoat for the tremendous upheaval of that month, and found it in Gomułka and his two principal associates. The new leaders had of course also been Gomułka's colleagues, but their excuse was that though they had seen Gomułka's faults and mistakes they were powerless to prevent them, still less to remove him from his office. Not only was he (in General Moczar's words) a "patriarch" as well as an "autocrat," he had also, by means of organizational devices, made himself immune from removal — a situation described at length by Cyrankiewicz.

Could fundamental decisions be changed, since after all one had the power to raise matters at meetings of the Political Bureau? Could one represent there opinions, bring influence to bear or persuade? In a larger set of people it was impossible since it roused the egotistic sensitivity of Comrade Gomułka and offended his sense of authority, which allegedly suffered when a different opinion was expressed. It led to rows about prestige or, what is worse, when the category of social welfare measures was concerned, to the accusation of popularity seeking. . . . The expression of differing opinion led nowhere, and only brought . . . personal alliances into play again. . . . (*Nowe Drogi* [Special Issue], p. 201)

Let's talk in real terms, comrades. If political-organizational configurations which existed in the last few years had allowed, one certainly could have made changes also before the VII Plenum [of the Central Committee on 20 December]. If not personnel changes, then at least changes in social policy. But this was, in my opinion, impossible to achieve; nobody could have done it, from the Political Bureau downwards. . . .

After all, comrades, after the tragic December week, at the Saturday meeting of the Political Bureau on 19 December, held already without Comrade Gomułka, which preceded the VII Plenum, when nobody was prevented from speaking even three times, precisely in order to let all attitudes, differences and nuances come into the open, the meeting of the Bureau lasted seven hours before decisions were taken. . . . There was a seven-hour meeting, a proposal was made to summon a plenum for Sunday and nominate Comrade Gierek as First Secretary. You can guess, comrades, that it would not have been necessary to discuss things for so long if there had been unanimity concerning the immediate summoning of the plenum. . . . And what would a meeting of the Political Bureau have looked like under Comrade Gomułka's leadership, in let us call it a normal situation, that is before December, if one of us who had a definite view of the situation made the matter clear . . . ? (*Nowe Drogi* [Special Issue], pp. 207-8)

Our problem is not to allocate responsibility for the December debacle but rather to explain how the enormous power which Gomułka apparently wielded as the First Secretary collapsed at the end of that black December week. The power and authority of the leader of a Communist state may rest on three different foundations. The first is the personal charisma, prestige or popularity he enjoys among the population at large or its crucial sections such as the workers and the intelligentsia.[6] When he returned to the post of First Secretary of the PUWP Central Committee in October 1956, Gomułka's personal mass support was enormous and probably equal to no other Communist leader's except Dubcek's. His prestige could be seen in the striking way he stemmed the anti-Communist wave in the January 1957 parliamentary elections, virtually single-handedly. The subsequent consolidation of the Party's rule, the abandoning of many hoped-for reforms, and Poland's return to the fold of the Soviet bloc lost Gomułka much of that popularity. It was eroded still further by bitter quarrels with the Catholic Church in the 1960's, by the conflict with students, writers and intellectuals in 1968 and, as far as the working class was concerned, by the stagnation in their living standards during the 1960's. The price changes of 13 December were the last straw. Admittedly they were a government measure, and it was the head of the government, Cyrankiewicz, who vainly appealed to the demonstrators to return to work. But it is almost certain that a public personal intervention by Gomułka would not have made any difference at that time. He simply no longer had the authority to move the masses by exhortation.

The second foundation of the power of a Communist leader is the devotion, loyalty or discipline he can command over the activists of the Communist Party and its elite, who themselves control the whole governing apparatus. In 1956/1957 they rallied round him (except for extreme Stalinist and "revisionist" elements) because he saved the system of Communist rule from collapse and quickly restored its normal functioning. This was enough for a long time to give him a firm hold over the Party without packing the leading bodies of the Party with his

---

[6] For various reasons in Communist states peasants and white collar workers (employees of economic enterprises, petty bureaucrats, etc.) rarely exercise the political influence the other social strata have.

own men. Between October 1956 and the Party Congress of March 1959 Gomułka directed the Party through a Politbureau and a Secretariat in which he had only three personal followers, a Central Committee which had been handpicked by his Stalinist predecessor Bierut in 1954, and only a slightly altered central and regional Party apparatus. Afterwards, though there were various changes, they never amounted to a thorough purge. Gomułka never built up a large personal following in the Central Committee or the Party apparatus; he was content to tolerate men of various backgrounds and shades of opinion provided they accepted his moderate, "centrist" line and loyally carried it out. The fact that, while so many members of the Party elite had meekly submitted to *force majeure*, he had opposed Stalin, suffered disgrace and persecution, and emerged from them unbroken to lead the Party again in 1956, gave him a sort of moral superiority over most of his colleagues and subordinates and inspired genuine respect and admiration.

In this second area of Gomułka's support an erosion of his authority also occurred, though it was not so rapid or so general. Much has been written in the West in the development of factions within the PUWP in the 1960's and there is no need to repeat it.[7] The special issue of *Nowe Drogi* of May 1971 confirms it and offers fascinating additional insight into contrasting attitudes and currents of thought among the Polish Communist elite. While the Politbureau report, as befits an official document which expressed a composite judgement of different groups represented in that body, is rather judicious, the speeches and written statements reveal significant differences. A large group of speakers clearly voiced the frustration that the economic system, despite countless changes and reforms, seemed unable to deliver the goods, whether judged by the rate of economic growth or technological progress or the improvement in the standard of living. To them Gomułka and his closest associates appeared inadequate for the task and his past merits irrelevant to the job at hand. The governmental and economic elite clearly resented the close supervision and minute interference of the Central Committee's Economic Department controlled by Jaszczuk. Then there were a number of important vested interests who were hurt by the Gomułka-Jaszczuk reforms. The running down of coal

---

[7] See especially Hansjakob Stehle, *The Independent Satellite*, Ch. 2 (London, 1965); Adam Bromke, *Poland's Politics*, Ch. 10 (Cambridge, Mass., 1967); and Nicholas Bethell, *Gomułka*, Ch. 16 (London, 1969).

mining on the ground that it had no future deeply offended the Silesian lobby in the Central Committee. Shipbuilding, the aircraft industry, oil prospecting in the Rzeszów region, cotton weaving in Łódź, and a number of other interests saw themselves threatened by the strategy of investing in "industries with a future." The concentration of investment on a few industries demanded by the concept of "selective development" dashed the hopes of Party secretaries of many cities and backward regions whose capital needs, whether for communal services or industrial production, were unlikely to be met for years.

But rather different voices could be heard as well. These were concerned with Gomułka's excessive concentration on economic issues, on his neglect of ideological issues, his toleration of "revisionist" elements in the higher echelons of the Party and the government, his passivity towards reactionary diversion inspired by imperialist circles in literature and science, and his failure to entrust the running of the country more to the care of those Party activists who had participated in the underground struggle against the Germans and could find a common language with other "patriotic" elements in the country. Although the March 1968 events were referred to rather seldom and discreetly during the February 1971 Central Committee session, they had been a turning point in Gomułka's political position. Taking advantage of a student demonstration (perhaps deliberately provoked), the same elements in the Party unleashed a campaign against "Zionism" and "revisionism," which resulted in a large-scale purge of the Party, governmental and intellectual elite, and the exodus of a large part of the small Jewish minority from the country. There is no evidence that Gomułka ever ordered or sanctioned the campaign; it originated not in the Central Committee Secretariat, but in the Warsaw City Party committee. When Gomułka eventually acted, it was to restrain the excesses of the campaign and to correct its abuses. But his temporary impotence and the hostile reception he got from a mass rally of Party activists on 14 April 1968 revealed that he no longer commanded the wholehearted loyalty of the Party and that many activists wished him to go. His long, televised speech was punctuated by catcalls and the shouts of "Gierek," although one suspects that the hecklers did not shout "Moczar" only for tactical reasons.

Finding the second foundation of his leadership shaken in spring 1968, Gomułka was forced to rely more than he had ever done before on the third traditional instrument of a Communist leader's power — the control of the Party's leading bodies through his power of appointment. At the November 1968 Party Congress Gomułka propped up his weakened authority in two ways: First, he strengthened his grip over the economy in order to enforce more effectively policies such as selective investment, modernization of plants, the material incentives scheme and so on. This was done by increasing the power of the Central Committee's Economic Department with Jaszczuk in charge. It was at the Congress that Jaszczuk became a full member of the Politbureau and thus acquired the necessary political standing. Possibly Gomułka intended also to build up Jaszczuk as his potential successor and a rival of Gierek and Moczar, who had been the leading contenders up to then. Cryptic remarks about Jaszczuk's "limitless ambitions" made at the February 1971 Central Committee session seem to confirm it, as does the vehemence of the attacks on Jaszczuk by both the Gierek and the Moczar group.

Gomułka's second tactic was also organizational and was intended to check the growing influence of his two potential successors at the Central Committee and the Politbureau/Secretariat levels. A group of youthful Party activists, a whole generation younger than Gierek and Moczar, were nominated for the Central Committee; a few of the younger men were also promoted to the Secretariat and Politbureau. Kliszko, as the executive of Gomułka's cadre policy, justified this at the November 1968 Party Congress by the need to secure a more adequate representation for the post-war generation of Party activists who constituted a large and growing proportion of the Party cadres. And in an apparent move to check Moczar's influence the Rzeszów provincial Party secretary Kruczek was also made a Politbureau member.[8] The composition of the Politbureau after the 1968 Congress, which is highly significant for the understanding of Gomułka's downfall in December 1970, was as follows:

Full (voting) members: Gomułka (S)
Jaszczuk (S)
Kliszko (S)   the Gomułka group or
Loga-Sowiński   so-called "inner
Spychalski   leadership"
Strzelecki (S)

---

[8] Kruczek once had the reputation of being strongly pro-Russian and Stalinist, and Gomułka had made an unsuccessful attempt to dislodge him from his post after October 1956. Moczar's veiled attacks on the Communists who had sought

Cyrankiewicz
Gierek
Jędrychowski
Kociołek
Kruczek
Tejchma (S)

Deputy (alternate) Jagielski
members: Jaroszewicz
Moczar (S)
Szydlak

Secretaries of the Central Committee: those with (S) after their name and also Olszowski and Starewicz.

In this way, for the first time since Gomułka's return to power, the largest group in the Politbureau and exactly half of its full members consisted of Gomułka and his wartime associates and friends. Had it ever come to an open split in the Politbureau, and of course Gomułka's authority and personality made this most unlikely, it needed only one man from outside the Gomułka group to give them the necessary authority.[9]

* * *

Let us now analyze the situation immediately preceding Gomułka's downfall in the light of these "political-organizational configurations" (as Cyrankiewicz called them). The Politbureau which met on 19 December 1970 did not include Gomułka (who was in hospital) and Gierek since the major issue to be decided was whether Gierek should replace Gomułka. Although agreeing to call the Politbureau the previous day Gomułka had made it clear that he considered his policy of

---

shelter in the USSR instead of fighting the Germans in the underground in Poland opened him to the charge of being "nationalist" and potentially anti-Russian.

[9] In the Secretariat the Gomułka group included Starewicz and hence had a majority of five to four. But, as was said at the February 1971 Central Committee meeting, the Secretariat never met as a body; the Secretaries attended Politbureau meetings, whether they were formally its full or deputy members or not.

repression until order was restored to be absolutely correct.[10] Those who questioned that view had no alternative but to try to replace him. Had Gomułka been well and present at the Saturday meeting, there is little doubt that he would have forced through his viewpoint and that the move to replace him would have failed. In his presence the opposition would have lacked courage as well as the votes and the attempt might not even have been made. The most Gomułka might have agreed to was some small conciliatory gesture to lower the tension in the country, perhaps just the kind of a wage rise for low paid workers and a rise in family benefits and old age pensions which the new leadership announced soon after 20 December.

Gomułka's mild cerebral haemorrhage transformed the situation and gave the opposition a chance. Not only was he no longer there to preside over the Saturday meeting (the opportunistic Cyrankiewicz took his place instead); his disability at such a critical moment was disastrous and clearly called for a speedy remedy. The difficulty facing the opposition was that, as long as the Gomułka group stuck together, the opposition had no clear majority of the voting Politbureau members even if they were in a majority at the meeting. The Gomułkaists held out for seven hours before the decision to ask for Gomułka's abdication in favour of Gierek was reached. Cyrankiewicz and Kliszko were asked to call on Gomułka at the hospital and to obtain his resignation. Once it was given in writing and the matter was reported to the Politbureau, a plenary meeting of the Central Committee was summoned for the following day.[11] The Politbureau, now under Gierek's chairmanship, proceeded to reconstitute itself and the Secretariat. The fact that of the Gomułka group only one man — Loga-Sowiński, the Chairman of the Central Council of Trade Unions — found himself in the new Polit-

---

[10] Kliszko doubtlessly pointed out, as he did at the February Plenum, that the strong-hand policy had been successful since street demonstrations in the Gdańsk-Gdynia area had ceased and work had resumed by Friday, and the Szczecin outbreak had changed its character to a peaceful occupation strike. On the other hand, Gomułka's opponents could have cited the wide-spread work stoppages throughout the country and the meetings being planned for Monday in a number of cities. It was of course impossible to tell whether the successful use of armed forces in the coastal cities would or would not have acted as a deterrent to street demonstrations elsewhere.

[11] In the material published in the special issue of *Nowe Drogi* the argument in the long Politbureau session was said to centre on the need to call the Central Committee so soon, which Strzelecki in particular was said to have opposed (see pp. 208, 221). If this was in fact the case, it was clearly an indirect dispute over succession. Without a formal election by the Central Committee

bureau suggests that it was he who broke the seven-hour deadlock by voting for Gierek. The other members of the Politbureau and Secretariat were confirmed in their posts or promoted and five new members were elected. The new composition of the two leading Party bodies after the 20 December Central Committee meeting was as follows:

Full members of the Politbureau:	Babiuch (S)
	Cyrankiewicz
	Gierek (S)
	Jaroszewicz
	Jędrychowski
	Kociołek (S)
	Kruczek
	Loga-Sowiński
	Moczar (S)
	Olszowski (S)
	Szydlak
	Tejchma (S)
Deputy members of the Politbureau:	Jabłoński
	Jagielski
	Jaruzelski
	Kępa
Additional Secretaries:	Barcikowski and Starewicz[12]

Once Gomułka had formally resigned and the Politbureau had agreed on the other changes, there was nothing for the Central Committee to do except to ratify the changes unanimously. For the reasons already mentioned, Gomułka's prestige in the Party elite had already sunk low before the December events. The clumsy way the price changes were introduced, and its terrible political consequences destroyed his prestige completely. He had, in any case, only a handful of personal followers to defend him and the leading ones fell with him. The Party elite must

---

Gierek would in effect have been only an acting First Secretary. Moreover, the postponement of the Central Committee meeting increased the chance of Gomułka's full recovery and his attendance at another Politbureau meeting where the Saturday decision might have been rescinded.

[12] Loga-Sowiński resigned from the Politbureau at the next plenary meeting of the Central Committee in February 1971, together with Kociołek. The rout of the Gomułka group was thus complete.

have hoped that the changes would relax tension and check new disturbances, and nobody more so than the large group of provincial and city Party secretaries in the Central Committee, since it was their headquarters which had been the primary targets of demonstrators both in Gdańsk and Szczecin. The election of General Jaruzelski, the Minister of Defence, to the Politbureau on 20 December implies that the army's high command, although they obeyed his orders, were unhappy about Gomułka's decision to use troops to quell the disorders. Their unfavourable reaction and possibly even warning that the loyalty of the troops could not be taken for granted in future clashes may have been another factor which strengthened the opposition's case against Gomułka. But it must be emphasized again what a close thing Gomułka's downfall was. It was not, strictly speaking, the riots that brought him down. Despite his enormous unpopularity in the country at that moment, despite the alienation of the higher and lower ranks of the Party elite, despite the determination of most of his colleagues in the leadership to get rid of him, it needed the fortuitous event of an illness at the crucial moment to seal his political fate.

*　　*　　*

A fascinating question, to which only a tentative and speculative answer can be given in the light of available evidence, is what role the Soviet leadership played in the downfall of Gomułka. There was, needless to say, no question of any blatant Soviet intervention in the leadership struggle within another ruling Communist Party. The last time such intervention occurred was to prevent Gomułka's election as First Secretary in October 1956, and it ended with a resounding fiasco. The lasting achievement of the "Polish October" was precisely the recognition by the Soviet leaders of the sovereign right of the Central Committees of ruling Communist parties to settle their leadership and policy disputes without overt Soviet pressure, with the proviso of course that such disputes did not endanger "socialism" in the country concerned (as they did in the Soviet view in Czechoslovakia). This principle, however, does not preclude informal consultations or the exercise of subtle behind-the-scenes influence; no great power is likely to be wholly indifferent to vital decisions taken in a neighbouring or allied country.

Until 1968 Gomułka was so well entrenched in his position that there was neither any need nor any opportunity for the Soviet leaders to exercise influence on his behalf. In any case he was, after 1957, a firm friend of Khrushchev, and following the latter's downfall he established close relations with Khrushchev's successors. He became an elder statesman of the Soviet bloc, whose views were sought by other Communist leaders and carried weight at international conferences of Communist parties. All this could not but raise his status in the Polish Party. As has been noted, however, the events of March 1968 damaged his authority severely by demonstrating to the PUWP elite and the Soviet leaders that there were forces within the Polish Party capable of acting independently, without the orders and against the wishes of the First Secretary. Who knows what might have happened at the V Congress of the PUWP in November 1968 if the Czechoslovak crisis had not occurred, if Gomułka had not loyally supported the Soviet invasion, and if Brezhnev (who was very much in evidence at the Congress) had not made manifest his appreciation of Gomułka in such warm terms? Perhaps the surprising fact that General Moczar was not promoted from deputy to full member of the Politbureau, while the relatively obscure Kruczek jumped straight from being a member of the Central Committee to full membership of the Politbureau reflected Gomułka's gratitude to the Soviet leader. Ironically the man who at first owed his tremendous prestige and popularity to his bold defiance of Khrushchev and his colleagues may eventually have come to depend, to some extent, on the good will of Brezhnev and the rest of the Soviet Politbureau.

How did the Soviet leaders react to the December crisis in Poland? They naturally kept in close touch with the Polish situation. The Foreign Minister Jędrychowski, a Politbureau member, flew to Moscow on the first day of the Gdańsk upheaval and thus had a chance to discuss the situation with the Soviet leaders. At that stage it was still a local disturbance, confined to one city, and the Soviet leaders may have merely stressed that the policy of détente they are actively pursuing in Europe required a quick and lenient settlement of the conflict. Jędrychowski returned to Warsaw the same day, but his place was taken by Jaroszewicz, who flew to Moscow to attend a meeting of the CEMA Executive Committee, which lasted from 15 to 18 December. He was thus in an excellent position to consult with the Soviet leaders during the crisis. The escalation of the disturbances no doubt worried them; according to rumours afterwards widely circulating in Warsaw, on 18 December Brezhnev sent a telegram to Gomułka advising him to seek a peaceful solution of the conflict. Although Gomułka apparently did not disclose the telegram to his colleagues, the Soviet message could have been conveyed informally to other Politbureau members by Jaroszewicz. Once it was clear where the Russians stood, the opposition to Gomułka's tough line policy must have been emboldened, and perhaps their demand for a Politbureau meeting to discuss the situation was voiced because of the Soviet attitude. On Saturday, 19 December, when Gomułka's fate hung in the balance for seven hours, the Soviet leaders could have indicated that they wished Gomułka to stay as First Secretary. Had they done so, the opposition to Gomułka would have lost supporters and the deadlock might have ended differently. In addition to his illness, the Soviet leaders' failure to act sealed Gomułka's fate.

*   *   *   *

Why then did they fail to act? Obviously the possibility of further clashes between workers and the army must have concerned them deeply since a large-scale confrontation carried at least an element of risk that it might get out of hand and necessitate Soviet intervention. Like the Hungarian and Czechoslovak invasions, such an intervention would have been a severe blow for their Western détente policy. It would also have weakened the European flank of the Soviet Union in case of a conflict with China, and have provided the Chinese — then still extremely hostile to the Russians — with a great propaganda weapon against the USSR.[13]

The Soviet leaders, however, may have had other and more positive reasons for wanting Gomułka to go than simply the fear that his intransigence, and his very continuation in office, was doing nothing to calm the inflamed passions of the Polish working class. Even without direct evidence, one wonders if the trend of Polish economic policy, pursued so vigorously by Gomułka and Jaszczuk, had been wholly palatable to the Russians. Although Polish foreign trade with the USSR had been growing steadily, the pattern of exchange was changing. The Soviet Union was ceasing to be Poland's sole supplier of industrial equipment, as it had been in the 1950's and early 1960's, and increasingly Poland was turning to the West for machinery and plants to develop the new branches of industry (motor cars, chemicals, electrical goods and electronics) which were to diversify and modernize the country's

---

[13] Interestingly, on 31 December 1970 China was taken severely to task in an editorial article in *Pravda* for fabricating stories about the concentration of Soviet armed forces on the Polish frontier when the disturbances broke out, and for playing an active role in changing the Polish Party leadership. Even the Western bourgeois press (*Pravda* wrote) made no such scurrilous allegations against the Soviet Union.

industrial structure. On the other hand a more realistic calculation of costs of production led to the restriction of output, export and investment in many traditional, mainly outdated and inefficient industries where the Soviet Union was the main importer or supplier of equipment.[14]

There was not much that the Russians could do to reverse this trend of Polish economic policy while Gomułka and Jaszczuk were in charge; what they could and did do was to stop them from pursuing their policies through the Council for Economic Mutual Assistance. In 1967 Gomułka resumed his campaign for greater economic integration within CEMA, which he justified by the need of the whole Communist camp to catch up with the West in the pace of technological revolution.[15] The chief advantage of the integration he envisaged to Poland was that multilateral clearing arrangements would have provided Poland with transferable rubles for purchasing technologically advanced equipment in the West, and with guaranteed markets in CEMA countries for the large-scale output of goods produced with this equipment. The Russians did not oppose integration outright but refused to move quickly. While Gomułka wanted to reap the benefits of integration already in the 1971-1975 economic plan, the other Communist states led by the Soviet Union mostly took the line that specialization and convertibility

---

[14] See Jaroszewicz's critique of this aspect of the Gomułka-Jaszczuk policies at the February Central Committee session (page references are to the *Nowe Drogi* Special Issue):
"The advantages flowing from specialization and production co-operation, from the long-term export of important equipment and machines from Poland to the Soviet Union, were not fully appreciated; we also did not take advantage of [Soviet] aid to realize investment tasks although such possibilities existed and although we took advantage of such possibilities in the 1950's. . . . Mechanical, pseudo-scientific determination of profitability criteria of export production led to the restriction of the traditional export, which had secured considerable foreign exchange earnings, before conditions arose for replacing it by new, more profitable export. . . ." (p. 159)
"The necessity to reconstruct our industry, the purchase of machinery and equipment and also some plants require the resumption of the import of complete equipment of industrial enterprises both from the Soviet Union and other socialist countries. . . ." (p. 163)
See also attacks on Jaszczuk for trying to wind up oil prospecting in the Rzeszów region as uneconomic, partly because it was carried out with obsolete Soviet equipment (p. 100); and for questioning the future of shipbuilding, which produces vessels mainly for the Soviet Union (pp. 198-199).

[15] See his speech in Moscow during the anniversary celebrations of the October Revolution, reprinted in Władysław Gomułka, *Przemówienia 1967* (Warsaw, 1968), especially pp. 307-308. He made many similar speeches in 1968 and 1969.

could only be a long-term process, which needed decades rather than years to achieve. The April 1969 meeting of CEMA made their attitude clear. Changing tack towards bilateralism in despair, Gomułka tried to secure at least some immediate help for the ambitious Polish economic plan by obtaining credits and securing greater outlets for Polish machinery. He conducted a series of high-level talks with CEMA leaders, but (significantly perhaps) only Rumania responded at all warmly to Polish advances. Probably Gomułka's decision to open nego- tiations with Bonn to settle the Oder-Neisse frontier problem, without all the other traditional conditions for normalization of Polish-West German relations, was a response to failure of his CEMA initiative. Certainly a resumption of diplomatic relations with West Germany was a pre-condition of closer economic cooperation, and West Germany was a potential source of modern industrial equipment and investment credits. For political as well as economic reasons the prospects could not have pleased either the Soviet Union or East Germany.

Gomułka was probably so strongly wedded to his dream of taking Poland over the threshold of technological revolution in his own life- time that he remained undeterred by the lack of CEMA support. He merely decided that if sufficient external help was not forthcoming, the country must bear the burden of the new phase of industrialization, and proceeded to tighten still further the belt of the already neglected Polish consumer. Professor Pajestka's trenchant criticism of the "guiding idea," as he called it at the February Central Committee meeting, has already been mentioned and, as has also been shown, the sacrifices of the consumers' interests has been one of the main targets of attacks on Gomułka since Gierek assumed power. But Gomułka did something else to release resources for his modernization programme, which directly concerned the Soviet Union. He decided to wind up the Polish aircraft industry which supplied military planes primarily for the Rus- sians, and formed a part of the Polish contribution to the defence needs of the Warsaw Pact. He could even have hinted that further economies in Polish defence expenditure would have to follow. Such drastic action could be justified by Bonn's acceptance of the *status quo* in Central and Eastern Europe and the good prospect for a lasting détente with the West. Apparently, however, Gomułka and Jaszczuk sought rather to justify it on economic grounds. Aircraft production, they argued, was absurd in a small country like Poland and its export was uneconomic.[16] This could be regarded as a form of economic nationalism which set the interest of one country above the general defence interest of the Soviet bloc.

Gomułka's handling of the disturbances in Gdańsk, Gdynia, Elbląg and Szczecin and the possibility of further outbreaks of this sort was probably the major, but by no means the only reason why the Soviet leaders deserted him in December 1970. Before they did so, of course, they had to make sure that his successor did not harbour any dangerous ideas and that he was willing to acknowledge and expiate Gomułka's sins towards the Soviet Union. They also had to be certain that the new Politbureau included men they knew well and could trust, and that these new recruits would possess sufficient influence. Gierek was the only man acceptable both to his Polish colleagues and to the Soviet leaders, but he had spent his early years in France and in Belgium and had not been in close relations with the Russians after his postwar return to Poland. If he were to be First Secretary of the Party, then the Prime Minister — the number two man in the Communist power hierarchy — had to be someone they knew better than Gierek. Jaroszewicz fitted the specification well. During the war he had served as a political officer in the Polish army in Russia. He had been Deputy Premier and Poland's representative on the CEMA Executive Committee under Gomułka, and had had close contacts with the Soviet leaders. His responsibilities kept him in Moscow much of the time, and by a stroke of fortune he found himself there between 15 and 18 December. It is impossible to say whether there was a specific "deal" over the Premiership for Jaroszewicz, and whether it was arranged before or after Gierek managed to obtain a majority in the Politbureau. There was, however, a curious delay between *Pravda*'s announcement of the new Polish Politbureau and Secretariat on 21 December and the publication of Brezhnev's warm congratulations to Gierek on 22 December. During the intervening day secret talks could have taken place between the two leaders and some of their colleagues which fully satisfied the Russians. Jaroszewicz was by no means the obvious candidate for the premiership. Jędrychowski, a full member of the Polit-

---

[16] Five speakers commented adversely on the decision at the February Central Committee meeting. They included Cyrankiewicz, Kruczek, a leading technological expert, the commander-in-chief of the Polish air force, and the secretary of the Party committee in the chief aircraft factory; see *Nowe Drogi* (Special Issue), pp. 127, 205, 250, 310-312, 166.

bureau, and with long experience on the Planning Commission and at the Ministry of Foreign Affairs, might have had a stronger *prima facie* claim. If a real change was desired, the most outstanding of the younger Party leaders, Tejchma, could have been appointed. However, on 23 December Jaroszewicz became Prime Minister and in his first speech to the *Sejm* declared:

The unshakeable foundation of our [foreign] policy is friendship, alliance and cooperation with the states of the socialist commonwealth. We attach particular importance to the development of fraternal friendship and all-sided cooperation with the Soviet Union. They are based on an alliance tested for twenty-five years, which we shall steadily strengthen and deepen. . . . We shall strengthen the Warsaw Pact and develop and deepen the cooperation of socialist countries. We shall consolidate the defensive capacity of People's Poland.

On 5 January Gierek and Jaroszewicz went on an official visit to Moscow; the official communiqué issued at the end of the visit stated that the parties to the talks "expressed their mutual desire to deepen political, economic, scientific, technical and defence cooperation, both bilaterally and multilaterally, within the framework of the Warsaw Pact and the Council of Economic Mutual Aid." The theme of "strengthening friendship," "tightening links" and "increasing cooperation" also ran through several speeches reported in the special issue of *Nowe Drogi*, including Gierek's, and was included in the report of the Politbureau to the February 1971 Central Committee meeting. Needless to say the aircraft industry was reprieved, and the traditional pattern of Soviet-Polish trade began to show signs of re-emerging during the same year. The heavily revised economic plan for 1971-1975 puts the emphasis on consumption, agriculture, housing, and traditional light and heavy industry, and effectively gives up the concept of selective development and the dream of a new industrial revolution on the basis of Western technology.

Gomułka's downfall in 1970 bears some resemblance to his downfall in 1948 though of course history never repeats itself exactly. In 1948 Gomułka fell because he had opposed Stalin over collectivization of agriculture, the setting-up of the Cominform and the expulsion of Tito from it, misdemeanours which in due course earned him the stigma of "rightist-nationalist deviation." In 1970 he fell because he would not take the Soviet leaders' advice on how to handle a political crisis which had serious implications for the Soviet Union and also perhaps because his economic policies began to be tinged with nationalism. In both cases he dragged down with him only a small group of personal friends and trusted colleagues from the wartime underground period. This highlights his essentially lonely position in the Party. He was incomparably stronger in 1970 than in 1948, and it needed a tremendous popular upheaval, in addition to a palace revolution, to depose him. Finally, he was treated much more kindly in 1970 than in 1948. He was criticized but not disgraced, and his past achievements were acknowledged by his successors. The Soviet leaders might themselves have insisted on restraint and moderation towards the man to whom, on 6 February 1970, the USSR Supreme Soviet awarded the order of Lenin on the occasion of his sixty-fifth birthday "for his outstanding services to the development of fraternal friendship and cooperation between the peoples of the Soviet Union and Polish People's Republic, for the strengthening of peace and socialism, and for many years of active participation in the world Communist movement."

December 1970: The Turning Point

MIECZYSŁAW F. RAKOWSKI

Almost two years have passed since the Polish nation, together with its friends throughout the world, was shocked by events which began on the Baltic coast. Exactly a week after the signature in Warsaw of the historic treaty between Poland and the Federal Republic of Germany, demonstrations by workers occurred in four cities: Gdańsk, Gdynia, Szczecin and Elbląg. Within a few hours, the peaceful demonstrations had changed into bloody clashes with the forces of law and order and the army was brought into action against the workers. The political atmosphere throughout the country underwent a sudden deterioration. The street clashes on the coast created a political crisis within the Party, as well as at all levels of government power. The developments were pushing the nation towards the brink of disaster. Each subsequent day deepened the internal crisis and foretold serious international implications.

The fatal sequence of events was interrupted in the afternoon of 20 December. The VII Plenum of the Central Committee of the Polish United Workers Party, conferring that day, appointed new national political leaders. At the head of the Party stood Edward Gierek, the then first secretary of the PUWP provincial organization in Katowice, an ex-miner who had spent many years of his life in the coal mines of France and Belgium. Gierek brought to the Party leadership the experience of a man who had had many years of direct contact with modern technology. His biographers should also note that the present leader of the Party was born in the western part of Poland. That part of the country has always been technically and culturally more developed than eastern and southern Poland. A man's early economic and cultural environment influence his later behaviour, a fact which could stimulate interesting analyses of the lives of past Polish leaders, including those of the inter-war period. This is, however, a separate subject.

In the December events the material and moral losses were terrifying. Forty-five people lost their lives and 1,165 were injured, including 564 civilians. In the course of the demonstrations and street battles fourteen public buildings were set on fire and 220 shops were either destroyed or looted. Communications systems and housing were also seriously affected. To the material losses, estimated at several million złotys, must be added the many millions lost by the national economy as a result of the strikes which took place in the first months of 1971.

Losses of a moral and political nature were immeasurable. Polish society emerged from the December events frustrated, embittered and disillusioned with the authorities. December seriously reduced the confidence which the average citizen had had in the Party and its slogans. The restoration of confidence, without which effective functioning of any authority is scarcely imaginable, became the main task facing the new leaders. It was not easy, since the lack of confidence was based not only on the facts and experience of the dramatic week, but also on experiences accumulated during the years preceding the December drama.

*   *   *

The post-war development of Poland, which had embarked upon the path of revolutionary changes in the years 1944-45, did not take place without conflict. This is certainly a banal observation, but one worth remembering. No thinking person can disregard the achievements of the Polish revolution. We Communists have done far more in these twenty-odd years than the Polish bourgeoisie had done in the inter-war period. Our ideas and our determination caused post-war Poland to emerge from the immense socio-economic backwardness in which it had remained throughout the inter-war era. The transformation of Poland from a poor and backward country into an industrial and agricultural country considerably improved the Polish national outlook and strengthened our position in the community of European nations.

Foreign policy also played a very positive role in raising Poland to a position which it had not held before the war. The originators of this policy concentrated from the start on actions aimed at putting out the fires of unrest which had burned since 1939 on almost all of Poland's frontiers, but particularly in the east. The policy of alliances which People's Poland employed vis-à-vis its neighbours, while giving priority to its relations with the Soviet Union, resulted in a strengthening of our position in Europe and in an increase in Poland's influence among the peoples of the world. Post-war Poland is not, as was sometimes the case in the past, a nation which can be manipulated by outsiders.

The extent of Polish territory, its population, its industrial potential and its central position in Europe all contribute to Poland's being a valuable ally of the Soviet Union. It seems that this aspect of the Polish-Soviet alliance is seldom appreciated in Western political literature. Even now, authors writing about Eastern Europe are too often willing to analyze the relations in terms relevant to the Cold War era.

The realization of the programme, promising a socio-economic trans-formation of Poland, put forward by the Polish left-wing camp, took place in exceptionally difficult and complex circumstances. The Poland of 1945 was devastated. The Nazi invaders had killed off the flower of the Polish intelligentsia. In Warsaw alone, several hundred thousand young people had lost their lives. These able young people were missing when we began rebuilding our country. The animosity of the Polish bourgeoisie towards socialism meant that the new authorities had limited possibilities for using the experience gathered by the social group termed "old," i.e., the pre-war intelligentsia. This animosity influenced wide circles of society, and the years 1944-47 saw the classic symptoms of civil war throughout Poland.

In such a situation, the new authorities had to rely on people who were trustworthy and totally dedicated to the socialist cause. There was no shortage of these people. They came mainly from the worker and peasant classes and brought to the revolution enthusiasm and a readi-ness for sacrifice. Those were extremely valuable attributes, but these people did not possess any experience in government. Although the new authorities were teaching others, at the same time they themselves were learning; and to learn is to commit errors. An additional element which facilitated mistakes and which pushed the new authorities into sectarian positions was the above mentioned animosity of the bour-geoisie. In the immediate post-war years, the creators and executors of the revolutionary programme felt threatened and encircled.

The state of mind of the new leaders in those early years is one of the subjects to which insufficient attention has been paid in Polish poli-tical literature. It must be considered, however, if we want a better understanding of the winding path followed by the socialist revolution in Poland.

This subject brings us to another matter, and that is the Stalinist era in Poland. It is no coincidence that in looking into the past, one should begin with an attempt at a sociological characterization of the new authorities. One cannot analyze the ideas and practices pertaining to Stalinism in isolation from the whole complexity of the development processes which appeared in the first years of People's Poland. Similarly, one cannot treat the Stalinist era in Poland as a continuous stream of perversions and errors. At the same time that dogmatic and sectarian ideas ruled the Party and the whole political life of the nation, the Six Year Plan shook the old social systems and created a base for the further industrial development of Poland. At the same time that mistrust gave birth to a policy of repression in relation to innocent people, both Communist and anti-Communist, an authentic promotion of the worker and peasant classes was taking place. Millions of peasants' and workers' sons filled the halls of the universities. Let us note the fact that the youth of that day, today constitutes the core of the ruling cadre.

As on the coast, in 1956 the workers of the Cegielski plant took to the streets, their demands being predominantly economic. There is no doubt, however, that the demands had a deep political motivation. In March 1956, at the XX Congress of the Communist Party of the Soviet Union, Nikita Khrushchev came out with a violent attack on Joseph Stalin. This attack, made in a speech to a closed session of the XX Congress soon became known to practically everyone in Poland. At the time, although emphasizing the need for moving away from Stalinist practices, the Party was not convinced that it was really necessary. It was the "Cegielski" workers who precipitated the retreat from Stalinism. Attempts to halt this process were to no avail.

In the second half of October 1956, at the famous VIII Plenum of the PUWP, the post of First Secretary was again assumed by Władysław Gomułka. Gomułka had been accused in 1948, as had been many other activists, of taking a right-wing, nationalist stance. He had been deprived of all official functions and was imprisoned. On once again taking over the post of First Secretary, Władysław Gomułka came forward with a fiery denunciation of Stalinism, and firmly condemned the use of force against the workers in Poznań. He declared that they had fought for valid issues. Fourteen years later, on hearing of the workers' demonstrations in Gdańsk, this same politician, with no hesitation, decided that the only response should be the use of force. And force was used. Whatever may have been his justification, the incontestable fact remains that this decision caused still more workers' blood to be shed in the history of People's Poland. Gomułka did not want to, or perhaps could not, discern the socio-economic sources of the discontent which had pushed the workers of the coast into taking dramatic action. Instead, he blamed anti-socialist elements for the demonstrations. Luckily for both the country and the Party, this thesis was emphatically rejected by the new leaders of the Party.

Both the events in Poznań in 1956 and further developments within the Party were carefully followed by the whole society. It accepted the decisions of the VIII Plenum of the Central Committee with enormous relief and great satisfaction. Władysław Gomułka had the complete confidence of the enthusiastic Polish people. The Party could indeed be content for at its head stood a leader unchallenged by anyone. Although society did not forget about what had happened on the streets of Poznań, this had no negative effect on the people's attitudes towards the tasks formulated by the VIII and subsequent plenary meetings of the Central Committee in the area of building socialism. The people undoubtedly understood the dramatic web of internal and external causes which had led to the explosion.

* * *

If, then, we state that the crisis of confidence, which occurred in December 1970, was based on the sum of experiences gathered by society in the period preceding the events on the coast, we do not mean what had happened in 1956 in Poznań, but the phenomena which had affected our lives in the 1960's.

The first few years of the new political course gave no indication of the complications which were to follow. The society continued to endow Gomułka and his team with complete confidence. It was ready to accept as inevitable various deviations from the principles formulated at the VIII Plenum. There came a time, however, when these changed from merely quantitative to qualitative. In the mid-1960's Poles began to change their perspective. It was realized that the Party leadership was beginning to neglect the main task of a socialist state: to strive constantly towards a greater satisfaction of the growing needs of the masses. The disproportion between the growth of the means of production and that of everyday consumer goods increased annually. The production of consumer goods was disregarded more and more, and demands for an increase in the production of these goods were described as either revisionist or yielding to petit bourgeois incitement. Anyone who urged that the Party and government leadership show a greater interest in the production of consumer goods was inevitably reminded of the pitiful conditions in which millions of Poles had lived between the wars. Two facts were ignored: first, that socialism had awakened aspirations in the field of consumption; and second, that the majority of the Polish population consisted of young people (over 50 per cent of the population of Poland is under thirty). These people, having grown up in the post-war era, were not impressed by references to the pre-war past, the streets full of loitering unemployed, the miserable farm workers' living quarters, the pitiful housing conditions, etc.

The economic policy of the 1960's had a direct influence on the trend of real wages. Although the wage fund grew from year to year, it was mainly the result of an increase in the national economy's labour force. The average real wage increased very slowly. According to the Main Census Bureau, the annual increase in real wages during the years 1965-1970 was less than 2 per cent. This means that, in practice, millions of working people felt no improvement in their material condition. Gathering strength in society was the view that the Polish economy was stagnating.

The economic policy caused delays in certain areas of the national economy; delays which began to have a negative effect on social development. The classic example was found in the housing situation. Often the waiting period for an apartment was eight or even ten years, meaning that, in effect, many young people had to give up the idea of starting a family. There is no need to stress that such a situation made people annoyed with the policy of the People's State. Not only were there far too few apartments being built — building standards were incredibly low. The construction of new hospitals, cultural institutions, gymnasiums, etc. were also drastically limited.

The planning methods and the reputation of the national economy left much to be desired. The Party and government leadership, in spite of constant emphasis on the need to modernize, was unable to formulate a general concept of how to direct a modern state. Sudden industrialization had given rise to new economic structures which were being forced into old, "tried-out" organizational frameworks. It must be added that up to 1970 almost all major decisions in the sphere of economic policy were either one-man decisions or were undertaken in an atmosphere which precluded any argument.

The phenomena mentioned above meant that not only the ordinary workingman, but also the Party and government personnel and men of learning and of the arts could not see a future for themselves. Dislike of, and lack of confidence in, the political leadership of the nation increased. Social activity declined; individual dynamism and that of whole social groups was sharply reduced. Individual initiative, one of the main driving forces of social development, was being systematically blocked. In many centres of power, democracy was becoming merely an empty slogan. Routine and bureaucracy had crept into the political parties and social organizations.

It is quite understandable that those phenomena deepened the state of frustration. They gave rise to an ideological vacuum, which in turn was conducive to the emergence of views alien to socialism and Polish *raison d'état*. The political life of the nation became uncertain and full of surprises. Various immature or already dated ideas began to appear — ideas such as the emphasis on Poland's heroic past. During this period, a political observer could well have come away with the feeling that some people considered this constant reference to the past as an effective cure for all the ills then besetting Poland.

These, then, were the trials and experiences to which the citizens of People's Poland were subjected in those years. It was during that time that the citizens collected observations which bred in them a mistrust of any governing group.

Given the situation described above, the demonstrations on the coast appear as the logical result of a certain process. They did not surprise astute observers of Poland. It was well known that the policies of the leaders were building up a store of dynamite, and that it would take a mere spark to cause an explosion. This spark turned out to be the increase in the price of food, brought in two weeks before the Christmas holiday. When the subject "December events" comes up in conversation, visiting foreigners usually ask what the reasons were for the decision and why it was brought into effect at just that time. It seems that the decision was a logical consequence of the policies realized in the latter half of the 1960's. Theoretically speaking, the decision symbolized the apogee of the puritanical concept of socialism. This concept was represented in the Polish Party by the generation of the leading team, which had matured politically in the 1930's. At that time, this generation had adopted a view of socialism from which it did not want to, or else was unable to, depart in the 1960's. It was inevitable that this view would at some point clash dramatically with society's concept of the subject and form of modern socialism. The time and place of the clash was incidental.

It is significant that the policies of the Party and the government (formulated under the overwhelming influence of the First Secretary of the Central Committee of PUWP, Władysław Gomułka) were criticized in such a drastic manner by workers who, materially and culturally, stood at the forefront of the Polish working class. The determination with which the dockyard workers acted, and the demands made by them, show that it was not merely a matter of protest against the increase in prices. The working class on the coast was protesting against the political course which had led to the events before December. The shipyard workers were demanding only that a new policy be adopted which would open broad and feasible prospects for the millions of people in our country. The demands of the demonstrating workers were exclusively socialist in character.

* * *

This fact certainly helped the new leadership in drawing up a programme which boldly and bravely pointed at the weaknesses in Poland, and which equally boldly outlined ways of emerging from the political crisis. The programme, whose individual elements we shall consider later, was drawn up and presented to the nation first at the VIII Plenary Session of the Central Committee (6-7 February 1971) and then at the VI Congress of the PUWP (December 1971). The programme is characterized by a concrete formulation of the issues and problems; it does not contain empty and unnecessary words. An analysis of that programme allows us to remark that December 1970 was undoubtedly a turning point in the post-war history of Poland. The programme formulated by the Party after that time also became the basis for actions aimed at restoring Polish confidence in the political and economic leadership. Today, with the perspective gained by almost two years, one can classify these actions, divide them into stages, and discern the main themes.

In the first half of 1971, the Party and government leadership concentrated their efforts almost exclusively on the elimination of the causes which bred political and economic instability. The numerous strikes, including the so-called second Szczecin strike and the strike of the textile workers in Łódź, were clear examples of the lack of stability and of continuing social tensions. The return of food prices to those in effect prior to 14 December 1970 should be considered as one of the most important moves in the early period. The decision contributed considerably to restoring calm. This period also saw the first serious corrections in the system of wages, with special attention paid to the lowest income groups. Government and trade organizations brought about substantial corrections in the sphere of supplying the market with consumer goods. The import of these articles was considerably increased.

How can one characterize the essence of the economic policy carried into effect in the first half of 1971 and in the following months? It seems to have been based upon a relaxation of the restrictions which had been forced upon this policy in past years. Experience shows that this method brings concrete, exceedingly positive results. This, of course, does not mean that our economy is not still in need of basic reforms, especially in the field of management.

In attempting to grasp the most characteristic quality of the post-December policy, one ought to look for it primarily in the psychological sphere. The leadership of the Party began to make efforts aimed at convincing public opinion that the basic object of the Party is man and his needs today, as well as those he will voice tomorrow and the day after tomorrow. An aim thus formulated is certainly no revelation, but one should bear in mind that, in the pre-December period, Polish society was not convinced that such a goal was visible to the people responsible for the development of the nation. The popular slogan, "everything by people, for people," which appeared in 1971 could, of course, only be accepted positively by the masses in the event of its being supported by concrete moves.

The main force in restoring the confidence of the people in the country's leadership was, and remains, the Party. Action takes place on two levels — the personal and the politico-organizational. Considerable personnel changes were introduced in 1971 in many important positions within the Party and the government. People who did not possess the confidence of the masses, who were bureaucrats, inefficient organizers, etc., were dismissed. New people appeared in many responsible positions: they were recruited primarily from the post-war generation, extremely well educated, dynamic, full of initiative.

The style of the Party's work also began to undergo change. The leaders of the PUWP brought in a permanent method of seeking the opinion of the people concerning more serious problems through the mass media: The Party and government leaders' proposals are discussed in the press, on radio and on television and the public is requested to make known its views. The Party, in attempting to increase efficiency in the work of the national administration, abolished several thousand past decisions and decrees during 1971. Rules which had been characterized by a mistrust of the citizen were removed and the stiff regulations concerning tourism were relaxed.

In its efforts to limit as much as possible the margin of error in decisions, the leadership of the Party raised the rank and improved the role of experts in economic and community life. It is now regular practice for the leaders of the Party and the government to consult the opinions of the experts. It was the experts who were entrusted with the task of preparing a report on the state of education. They were also entrusted with the presentation of proposals concerning the modernization of the systems of management and of the general direction of the nation. For six months, two hundred experts were engaged in an enormous task. They carried out a critical analysis of problems existing in Polish life, and formulated definite proposals. Many of these have been already brought into the programme of action presented at the VI Congress; others are awaiting realization.

The new style of the Party's work was immediately and positively noted by the entire nation. This was for two reasons: first, it was a new phenomenon in Poland, and secondly, the internal life of the Party, its style and its methods have a direct influence on the functioning of the machinery of state. It is an undeniable fact that there exists a close link between, for example, democracy in the Party and democracy in the nation. It is thus understandable that everything that takes place within the Party is carefully observed by all of society.

* * *

Nearly two years' experience of our policy shows that, above all, further improvements in the standard of efficiency of the Party's methods are required in order to minimize the distance separating us from the highly developed nations. Too much of a routine bureaucratic approach to both people and problems is still in evidence in the daily activities of the Party, the force which delineates the main directions of the nation's development. We possess a progressive programme, but there are still too many Party members who do not deserve to be called progressive individuals. The leadership of the Party is aware of these problems and is striving to solve them.

Long-term aims have by now been formulated. Leading circles in the Party were fully aware of the need for a complex programme of action: on the one hand, guaranteeing the nation the maximum development possible in the economic sphere, and on the other hand, ensuring a constant strengthening of the nation and the Party. The thesis of the unity of social and economic tasks became the starting point in the elaboration of the programme of action. In the past this unity had been brutally violated, resulting in enormous social harm. In the programme submitted by the Party, the economic concepts were adapted to Polish needs and possibilities; activity in the area of social policy is being similarly adapted.

The programme presented at the VI Congress of the PUWP takes into consideration all of these principles. It suggests to Polish society that it actively join in in the realization of difficult, and often complicated, tasks. The programme states that we shall be consuming the fruit of this activity immediately, since the centre of concern is not an abstract human being, but real people and their needs.

It is impossible to discuss in a brief outline all the important aims and proposals included in the programme. In order to give an idea of the subject, however, a few of the major proposals shall be mentioned. A leading place must be given to the tasks of increasing the standard of living and of modernizing industry, and to those aimed at updating the system of planning and management. The programme also points out the necessity of correcting as soon as possible the current lack of housing. After the Congress, the *Sejm*, on the initiative of the PUWP, passed a twenty-year programme of housing construction. In relation to the present housing situation, this programme foresees the building of a second Poland in the course of the next twenty years. Plans are being realized concerning the production of an inexpensive car, awaited by millions of Poles, and the construction of autoroutes has been started. In accordance with the ideas and proposals included in the programme, concrete steps are also being taken to realize the principles of socialist democracy.

On the second anniversary of the December events, one must answer two questions: Where does Poland find itself now? How has the Party availed itself of this two-year period? We can say with a clear conscience that, irrespective of the weaknesses appearing in our activities, the Polish Party has not been idle. The Party forced itself to make an enormous effort to understand the complexities of social development. It gave the masses a convincing reply to the question of what the chances are of quickly eliminating the accumulated delays, and of thus rapidly improving the material and cultural well-being of the working masses. Polish society today possesses a perspective; this in itself has brought about extremely positive effects.

January 1971 marked the beginning of another Five Year Plan of Poland's socio-economic development. The results of the first two years of the plan encourage optimism. The dynamism of economic development has been greater than expected, and better results than were planned have been achieved in all spheres: in production, in the increase in the standard of living, in consumption, in agricultural production, in real wages, and in the solution of many pressing social issues (old age pensions, retirement pensions, sickness benefits, etc). In many instances, these results have surpassed all expectations.

The post-December development of Poland has shown that our nation has at its disposal immense material and spiritual reserves. The heart of the matter lay in finding the key which would open the door to these treasures. After December 1970, this key was found. The Party will retain this key and will be able to make effective use of it only as long as it does not lose its creative dynamism and its constructive criticism. Nothing as yet points out to the fact that the leading circles in the Party and its numerous active members are ready to rest on their laurels; it is too early for that.

In the spring of 1971 in one of my articles I wrote that the Polish nation reacted to the events on the coast with sadness and pain, and had granted the new leadership its confidence "on credit," on the condition that promises made in December be fulfilled. The experiences of the last two years permit the following observation: Due to the consistent realization of these promises, the conditional confidence has been replaced by an authentic one. This is an enormous success for Polish socialism. Its further development and new successes depend upon the extent to which the Party will be able to face the complicated problems presented to us every day by the constantly changing reality- in Poland and that around us.

Political Change Under Gierek

VINCENT C. CHRYPIŃSKI

On 14 December 1970 dock and shipyard workers of Gdańsk started riots which rapidly spread to other coastal cities and came close to engulfing the entire country. The Communist regime of Poland has never had to face a movement of civic protest on this scale, and it resorted to exceptional measures to contain it. At one stage, the police and army were given orders to shoot. The causes of this civil strife cannot be reviewed here,[1] but it is obvious that the unrest manifested a significant erosion of support once enjoyed by the Gomułka regime. It is worth repeating that at the centre of the trouble was the proletariat, the class in whose name the Party claimed to rule and whose interests supposedly it was to protect.

The climax of the crisis was reached with the dramatic transfer of leadership to Edward Gierek on 20 December 1970. The ouster of Gomułka and his closest associates (Kliszko, Spychalski and Strzelecki) from the Politbureau, while certainly an outcome of a power struggle at the top,[2] served as a manoeuvre to appease an angry populace. Gomułka and Company, the chief architects of the "mistakes," were sacrificed as scapegoats to rescue the ruling elite and to save the myth that the "system is good, only the people are bad."

The reshuffling in the Politbureau was accompanied by a number of economic concessions to the population in order to strengthen the effect of personal changes and to curb the workers' unrest. The measures achieved their immediate objective: they put an end to violence. The termination of open rebellion, while easing the stress on the new team, did not resolve the problems they had to face. Not the least of these was the task of readjusting the balance of power in the new ruling group.

Gierek had been cautious in consolidating his position, but ultimately he succeeded in overthrowing not only former supporters of Gomułka (Loga-Sowiński, Kociołek, Cyrankiewicz and Jędrychowski ousted from

---

[1] For an evaluation see V. C. Chrypiński, "Poland," in *The Communist States in Disarray, 1965-1971*, Adam Bromke and Teresa Rakowska-Harmstone, eds. (Minneapolis: University of Minnesota Press, 1972), pp. 95-120. See also Adam Bromke, "Beyond the Gomulka Era," *Foreign Affairs*, April 1971.

[2] Zygmunt Bauman, "Twenty Years After: The Crisis of Soviet Type Systems," *Problems of Communism*, XX, No. 6 (Nov.-Dec. 1971), 46.

the Politbureau, and Starewicz from the Secretariat), but other actual and potential rivals as well. Perhaps most significant was the defeat of Mieczysław Moczar, the leader of the so-called "partisans," who in the 1960's had been the second most prominent figure (after Gomułka) on the Polish political stage. Gierek chipped away at his standing in piecemeal fashion. At first he was stripped of his Secretariat duties as an overseer of the security apparatus, then demoted to the politically insignificant post of Chairman of the Supreme Chamber of Control, and later was forced to resign altogether from the Secretariat. At the VI Party Congress, in December 1971, he was dropped from the Politbureau, and finally, in May, removed from the chairmanship of the large veterans' organization, ZBOWiD. In other shake-ups, in December 1971 and March 1972, Stefan Olszowski and Józef Tejchma, while remaining in the Politbureau, were transferred from the Party Secretariat to the Council of Ministers.

The demotions and transfers opened the way for the introduction of new men in leading organs of the Party. As might be expected, Gierek used his powers as First Secretary to extend his influence. The number of Central Committee members elected at the VI Party Congress in December 1971 was raised from eighty-seven to one hundred fifteen, and the number of candidate members from ninety-one to ninety-three. Of the one hundred fifteen members, only forty-nine (i.e., 37.4 per cent) remained from the previous Central Committee. Among the candidate members the turnover was even higher since sixty-eight (i.e., 73 per cent) of them were newly elected.[3] In many instances the elevations were traceable to earlier association with Gierek (e.g., Drożdż and Lejczak), or were accorded to people whose major leap in the Party hierarchy took place under Gierek's tutelage (e.g., twelve voivodship secretaries). The new members represented a certain variety of political viewpoints, but on the whole they were more attuned to Gierek's style and to policies he promoted. This was clearly demonstrated in the subsequent selection of top Party leaders.

The two leading Party bodies, the Politbureau and the Secretariat, were also slightly enlarged and are presently composed of twenty men. Allowing for dual membership, of which there are six cases, there are fifteen Politbureau positions (including four deputy members) and

---

[3] Ewa Celt, "The New Central Committee of the PUWP," *RFE, Poland/23* (1 August 1972), p. 2.

eleven members of the Secretariat, of whom eight are secretaries. Of these twenty topmost leaders, only seven were in the Gomułka elite (Gierek, Jagielski, Jaroszewicz, Kruczek, Olszowski, Szydlak and Tejchma), while the rest have risen to the highest echelons of Party leadership under Gierek's patronage. The nucleus of the entire group consists of those individuals who are full Politbureau members and also occupy posts in the Secretariat (Gierek, Babiuch, Szlachcic and Szydlak). Interestingly, all of them demonstrate evident similarities of background and experience. In addition, all were at some time associated with Gierek's Silesia.

Gierek proved himself quite adept at partisan manoeuvring. The changes he engineered not only strengthened his hand, but also led to the creation of a more cohesive and better ruling team. Its members are, on the whole, relatively youthful (with the average age of the entire group below fifty) and well educated (five have PhD's, eight have M.A.'s, three hold various other academic degrees, and the remaining four have studied for at least two years at Party colleges). All of them are specialists in certain areas of Party (fourteen) or government work, and all were exposed to foreign experience, including seventeen who have visited non-Communist countries on one or more occasions. The longest exposure to other systems was experienced by Gierek, who lived for more than twenty years in Western Europe, and Zdzisław Grudzień, Candidate Member of the Politbureau, who was born in France and returned to Poland at the age of twenty-two.

In matters of policy — although a spectrum of attitudes may be found among the leaders, ranging from the conservative approach of Kruczek to the more liberal tendency of Tejchma — the members of the leading Party bodies exhibit no significant differences in their philosophy or strategy.[4] As a group they might be dubbed "pragmatists," whose primary interest lies in the building of socialism not through revolutionary measures and sharpening of social conflicts, but through improvements in the living standards of the population.[5] Consequently, their first priority is the betterment of the Polish economy. In this respect they give less consideration to the ideological aspects than to everyday practical issues. Naturally, they are bound by the prerequisites

---

[4] Adam Bromke, "A New Political Style," *Problems of Communism*, XXI, No. 5 (Sept.-Oct. 1972), 1-19.

[5] Jan Szydlak, "Głowne zadania w pracy ideowo-wychowawczej," *Nowe Drogi*, No. 7 (July 1972), p. 44.

of Marxism-Leninism and their posture does not imply criticism of the political system, but rather reflects their desire to increase its efficiency. Similarly, their attitudes toward the Soviet Union are marked not by the quasi-religious zealotry of early Communists, but by the sound recognition of geopolitical realities.

More should be known about relationships within the top Party forum before expressing judgement as to the extent of Gierek's control over the new leadership. It would appear, however, that his dominance is well established and there is, at present, no competitor on the horizon to offer a serious challenge to his position. Nearly every statement of his colleagues contains some reference to the First Secretary, and — what is more important — he obviously has a decisive voice in the crucial field of personnel policy. The recent appointment of another of his Silesian protégés, Maciej Szczepański, to head Polish Radio and T.V. (a highly important instrument of ruling) is an outstanding example of Gierek's influence. The stability of the current situation is enhanced by an absence of manifested differences, which in the past polarized the ruling group into a variety of conflict-prone coteries. Thus, there are no more distinctions between "young" and "old," "partisans" and "Muscovites," Jewish and non-Jewish, etc. elements which previously had offered potential grounds for factional infighting. There is no doubt that the memory of December 1970 also increases the consolidation of the ruling structure.

Yet, after all this has been said, caution is still advisable in adopting a static view of the Polish elite. Needless to say, not all of its members share identical views on tactical approaches to problems of socio-economic development and political rule. As long as Gierek's tactics work, success will cement the unity of the ruling group. It is, however, quite conceivable that in the future, difficulties, especially in the economic sphere, may appear and expose belligerent inner opposition. It is also possible that in times to come some ambitious men may raise pretensions to leadership. For understandable reasons individual aspirations are not amenable to investigation. The evidence in this area is too scanty to do anything more than draw attention to the fact that the potential for personal clashes does exist, despite the placid facade of a relatively homogenous leadership. The very fact that a number of top officials demonstrated the ability for political machinations indicates that any presumption of unflinching loyalties would be misplaced. If, when, and how their predilections 'may be translated into actual power play must remain a matter of conjecture.

The reshuffling at the top was accompanied by concerted efforts to revitalize the Party which after the December debacle was in a state of paralysis. As might be expected, the greatest thrust was directed toward Party cadres whose middle- and lower-level elements were slow in adjusting themselves to the policies and styles of the new leadership. Some of the recalcitrant *apparatchiks*, including twelve voivodship secretaries, were replaced by new men, and the rest whipped up to a better implementation of decisions from above and to a more vigorous exercise of the "leading role" of the Party.[6] The principle itself was refurbished and strongly reaffirmed.[7]

The leadership also began to cleanse the Party down to its base and to tighten discipline among rank and file members. The operation was started in early 1971 and took a form of mass "verification" of membership cards and of individual talks, especially with Party activists, comprising about one-third of the entire membership, i.e., around 750,000 persons. By August of 1971, interviews had been conducted with about 1,200,000 members and reached over 91 per cent of basic Party units.[8] Ostensibly, the purpose of the screening was to find out more about people assigned to important administrative and economic positions and to determine whether the tasks given to them were compatible with their abilities. In practice, it resulted in personnel changes in various posts, and even in expulsions from the Party. In 1971 alone, close to 100,000 persons were removed from the Party rolls. The purge continued well into 1972, but in June of that year Gierek indicated that it might be drawing to a close.[9]

In order to rally the general membership to loyal support, the leaders greatly intensified the ideological campaign. In May 1971 the Secretariat issued special directives on the subject, outlining the main principles and methods of theoretical schooling. The fact that a leading

---

[6] See series of articles in *Nowe Drogi*, opened by Zygmunt Stępień, "Węzłowe problemy polityki kadrowej," No. 4 (April 1972), pp. 40-51.

[7] Tadeusz M. Jaroszewski, "Kierownicza rola partii etc.," *Nowe Drogi*, No. 3 (March 1971), pp. 107-22; also Adam Łopatka, "Kierownicza rola partii wobec państwa," *Ideologia i Polityka*, No. 5 (May 1971), pp. 15-24.

[8] Edward Babiuch, "O niektórych problemach rozwoju i umacniania partii," *Nowe Drogi*, No. 9 (September 1971), p. 8.

[9] Speech at a conference of the Party's central actif, *Nowe Drogi*, No. 7 (July 1972), p. 58.

Party body addressed itself to the problem — in previous years it had been handled by the Central Committee Ideological Commission — signified the importance attached to the issue. A new program of training was prepared,[10] and a number of textbooks and other teaching materials were issued to instructors whose number and quality were carefully evaluated. In short, the Party was readied from top to bottom to implement Gierek's policies.

* * *

Naturally, Gierek could not wait until the Party was in shape to carry out his plans. He had to act immediately. He did, and his initial performance was highly effective, for he not only restored order in the Baltic provinces and got the strikers back to work, but also gained the support — if only qualified — of other segments of the population. The methods he used were of the "carrot and stick" variety. On one hand, he offered the masses significant improvement in economic well-being (higher wages, lower food prices, end of compulsory deliveries) and made some concessions to popular sentiments (rebuilding of the old royal castle in Warsaw, compromises with the Catholic church). On the other hand, he served a stern reminder that the Party would not hesitate to use force to protect its position (harsh sentences for the brothers Czuma and others).

While Gierek's stopgap measures were, on the whole, very effective, he was unable — or unwilling — to produce more fundamental social and economic reforms. The only significant exception was in the agricultural policy, where a number of decisions (e.g., the settlement of property rights) represented a basic change in the attitudes of Communist rulers and demonstrated their appreciation of agricultural problems.

There is no doubt whatsoever that Gierek's ambitious plans for improving the living standards of the population depend upon the performance of Polish agriculture. This point of view is backed by enough evidence to have gained acceptance among the ruling elite. Nobody, after all, would deny that in Poland foodstuffs form a very high percentage of general consumption and that every increase in income, especially among lower-paid groups, results in a disproportionate rise in demands for victuals. Since the 1971-75 economic plan envisages

---

[10] "Tematyka szkolenia partyjnego w roku 1971/72," *Ideologia i Polityka*, No. 7-8 (July-August 1971), pp. 179-181.

a 17-18 per cent growth of real wages, the food supply during this period must expand by about 35 per cent. Consequently, the global production of Polish agriculture should be enlarged by about 18-21 per cent.[11]

In attempting to reach this high level of development — higher than ever before — Gierek once again revealed his pragmatic approach to current issues. Instead of resorting to emotional appeals or to administrative means, he decided to induce individual farmers (who manage about 83 per cent of all usable land) to greater productivity by granting them better security and profitability in pursuing their occupation.

For a variety of reasons, born out of World War II and post-war political transformations, about one million farmers held and cultivated their farms without any formal certification of their property rights. Although this state of affairs was well known to the authorities, they decided to keep the problem unsettled. Probably they had hoped that collectivization would solve the whole issue. Gierek put an end to this disturbing situation, and by virtue of laws passed by the *Sejm* on 26 October 1971 these farmers became rightful owners of their land. The same bills also eliminated most of the impediments in regard to the sale and inheritance of land. Another important move in the direction of increasing the farmers' security was the inclusion, since 1 January 1972, of the inhabitants of villages (altogether about 6.5 million persons) in the national health service. Although there exist serious doubts whether the present medical network is ready for the task, the grant plays a very important psychological role by doing away with unjust discrimination against the rural populace.

A second group of measures was oriented toward increasing the profitability of farming. Here, the new leadership made a great many sensible decisions, including a fundamental revision of Gomułka's autarchic policy in grain production, which in the past had barred the way to an increase in animal breeding. In addition, the new authorities abolished compulsory deliveries, raised the procurement prices, changed the taxation system, facilitated credit as well as purchases of fodder, fertilizers and other necessary supplies, etc., giving farmers a material interest in increasing agricultural output.

Although it is still too early to speak definitely about the improvements brought about by the new policies, the authorities seem to be

---

[11] Kazimierz Barcikowski, "Aktualne problemy polityki rolnej," *Nowe Drogi*, No. 11 (November 1971), p. 4.

satisfied with the progress. Speaking at the Party conference in June 1972, the Chairman of the Planning Commission, Jagielski, stated that "auspicious tendencies, especially in animal production" are well established and that expected deliveries of milk and meat products are expected to be higher than originally anticipated. He also announced that procurement payments to farmers had increased 40 per cent.[12]

It appears that the innovations introduced by Gierek have produced desirable results. Naturally, future developments will be conditioned by the actions of the Party leadership. If the present policy is only a temporary concession forced upon the ruling group by the shortage of food on the market, one might expect a sudden reversal and new attempts for socializing agricultural production. Constant talk about "creating conditions for socialist transformation of the country-side" surely indicates this possibility. The farmers are aware of it and fear that the officials "will think again and will slow down good changes."[13] If, however, all these official and unofficial statements are just lip service paid to old shibboleths, individual farming will for many years provide food for the Polish people.

*   *   *

The quest for a fresh approach with which Gierek is attempting to solve agricultural problems, was not paralleled in other areas of the national economy. The crucial issue of economic reform was generally ignored, although it is obvious that the ambitious social goal for 1971-75 (jobs for 1.8 million people, 1,080,000 new apartments, 600,000 automobiles) cannot be achieved without far-reaching changes in the entire system of planning and management. Thus far, however, the new leadership has not unveiled any far-reaching concepts. Instead, it has concentrated on frequent reiteration of already known objectives and on urgent appeals for greater productivity. No wonder that some chronic ills of the economy still remain and that people are afraid of a new crisis that might destroy the precarious stabilization. Recently announced price increases for postal and telephone services started wide-spread rumours that the cost of foodstuffs would follow the trend. In order to defuse the tension, the leaders decided, on 30 October, to prolong the present price

---

[12] Mieczysław Jagielski, "Aktualne zadania gospodarcze etc.," *Nowe Drogi*, No. 7 (July 1972), pp. 26-27.

[13] "Poland: Important Changes in Agricultural Policy," *The Week in East Europe*, RFE, No. 72/21 (18-24 May 1972), p. 9.

freeze for basic food articles until the end of 1973. A similar observation of ambiguity may be applied to other fields as well. Trade unions are a case in point.

During the December crisis, the workers challenged the authorities with two kinds of demands: more material benefits and more voice in the management of production. Once again — and quite rightly — a movement for better living conditions was coupled with a desire for some kind of political protection. The "Strikers' Postulates," put forward by the dockers of Szczecin, strongly pressed for "immediate and legal elections" in trade unions and workers' councils.[14] Gierek sensed the urgency of the requests and incorporated them into a solemn declaration of intent with these words: "I promise you that we will go much further. I promise you that we will go further in respect to bringing the workers to rule the country — you can be sure of this."[15] More assurances of the same type, this time specifically referring to the internal democratization of trade unions, were given by Gierek at the VIII Central Committee Plenum in February 1971.

But the promises were never implemented. The Congress of Trade Unions, which was to take place about the middle of 1971, was postponed until 13 November 1972. In the meantime the vast organization, with about 20,000 paid functionaries, was assigned to the most reactionary member of the Politbureau, Władysław Kruczek. No wonder that the primary task of the unions was — as before — to mobilize and control workers in the interest of maximizing economic production. Such a position was based on old arguments claiming that it was incorrect to ascribe to trade unions the traditional role of major defender of workers' interests, since in a socialist state this concern rests with the entire political system. The unions act only as "transmission belts" between the "vanguard" and the masses.[16]

It would be unfair, however, to stop at that and leave readers with the impression that all demands of the rioting workers went unheeded. As indicated above, many of the 1970 grievances were settled by executive fiat, and many others were to be taken care of in the future. The food prices were frozen at the pre-December level, and real wages increased

---

[14] Ewa Wacowska, ed., *Rewolta szczecińska i jej znaczenie* (Paris: Instytut Literacki, 1971), p. 26.

[15] *Ibid.*, pp. 35-6.

[16] Krysztof Ostrowski, *Rola związków zawodowych w polskim systemie politycznym*, Ch. II (Wrocław: Ossolineum, 1970).

by about 5 per cent, with another 3.5 per cent rise provided for 1972. At the same time a greater concern was shown by the new leadership to working and living conditions of the workers. Improvements in medical care, in a bonus system, more flexible holiday timing and other similar measures were widely introduced. A particularly significant step was made with the elimination of systematic shortages of food supplies, especially meat, whose consumption per capita increased by 3.4 kilogrammes in 1971, and was expected to rise by another 2 kilogrammes in 1972.[17] Also important was the improvement, though not very extensive, in housing conditions. In 1971, the non-rural population received 132,000 new dwellings, and a promise that in the future at least 50 per cent of all units constructed by building cooperatives would be assigned to workers.[18]

Nor is this all. Throughout 1971, the press and radio frequently reported the dismissals of managers as well as court actions started against administrators of state-owned enterprises in defence of workers' interests. While the ousters of officials under pressure from the workers were rather rare (most notorious being that of a director and his deputy in Wrocław), the lawsuits were very frequent, especially among the miners who number more than 420,000. The interesting aspect of these litigations is that they were not phoney plays set up by the authorities, but real complaints by injured parties who claimed violations of work contracts, unfair distribution of bonuses, managerial arrogance, etc. It was estimated that in 80 per cent of all cases the courts decided in favour of the aggrieved individuals.[19] Although it is tempting to speculate about the long-term implications of these occurrences, the fact remains that they actually help to quiet particular sources of dissatisfaction before they present a broader challenge to the ruling elite.

*   *   *

There is another area besides the unions where hopeful expectations have not been met: participation in the political process. On several occasions Gierek and other leaders expressed their desire to enlarge political opportunities for people outside of the Party. Since at the

---

[17] An interview with the Minister of Food Industry, Emil Kołodziej, *Polish Perspectives*, XV, No. 4 (April 1972).

[18] "Aktualne zagadnienia budownictwa mieszkaniowego," Special Supplement to *Gospodarka i administracja terenowa*, No. 3 (March 1972), pp. 7 and 9.

[19] *The Week in East Europe*, RFE, No. 72/38 (14-20 September 1972), pp. 13-14.

same time they announced their intention to strengthen the *Sejm*, the people hoped for liberalization of tight rules governing the elections. This was not done, however, and the electoral contest of March 1972 was run according to old rules. As before, the candidates were carefully screened, only one list was presented to the electorate, and the voters were given the same limited opportunity to express their preferences. As a result, the new parliament compared unfavourably with that which was elected in 1957, following the assumption of power by Gomułka. The number of unaffiliated deputies dropped from sixty-two to forty-nine, and Catholic clubs decreased from twelve to ten. Even if one takes into consideration the understandable rush to get popular confirmation of Gierek's intra-Party victory and the desire to remove the last vestiges of Gomułka's influence as soon as possible, the outcome was very disappointing.

Nor is there any persuasive proof of concrete measures to enhance the powers of the *Sejm*. Eloquent appeals to make it a "truly supreme organ of state authority"[20] found only partial application in practice. It is true that in comparison to the immediate pre-Gierek period, the number of speeches on the floor doubled, and the frequency of ministerial appearances (including that of the Prime Minister) trebled; it is true that the committees intensified their activities, held 517 meetings and passed 542 "desiderata"; it is even true that the deputies raised thirty-four interpellations (only one before) on a variety of subjects. But this is still not enough to claim that the "new quality of functioning" has been achieved.[21] Rather, it seems that an earlier observation of this writer still holds true, and that "the role of the *Sejm* amounts only to the 'petrification,' in the form of laws, of the Party directives."[22]

As if to counterbalance the lack of concrete changes in the system of representation, the new leadership made some friendly gestures toward the non-Party people. An independent Deputy, Mrs. Halina Skibniewska, was elected a Deputy Speaker of the *Sejm*, and an unaffiliated man, Professor Janusz Groszkowski, was designated by the National Unity Front as the chairman of its Presidium. About the same time,

---

[20] Andrzej Burda, "Instytucjonalne gwarancje praworządnosci etc.," *Państwo i Prawo*, CCVI, No. 8-9 (Aug.-Sept. 1971), 228.

[21] Kazimiérz Kąkol, "W kręgu problemów socjalistycznego parlamentaryzmu," *Prawo i Życie*, No. 1 (9 January 1972), p. 1.

[22] Vincent C. Chrypiński, "Poland's Parliamentary Committees," *East Europe*, 14, No. 1 (January 1965), 18.

the authorities made available regular information on Party and government activities. Short bulletins are now issued after each Politbureau meeting, and a government spokesman acts as a regular liaison between the Council of Ministers and the Press. Naturally, information available to the public is carefully selected.

A trait of dichotomy — though of a somewhat different kind — was also discernible in the state-church field. Immediately upon taking over, the new leadership expressed the desire to seek a normalization of strained relations with the Catholic church. The Episcopate responded positively, and early in March 1971 a meeting took place between Premier Jaroszewicz and Cardinal Wyszyński. Little was divulged of what went on behind closed doors, but the conference was followed by other consultations and by friendly gestures on both sides. The government made a number of concessions to the Church, including the transfer of title deeds to formerly German sacral buildings in territories gained by Poland as the result of World War II, the repeal of regulations demanding full inventories of church properties, and the issuance of building permits for the construction of new places of worship. A Catholic bishop was invited to become a member of the committee for the reconstruction of the Warsaw royal castle, and in October 1971, the authorities helped in organizing an airlift of a mass pilgrimage to Rome for the beatification of the Polish martyr of Auschwitz, Father Maksymilian Kolbe. Simultaneously, the new Party leaders sought to gain support in the lay Catholic circles by praising believers and non-believers as the co-authors of past achievements, by stressing equal opportunities for members of both groups, and by appealing to all for equal efforts in building the future of socialist Poland.

Parallel to these developments, the government established contacts with the Vatican aimed at the resumption of diplomatic ties. The negotiations are, as yet, not completed, but rumours claim that a Polish-Vatican agreement is close to conclusion. The optimism is mainly attributable to steps taken by the Vatican. Doubtless, most important was the June 1972 decision to acknowledge the Polish ecclesiastical administration in the so-called Recovered Territories. The Holy See hesitated for a long time to recognize Polish sovereignty over these lands, but the ratification of the treaty between Poland and West Germany cleared previous doubts. Equally significant for cooling emotional strains was another act of the Vatican. On 26 October 1972, Secretary of State Cardinal Villot notified Kazimierz Papee, Ambassador of the Polish exile government in London, that the Holy See considered his mission as terminated.

And yet everything is not quite as well as it seems. The incident of Zbrosza Duża, where in March 1972 militiamen demolished a provisional chapel, indicates that a real "normalization" of state-church relations still awaits the resolution of several important issues. The building of churches is among the most complicated and conducive to conflicts, since the government claims for itself the right to decide whether new constructions are justified by "religious social needs."[23] Also still outstanding is the complex question of the religious instruction of children, alleviation of taxes, and a score of others.

It is sometimes explained that the tenuous state-church relationship in Poland is due to the attitudes and actions of lower Party or administrative officials as yet not affected by the more liberal decisions coming from above. Perhaps it is true. It is hard to believe, however, that the elevation of Bolesław Piasecki (the leader of "progressive Catholics," who under all circumstances sides with the regime) to the membership of the State Council could be done without the approval of the Party leadership. The same might be said about the exclusion of Tadeusz Mazowiecki, a member of the Church-approved *Znak* group, from the roster of candidates for the *Sejm* elections.

*　　*　　*

The narration of Gierek's ambivalence requires an inquiry into its possible causes. The truth — or something near to it — is perhaps impossible, but several explanations seem to be quite plausible. Admittedly, Gierek is an intelligent and sensitive man, with a highly developed instinct for survival and a realistic grasp of matters close to him. There would seem little doubt that the traumatic experience of the Soviet intervention in Czechoslovakia in 1968 taught him an unforgettable lesson. It is not altogether impossible that he intends to introduce necessary reforms without any flourish of fanfares and without raising undue excitement at home and abroad. In fact, Jan Szydlak, a Politbureau member, indicated this tendency when during the *Sejm* debate on the economic plan for 1972 he said: "*Partial overhauls* (italics mine, V.C.) of planning and management will be introduced in 1972."[24] It is con-

---

[23] Alexander Skarżyński, "Principles of the Normalization of Church-State Relations," *Catholic Life in Poland*, No. 10/70 (October 1971), p. 35.
[24] *Polish Perspectives*, XV, No. 4 (April 1972), 52.

ceivable that many aspects of these "overhauls" have not yet been decided upon since commissions of experts, engaged to study and make proposals, have not completed their work. Naturally, Gierek also may fear the disturbances that accompany the process of liberalization and doubt his and the Party's ability to control its course.

It is no exaggeration to say that the most salient feature of the Gierek era is the ambiguity of domestic politics. The December riots triggered demands for a total renovation of relations between the rulers and the ruled, for an authentic popular participation in the process of governing and for a genuine expansion of political freedoms. But they also sensitized old reflexes of the authoritarian regime fearful about a loss of hegemony. Hence the duality of official policy. On one hand, the satisfaction of specific grievances, the opening of new participatory channels, the pruning of *nomenclatura* lists and appeals to all — including hitherto mistrusted "believers" and "non-Party people" — for collaboration; on the other, disregard of demands presenting a broader challenge of the decision-makers, the determination to preserve intact the Party's "leading role," and resolute attempts to keep the fundamental style of ruling free of any institutional or procedural restraints.

Such varied approaches reinforce the view that Gierek's rule is grounded in paradox. The two principles that chiefly account for this are mutually antagonistic because where real participation increases, the authoritarian rule must retreat, and vice versa. This is not to say that some sensible compromise cannot be tried. But in Poland the prospect is not very palatable to the ruling elite and thus future tensions are quite likely.

At present, Gierek maintains an equilibrium by conscious efforts to satisfy the material needs of the population. His policy is based on an apparent conviction that the December 1970 riots resulted from the privations of everyday life. Be this as it may, one must admit that Gierek managed to soften some of the most drastic irritants (e.g., meat supply) and started to work on problems whose solution would require more time (e.g., housing).

The preoccupation with the standard of living was supplemented by attempts to remove the causes of some specific discriminations. The achievements, though not complete, are worth recognition. As evidence one should mention again the extension of health insurance to the rural population as well as pending labour legislation that should eliminate the distinction, in terminology and in privileges, between "workers" and "office employees."

The new leadership also made several unorthodox moves in order to improve the performance of Party and government organs. By a 1971 decision, the thirty big firms gained the right to by-pass organizational channels and to enjoy direct access to the Central Committee and to Gierek personally. And the reform of Poland's administration, starting 1 January 1973 at the village level, indicates a change for the better in the country's government as a whole.

But if Gierek has largely, or even partly, resolved various problems at hand, he has progressed against many obstacles. Paradoxical as it may sound, not a few of them were caused by dogmatic elements within the Party and state apparatuses, which are often occupied by bureaucrats without necessary initiative and often without competence. The impediments are especially noticeable at the middle level, thus forming a barrier between the top leadership and the local cadres. Gierek is aware of the situation, and on several occasions gave vent to his worries, as, for instance, in the speech of 27 September 1971 in which he complained that many *apparatchiks* are just unable to work well.

Undoubtedly, Gierek is right. The myth of the ruling proletariat and the circumstances in which the Communists took over the government in Poland led to the recruitment of early cadres not from those best qualified, but from those who promised the greatest loyalty. While this situation could be justified in the past, its continuation nowadays cannot be vindicated and must result in harmful consequences. But Gierek is unable, or unwilling, to break with the past practice decisively. Thus, instead of firing unproductive people and sending them into retirement, he still favours the "carousel of cadres," which continues fruitless and expensive experimentation.

While no one should underestimate the evil capacity of the Party-government apparatus, more important for the future is the attitude of the general population. Surely, without massive popular support and involvement Gierek's chances for success are slim, especially in regard to his program of economic recovery. The majority of the people, however, seem to have no great confidence in the prospects,[25] with most of their doubts centring precisely on the country's economy. The pes-

---

[25] "Polish Confidence in Gierek," *The Week in East Europe*, RFE, No. 72/2 (6-12 Jan. 1972), Special Report.

simism manifests itself in a variety of ways: young people express little interest in ideological questions[26] or drift into a "parasitic existence"; intellectuals engage in discussions about "A Feeling of Success or a Feeling of Defeat?" or republish lamentations from the last Gomułka years;[27] workers start skipping their jobs.[28]

Gierek is attempting to remedy the ills by a peculiar "strategy of development,"[29] which emphasizes improved efficiency of performance of the new decision-making structure, and with appeals to the nationalistic sentiments of the population. It is doubtful, however, whether this strategy will work in the long run. More than efficient authoritarianism and psychic stimuli, Poland needs a basic form of the centralized bureaucratic system of government. It is not enough to introduce technical rearrangements of the economy, or to admit more people to sharing the symbols of authority. Real reform requires a break with old authoritarian tendencies and the acceptance of a genuine democratic participation with individuals convinced of their influence on the decision makers. Will Gierek do it? The chances are problematic.

[26] Bronisław Gołębiowski, "Młode pokolenie o sobie i swoich dążeniach," *Nowe Drogi*, No. 10 (October 1972), p. 147.

[27] E. G. Jan Szczepański, *Rozważania o Rzeczypospolitej* (Warsaw: P.I.W., 1971).

[28] According to *The Economist* (25 Nov.-1 Dec. 1972), p. 48, absenteeism in Polish factories increased, in 1971, by 4.6 per cent.

[29] Zwi Gitelman, "Beyond Leninism: Political Developments in Eastern Europe," *Newsletter on Comparative Studies of Communism*, V, No. 3 (May 1972), 41.

The Strategy of Development and Gierek's Economic Manoeuvre

ZBIGNIEW M. FALLENBUCHL

In the first half of the 1960's in Poland, as in all countries of Eastern Europe including the Soviet Union, it was increasingly more difficult to maintain the rates of economic growth at a high level. It became clear that the strategy of economic development, which had been introduced at the beginning of the 1950's, could not be expected to give satisfactory results in the future.[1] This was, using the current Marxist terminology, the strategy of extensive development. The process of growth depended on the increases in the quantity of the factors of production, particularly labour and capital. The increases in labour productivity were achieved as the result of heavy investment outlays. The ratio of capital to labour was increasing and the productivity of capital declining.

The system of economic management and planning, which after the short-lived period (after October 1956) of searching for new solutions returned to the traditional Soviet model with only relatively few modifications, was well geared to this strategy. Highly centralized and depending mainly on administrative commands, it could enforce a high degree of the mobilization of resources and their concentration in a few selected areas. It was not, however, able to ensure their efficient use.[2]

At the same time the entire industrial structure was also adjusted to the extensive pattern of growth.[3] It had been created during the Stalinist industrialization drive during the early 1950's, when an attempt was made to establish a basic industrial complex, composed above all of heavy industry, which would be capable of supporting the future

---

[1] A. Karpiński, J. Pajestka, "Ogólne zagadnienia polityki rozwoju ekonomicznego" in *Polityka gospodarcza Polski Ludowej*, Part I, 3rd ed. (Warsaw, 1965), pp. 41-43.

[2] Z. M. Fallenbuchl, "How Does the Soviet Economy Function Without a Free Market? *The Queen's Quarterly*, No. 4 (1965), reprinted in M. Bornstein and D. F. Fusfeld, *The Soviet Economy* (Homewood, Ill., 1966 and 1970).

[3] A. Karpiński, "Z perspektywy 23 lat kilka refleksji na temat rozwoju gospodarczego i polityki gospodarczej Polski Ludowej," *Gospodarka planowa*, No. 7 (1968), p. 2.

investment effort with the output of domestically produced producers' goods. A relatively high degree of self sufficiency was then desired not only for the completed industrial structure, but also during the process of constructing it.[4] This was the concept of building the industrial complex "from below," starting with the basic materials, such as steel and some "heavy" chemicals, in order to produce machines, equipment, and some intermediate products which would enable the production of as many consumption goods as possible within the country at some distant future date.[5]

The big investment effort of the years 1950-1953 caused not only severe disturbances in the process of growth but also some serious disproportions in the economy.[6] Because of the excessively wide investment front the length of the construction of individual projects increased and some projects were not completed on time. In industry only 131 new enterprises out of the planned 210 were actually completed as envisaged during the Six Year Plan period (1950-1955).[7] A large volume of resources was "frozen" in the unfinished investments. In order not to waste these resources, in the years 1956-60 the main stress was put on the completion of the previously started investment projects and on the elimination of the disproportions which had been created during the Six Year Plan. These efforts resulted in the petrification of the newly developed industrial structure. In the years 1959-1965 the main stress was on the expansion of the domestic fuel and raw material base, and during the Second Five Year Plan (1961-1965) more than 35 per cent of all industrial investments were allocated for this purpose. At the same time it became clear that in order to expand agricultural production it was necessary to increase the output of fertilizers and other chemicals, as well as agricultural machines.[8] The concentration of a very large proportion of investments in the most capital-intensive branches of industry left very few resources not only for the expansion

[4] R. Wilczewski, *Środki trwałe we powojennym przemyśle polskim* (Warsaw, 1971), p. 145.

[5] K. Secomski, "Polityka ekonomiczna w minionym 25-leciu," *Gospodarka planowa*, No. 7 (1969), p. 4.

[6] A. Karpiński, *Zagadnienia socjalistycznej industrializacji Polski* (Warsaw, 1958), pp. 69-100; S. Kuziński, *O czynnikach wzrostu gospodarczego Polski Ludowej* (Warsaw, 1962), pp. 71-72.

[7] Karpiński, *Zagadnienia* . . . , p. 69.

[8] Karpiński, Pajestka, "Ogólne . . . ," p. 23; G.U.S., *Struktura* . . . , p. 22.

of the production of consumption goods and housing, but also for the modernization of machines and equipment throughout the economy.[9]

The Third Five Year Plan (1966-1970) was expected to increase the role of intensive sources of growth. Four groups of changes were mentioned as pre-requisites: (1) changes in the structure of production; (2) the acceleration of technological progress; (3) the increased role of international trade and of the international specialization and cooperation; and (4) improvements in the system of management and planning.[10] However, none of these changes were introduced wholeheartedly and none advanced very far. As a result, time was wasted and the plan for the years 1966-1970, instead of introducing the intensive pattern of growth, further strengthened the adverse effects of the extensive pattern.

Despite the relatively high rates of growth the situation deteriorated during the second half of the 1960's. The planned rate of growth of national income (Marxist definition) of 6.0 per cent was achieved, but it was possible to do so only by increasing the rate of growth of investment from 6.8 per cent, as it had been planned, to 8.4 per cent. While the long-run declining trend in national income continued, labour productivity outside agriculture declined despite great increases in the capital stock: the average rates of growth of national income were 8.6 in 1951-55, 6.5 per cent in 1956-60, 6.2 per cent in 1961-65 and 6.0 per cent in 1966-70; the average rates of growth of capital stock at the 1960 prices increased from 2.2 per cent in 1951-55 to 3.2 per cent in 1956-60, 3.6 per cent in 1961-65 and 5.0 per cent in 1966-70; the average rate of growth of labour productivity, as measured by material production outside agriculture at the 1961 prices, increased from 4.2 per cent in 1951-55 to 5.7 per cent, but then declined to 4.8 per cent in 1961-65 and 3.8 per cent in 1966-70. The capital intensity of the process of growth increased rapidly. The average ratio of the share of accumulation in national income to the rate of growth of national income increased from 2.76 in 1951-55, to 3.44 in 1956-60, 4.11 in 1961-65 and 4.75 in 1966-70.[11]

---

[9] A. Karpiński, *Polityka uprzemysłowienia Polski w latach 1958-1968* (Warsaw, 1969), pp. 394, 400; J. Pajestka, "Z problemów wzrostu i podziału dochodu narodowego w Polsce Ludowej," *Gospodarka planowa*, No. 5 (1964), p. 4.

[10] Karpiński, Pajestka, "Ogólne . . . ," pp. 42-46.

[11] The author's own calculations based on G.U.S., *Rocznik statystyczny 1971* (Warsaw, 1971), pp. 2-3.

Despite all the measures envisaged in the Third Five Year Plan,[12] this was clearly the extensive pattern of growth, with three important consequences:

(1) If the rates of growth of national income and industrial production depend on increases in the labour force rather than in productivity, a decline in the rate of growth of the labour force must result in deceleration of growth.

(2) With capital intensity growing more rapidly than national income, increases in the share of accumulation in national income are necessary in order to maintain the rates of growth of national income; this policy has some definite limitations.

(3) During the period of rapid increase in employment outside agriculture, the productivity of labour is kept low because of the large inflow of labour, mostly unskilled, and real wages cannot increase. When the rates of growth of national income cannot be increased, or even kept at the same level other than by increasing the share of accumulation, current consumption can only increase by less than the rate of growth of national income. In both cases there is no room for more significant improvements in the standard of living.

There is still no shortage of labour in Poland and this situation is expected to continue for another decade. The number of people at the working age increased from 14.5 million in 1950 to 16.3 million in 1960 and 18.3 million in 1970, or by approximately 12 per cent in both decades. The number of people at the working age is expected to increase during the 1970's by 3.1 million, or 17 per cent, and reach 21.4 million in 1980. After this sharp acceleration, the growth will be very moderate during the following decade. The number of people at the working age is expected to increase by only 1.2 million, or less than 6 per cent, to 22.6 million in 1990.[13] During the 1970's increases in the labour force can, therefore, still provide an important source of growth. However, the transfer of labour from agriculture to non-agricultural occupations has now become a relatively capital intensive process:

---

[12] E. Szyr, "O większą efektywność inwestycji przemysłowych," *Nowe Drogi*, No. 5 (1966); The Political Bureau of the Central Committee of the Polish United Workers' Party, Głowne kierunki usprawnienia procesu inwestycyjnego, *ibid.*; K. Secomski, "Problematyka planu pięcioletniego na lata 1966-1970" in *Polityka gospodarcza Polski Ludowej*, pp. 105-125.

[13] K. Secomski, "Polska — 1970," *Gospodarka planowa* No. 11 (1971), p. 643.

The possibility of maintaining high rates of economic growth with the help of large-scale increases in employment has been reduced because of the exhaustion of those reserves of labour which could be utilized without greater difficulty. An important factor is also a reduction in the effectiveness of this policy. The transfer of labour has recently been taking place at the increasing social cost (the cost of urbanization, of the mechanization of agriculture, and so on), the declining economic and social effects and the adverse results in the field of income distribution. . . . In the early period an increase in employment outside agriculture did not require large investments for urbanization (a considerable number of the newly employed workers commuted to work or found some temporary accommodation) or large investments for the purpose of releasing labour from agriculture. At the same time new jobs outside agriculture were created at the cost of relatively low average outlays on directly productive investments because it was possible to increase the degree of utilization of existing productive capacities. In more recent years the situation has, however, changed. The outlays on all three types of investments, which are necessary in order to effect the transfer of one employee from agriculture to non-agricultural activities, have been increasing. . . . The transfer of population from agriculture to non-agricultural activities has become a very important factor behind the increasing capital intensity of the process of economic development in our country.[14]

With the rapidly increasing capital intensity, the rates of growth of the national income can only be kept at a relatively high rate by increasing the share of accumulation in the national income. The average share of accumulation (Marxist definition) increased from 23.7 per cent in 1951-55 and 22.7 per cent in 1956-60 to 25.5 per cent in 1961-65 and 28.0 per cent in 1966-70. It was 28.8 per cent in 1968, 28.2 per cent in 1970, and 28.0 per cent in 1966. These figures can only be compared with the share of accumulation of 28.5 per cent which was enforced in 1953, the last year of the great Stalinist industrialization drive. The share of accumulation of this size must be very close to the absolute maximum and it was probably excessively large at least in the 1966-1970 period, as it had been in 1953.[15] Once the maximum

[14] J. Pajestka, "Niektóre problemy strategii rozwoju ekonomicznego Polski Ludowej," *Nowe Drogi*, No. 7 (1969), pp. 23-24.

[15] Z. M. Fallenbuchl, "Investment Policy for Economic Development: Some Lessons of the Communist Experience," *The Canadian Journal of Economics and Political Science*, No. 1 (1963).

has been reached a reduction in capital intensity becomes the only way in which growth can be accelerated.

The impact of the extensive pattern of growth on the standard of living can be illustrated by the reduction in the share of the population's individual expenditures on consumption in national income. The average share declined from 69.6 per cent in 1951-55 and 69.8 per cent in 1956-60 to 65.8 per cent in 1961-65 and 62.4 per cent in 1966-70. The movement of the rates of growth of real wages in industry is also revealing. There was a decline in real wages in the years 1950-1953; the average rate at that time was −3.7 per cent. The decline was followed by a period of relatively rapid increases and the average rate of real industrial wages was 8.3 per cent between 1954 and 1958. The rate of growth declined, however, at the beginning of a new investment drive. The average rate was only 1.5 per cent in 1959-65 and 1.9 per cent in 1966-70. During this last five-year period the highest annual increases took place in 1966 and 1967 and the lowest in 1970.[16]

In this situation some drastic changes became absolutely necessary. They were not, however, easy to introduce because in Poland, as in all other East European countries, a vicious circle appeared.[17] In order to effect a switch from the extensive to the intensive pattern of growth, it is necessary to reform the system of management and planning, to introduce more realistic prices and more effective incentives. The economic reforms, as the Hungarian experience indicates, require at first a reduction in the investment drive in order to remove, or at least to reduce, the pressures which are usually associated with very high levels of investment activity. In addition, it is necessary to prepare some reserves, to reduce the degree to which the market is a sellers' market and to secure sufficient supplies of consumption goods, without which even the theoretically best system of incentives becomes useless.

At the same time it is impossible to introduce the intensive pattern of growth without some changes in the industrial structure which is geared to the extensive pattern and prevents, therefore, the introduction of a more intensive pattern in the short run. The relative importance of those branches of industry in which increases in labour productivity can only be achieved by heavy investment outlays must be reduced. In

---

[16] A. Karpiński, "Strategia rozwoju gospodarczego Polski w ujęciu perspektywicznym," *Gospodarka planowa*, No. 7 (1971), p. 394 and G.U.S. *Rocznik Statystyczny 1971* (Warsaw, 1971), pp. 17 and 588.

[17] J. Kleer, *Przez sześć krajów* (Warsaw, 1967), p. 167.

order to take full advantage of the economies of scale, the structure must be adjusted to the requirements of internation specialization and trade. The enterprises and industries which produce at limited scale, particularly those which persistently operate at a loss and have to be financed by the economy as a whole, should be reorganized or eliminated. Old and inefficient equipment and machines must be replaced and modern processes introduced.[18]

A reconstruction of this nature requires a large volume of investment. In order to effect it within a relatively short period of time and at a significant scale, it is necessary to increase again the share of accumulation in national income. A new investment drive is, however, incompatible with the requirement of reducing the pressures within the economy and increasing consumption, without which a successful reform cannot be introduced. Hence the vicious circle.[19]

The V Party Congress, which was held in 1968, attempted to find the ways and means of breaking away from this circle. The priority was given to structural changes, even if it meant maintaining or increasing the investment drive. Some modifications of the system of management and planning were envisaged but no large-scale reform.[20] The main stress was put on "selective development," i.e., on the development of certain selected branches of industry and commodities in which Poland was expected to become one of the major producers and the exports were to reach the highest world standards in respect of quality. This approach, basically undoubtedly sound, was spoiled by, first of all, selecting an excessively large number of industries and enterprises which were designated as specializing in production for export.[21] An

---

[18] J. Kleer, "Wybierać to znaczy rozwijać i ograniczać, *Polityka*, No. 19 (1969); G.U.S., *Struktura gospodarki narodowej* (Warsaw, 1969), pp. 122-123.

[19] Z. M. Fallenbuchl, "From the Extensive to the Intensive Strategy of Economic Development in the Soviet Union and Eastern Europe"; a paper presented at the Annual Meeting of the Michigan Academy of Arts and Sciences and Letters in April 1970, *Working Papers of the Department of Economics, University of Windsor* (mimeographed).

[20] "Problemy gospodarcze w tezach na V Zjazd PZPR," *Gospodarka planowa*, No. 10 (1968), pp. 1-4; "Doskonalenie struktury i organizacji gospodarki narodowej w świetle debaty zjazdowej," *Gospodarka planowa*, No. 1 (1969), pp. 1-6; J. Pajestka, "Proces doskonalenia systemu funkcjonowania gospodarki socjalistycznej w Polsce," *Gospodarka planowa*, No. 11 (1970), pp. 1-3.

[21] "Zakłady przemysłowe i branże specjalizujące się w produkcji eksportowej," *Handel zagraniczny*, No. 9 (1968), pp. 335-336; U. Płowiec, "Kierunki doskonalenia handlu zagranicznego w świetle tez na V Zjazd," *Handel zagraniczny*, No. 10 (1968), pp. 368-370.

even more important drawback was that the selection was made on the basis of the decisions of the central authorities, without taking into consideration the signals of the international market and true costs. The existing system of management and planning, together with distorted prices, made it impossible to make a fully rational choice. This was, in effect, the same method of the centrally planned structural changes in favour of industries which the planners regarded as "progressive" and, therefore, desirable, as that which had been applied in the past. In the early 1950's the industries producing producers' goods were regarded as "progressive" and their development at any cost and without regard for the comparative advantage of the country was accepted on an *a priori* basis as always conducive to rapid economic development. As has been pointed out by a Polish economist, priority was given in the majority of the socialist countries at that time to the development of the metallurgical, fuel, heavy machinery and transportation equipment industries which had been "leading" industries in the 1930's but lost that role in the 1940's and 1950's.[22] In the years 1959-1965 it was the domestic fuel and raw materials base which was selected for the priority development, again without regard for costs and comparative advantage. For the 1970's the envisaged structural strategy would take into consideration the factors which accelerate growth: "the strategy of developing the branches of industry which are based on the most advanced science, which are characterized by the most dynamic technological changes and which bring the greatest economic effects."[23] The petrochemical, electronic, precision and some other branches of the electromachine and chemical groups of industries were classified on an *a priori* basis as the most progressive industries.

In addition, the possibility of restricting consumption in order to increase the investment drive was overestimated, while the role of international trade in adjusting the structure of supply to the structure of demand and in the process of effecting the desired changes in the industrial structure was underestimated.[24]

The riots in December 1970 made it impossible to introduce the selective development at the envisaged speed and scale within the plan period

[22] L. Zacher, "Struktury dynamizujące postęp techniczny," *Gospodarka planowa*, No. 9 (1970), p. 24.
[23] Pajestka, "Niektóre problemy strategii . . . ," p. 29.
[24] H. Kosk, "Stare i nowe w handlu zagranicznym," *Życie gospodarcze*, No. 7 (1972).

1970-75. At first it even looked as though they had completely destroyed the possibility of breaking away from the vicious circle at the time when the situation remaining within the circle spelled complete stagnation.

* * *

In this situation Gierek's economic manoeuvre is extremely interesting. First of all, because of the explosive atmosphere, it was necessary to effect some immediate improvements in the standard of living. The wages and the pensions for the lowest income brackets were raised. The unpopular new system of incentive bonuses was withdrawn. The increase in the prices of food was cancelled, while the reduction in the prices of consumption goods of industrial origin was maintained.

These short-run remedies were fortified by formulating a doctrine which stated that "consumption must become the engine of growth" and that priority should be given to the requirements of social development over those of economic growth. The increase in consumption was supplemented by a number of measures in the field of social policy and by attempts to involve wider segments of the population in the process of economic decision-making.[25] As a result of all these measures, a considerable degree of support for the newly introduced economic policy was obtained.

In agriculture compulsory deliveries were abolished. The policy of restricting the development of livestock production, in order to reduce the import of grain, was changed. The prices of meat and milk were raised. There was an immediate expansion in the supply of various commodities required by the agricultural machines. An important social measure was the extension of medical insurance to cover the rural population.

These measures resulted in a substantial rise in the incomes of the rural population, which had lagged behind those of the non-agricultural population, with the dimension of the lag increasing during the 1960's.[26] It came as a surprise to the government that the farmers did not spend the increase in their incomes on consumption and the so-called "non-

---

[25] "Program na miarę społecznych możliwości i potrzeb," *Gospodarka planowa*, No. 17 (1971); W. Dudziński, "Konsumpcja a tempo rozwoju," *Życie gospodarcze*, No. 6 (1971).

[26] Z. M. Fallenbuchl, "The Impact of the Development Strategy on Urbanization: Poland 1950-1970," a paper presented at the Conference on Comparative Urban and Grants Economics at the University of Augsburg, F.R. of Germany, August 1972.

productive investment," i.e., housing, as should have happened in accordance with one of the fundamental dogmas of the Communist political economy on which the policies towards agriculture have always been based in Poland, in the Soviet Union, and in all other socialist countries in Eastern Europe.[27]

Directly productive investments in agriculture increased by 15 per cent in 1971, including a 45 per cent increase in the purchases of agricultural machines, while the expenditures of the agricultural population on consumption and "non-productive investment" grew by only 7 per cent. The "rural pressure" upon the market for consumption goods, the dangers which had been so much feared by the government, did not materialize.[28]

In industry a serious effort was made to reduce the discrepancy between the rates of growth of the production of producers' goods (Group A) and consumption goods (Group B). In Poland it is hardly possible to increase the rate of growth of consumption and real wages without increasing the rate of growth of the production of consumption goods. A country can, of course, specialize in the export of producers' goods and can import, in exchange, consumption goods. It is, however, doubtful that Poland has a comparative advantage in this field of specialization at present. A policy of this nature would, therefore, create a tremendous burden for the economy and would have an adverse effect on the rates of growth. As has been pointed out by a Polish economist, "the past experience shows clearly that more rapid increases in real wages were only achieved at the time when the pace of production of the so-called Group B was either higher or only slightly lower than that of the production of the commodities of Group A, which are mainly produced by the heavy industry."[29] During the whole post-war period the rate of growth of Group B exceeded the rate of growth of Group A only during the Three Year Plan of construction in 1947-49 and during the deceleration in the pace of industrialization in 1954-58. The Third Five Year Plan (1966-70) assumed a reduction in the difference between the two rates. While the actual rates were 9.8 per cent for Group A and 6.5 per cent for Group B during the period 1961-65, the

---

[27] Z. M. Fallenbuchl, "Collectivization and Economic Development," *The Canadian Journal of Economics and Political Science*, No. 1 (1967).
[28] G. Pisarski, "Rezultaty polityki aktywnej," *Życie gospodarcze*, No. 7 (1972).
[29] Karpiński, "Strategia rozwoju . . . ," p. 394.

planned rates for 1966-70 were expected to be 8.6 per cent and 6.6 per cent. However, the actual rates were 9.3 and 6.6 per cent and the difference between them instead of declining from 3.3 per cent points to 2.0 per cent points, decreased to only 2.7.

This was the usual pattern. The rates of growth of Group A tended to exceed the planned rates, while the rates of growth of Group B were either just equal to the targets or were below them. Whenever the plan was in danger, some additional resources were rushed for the expansion of the output of investment goods. In this way the volume of investment could increase. The planned targets in the priority sectors were saved by greater investment outlays and an increase in capital intensity. There was also present the effect of the deformity in the industrial structure. As the result of a prolonged period of priority in respect of investment allocations, heavy industry had some unused productive capacity and the output could expand there more rapidly than in the neglected light and foodstuff industries. These two industries usually had insufficient investment allocations. Their capital stock was more fully utilized, sometimes beyond the optimum level. It was old and often technologically backward, and decapitalization, i.e., non-replacement of the used-up capital, was "not a rare phenomenon."[30]

In 1971 the rate of growth of Group A was reduced to 8.5 per cent, while the rate of growth of Group B was maintained at approximately the same level as before (7 per cent)[31] and the difference between the two rates was, therefore, reduced to 1.5 per cent points. This objective has, however, been achieved not by a significant increase in the rate of production of consumption goods but by a reduction in the rate of production of producers' goods. A greater narrowing of the gap between the two rates, and especially an increase in the rate of consumption goods, was impossible without some changes in the industrial structure, which required investment and could not be made in the short run.[32] The adjustment of the structure of supply to the structure of demand could, therefore, be achieved only through international trade.

For this reason, the import of agricultural and industrial consumption goods was increased. The export of foodstuffs and of some consumption

[30] S. Marciniak, *Struktura produkcji a dynamika wzrostu gospodarczego* (Warsaw, 1972), pp. 76-77.

[31] Pisarski, "Rezultaty . . . ."

[32] Z. M. Fallenbuchl, "Some Structural Aspects of the Soviet-type Investment Policy," *Soviet Studies*, No. 4 (1965).

goods of industrial origin was reduced. There was, therefore, an increase in the supply of these products for the domestic market. This willingness to utilize imports to a greater extent than before in order to bridge the gap between demand and supply and to adjust the structure of supply was a particularly important feature of the policy which was introduced after December 1970. In 1971 imports increased by approximately 12 per cent, while exports increased by 9 per cent and the allocated national income increased by more than the produced income (8 per cent as compared with 7.5 per cent).

The policy of increasing imports more rapidly than exports was facilitated by three factors which were utilized for this purpose in 1971: (1) it was possible to increase imports from some socialist countries where Poland had accumulated some balances of assets in the previous years; (2) the import of consumption goods from the non-socialist developing countries expanded as the result of the acceptance of those commodities in repayment of the previously granted credits or in exchange for the currently exported producers' goods; (3) there was a favourable situation in the world market with respect to Poland's exports and imports. These three factors will not all be present in the future and the policy of increasing the import of consumption goods may not be feasible in the long run.[33] However, if the domestic production of these commodities accelerates, imports may become less crucial for maintaining domestic equilibrium.

At the same time attempts were made to increase domestic production by increasing the efforts of the workers and management and by better utilization of existing productive capacity. The restrictions on the expansion of employment and on the increase in wages by the enterprises were substantially reduced in order to ensure greater flexibility. The managers were authorized to add to their staff or to offer higher wages when an increase in production for the domestic market or for export was expected to result. A very strict control over employment and wages had been one of the taboos of central planning in Poland and the decision to reduce controls required considerable courage on behalf of the leaders. Again, the results of liberalization did not confirm the fears. Employment in the socialist sector of the economy increased only slightly

---

[33] "Rozwój obrotów z zagranicą w roku 1971," *Życie gospodarcze*, No. 13 (1972); W. Rux, "Polski handel zagraniczny w pięcioleciu 1971-75," *Gospodarka planowa*, No. 2 (1972).

above the planned rate (3.4 per cent as compared with 3.0 per cent). The wage increases were associated with increases in production, the value of which amounted to 29 billion złoty.

There was a considerably larger increase in real wages than in the previous years. The increase in 1971 was 5.3 per cent as compared with the average of 1.8 per cent for the previous ten years. It was higher than the planned 4.2 per cent.[34] The disposable income of the population increased by 60 billion złoty, or by 10 per cent. However, again contrary to the previously unquestioned dogma, the purchases of goods increased by only 8.5 per cent and the purchases of services by 5.0 per cent. On the other hand, the savings deposits and cash reserves of the population increased by about 15 per cent. In this way the equilibrium in the market for consumption goods and services was maintained.

The overall results in 1971 were moderate. The national income increased by 7.5 per cent which was above the average of 6.0 per cent for 1966-70. Gross industrial production (a rather useless indicator because it includes a lot of double-counting) was 8.1 per cent, slightly below the average for 1966-70 which was 8.2 per cent. Agricultural production increased by 3.7 per cent and was, therefore, above the average of 1.9 per cent for 1966-70, but this was by no means a spectacular increase as it was lower than the increases which had been achieved in 1966 (5.2 per cent) and 1968 (4.4 per cent) during the previous five-year period.

The most important and disappointing feature, however, was the lack of acceleration in the growth of labour productivity in industry. The increase in 1971 was 4.9 per cent — equal to the average increase for 1966-70. It was below the increases which had been achieved in the three last years of the Third Five Year Plan: 5.5 per cent in 1968, 5.2 per cent in 1969, and 6.7 per cent in 1970.[35] These results show that increases in labour productivity are not particularly affected by appeals to the workers in order to induce them to work harder even when these appeals are met, as to a considerable extent they were in 1971, with a rather favourable reception. These increases depend less on the psychological factors than on changes in the industrial structure, modernization of equipment and machines, as well as on improvements

[34] "Niektóre dane o bieżącej sytuacji gospodarczej i przebiegu realizacji planu," *Gospodarka planowa*, No. 12 (1971), p. 764.

[35] S. Chełstowski, "Wysoka stawka," *Życie gospodarcze*, No. 6 (1972) and G.U.S., *Rocznik statystyczny* 1971, pp. 3, 7, 9, 202.

in the methods of management and planning and the overall efficiency of the economy. It was not, of course, feasible to effect any changes in the industrial structure or to introduce a meaningful economic reform within a brief period of time. So far the government has relied mainly on appeals, on improving the image, and on promises in order to convince the workers (and the entire population) that a fresh start is being made. It has been trying to make alive again the expectations and hopes which had appeared after October 1956 and were subsequently frustrated by the return to the old economic strategy and system.

The success of the new policy in the long run will undoubtedly depend on the developments within the next few years and, for this reason, the plan for 1971-75 assumes particular importance. By a decree of the Council of Ministers of 3 February 1971 a Commission and seventeen committees of experts were formed in order to effect the reappraisal of the Fourth Five Year Plan.

The main feature of the revised plan is an attempt to achieve two objectives simultaneously: a substantial immediate improvement in the standard of living and an increase in national income which would exceed the increases achieved during the previous ten years. It envisages an increase in the national income of between 38 and 39 per cent over the plan period, as compared with 34 per cent and 35 per cent increases in 1966-70 and 1961-65. The increase in real wages is planned to reach 17 to 18 per cent, as compared with less than 10 per cent and less than 8 per cent in 1966-70 and 1961-65. The accelerated growth of the purchasing power in the hands of population is expected to be met by (1) an improved supply of consumption goods of industrial production from both domestic production and import; (2) an increase in foodstuffs which is expected to be induced by new agricultural policies; and (3) an accelerated housing programme.[36]

It is expected that the planned increase in the standard of living should provide an effective stimulus to increase productivity which would, in turn, result in higher rates of growth of output and income.[37]

In order to reduce capital intensity a special stress is put on increasing output without new investment. Not a new measure, it has been attempted very often before without much success. It was supposed

---

[36] K. Secomski, "Five Year Plan 1971-75," *Polish Perspectives*, No. 9 (1971), p. 5.

[37] *Ibid.*, p. 6.

to play an important role in the Second Five Year Plan (1961-65). The Political Bureau's paper on investment policy, presented at the V Plenary Meeting of the Central Committee in 1960, states that "the reserves of increased production in existing enterprises are not fully utilized and, for this reason, special attention should be given to this problem" as this is where "the largest possibilities of reducing investment outlays are present."[38] Its importance was also stressed in the Third Five Year Plan (1965-70). The Political Bureau's paper, presented at the VI Plenary meeting of the Central Committee in 1966, mentions "excessive requests for investment allocations, which are presented by the production units of the socialist economy, branches of industry and national councils of all levels" and points out that "it has been shown that the programme of new investments is often prepared without linking it with the analysis of existing reserves of productive capacities and without sufficient attention being paid to the possibility of replacing expensive investment outlays on the construction of new plants, with prolonged gestation period, by investments on the modernization and expansion of existing plants, which are usually cheaper and give results in a shorter period of time."[39]

In the past all efforts to accelerate growth by the use of "non-investment methods" failed and, on the contrary, the rates of growth depended to an increasing extent on the investment effort, as was pointed out by the V Party Congress and the subsequent discussions by the Central Committee.[40]

In the light of past experience it is questionable whether this measure should, indeed, be referred to as one of "the new elements in the policy for drawing out growth potential"[41] and whether it could be expected to be more successful this time, unless some far-reaching changes are made in respect to the development strategy, modification of the industrial structure and, above all, economic reform. At the moment the main stress seems to be on simply increasing the number of shifts. This

---

[38] Political Bureau of the Central Committee, "O zadaniach w dziedzinie inwestycji w latach 1961-65," *Nowe Drogi*, No. 7 (1960), pp. 43-45.

[39] Political Bureau of the Central Committee, "Główne kierunki usprawnienia procesu investycyjnego," p. 135.

[40] Political Bureau of the Central Committee, "Metody opracowania planu na lata 1971-1975 oraz zadania w dziedzinie zwiększenia efektywności inwestycji w gospodarce narodowej," *Nowe Drogi*, No. 7 (1969), pp. 5-7.

[41] Secomski, "Five Year Plan 1971-75," p. 7.

policy requires (1) the creation of skilled manpower to staff the second and the third shifts; (2) provision of necessary accommodation for the additional workers; (3) increased supplies of raw materials and power for the enterprises which are expected to increase the number of shifts; and (4) improved cooperation among the enterprises and various branches of industry.[42] Unfortunately, this policy cannot be introduced without substantial investment outlays. It is necessary to invest in housing, generation of power, expansion of the output of raw materials and in increasing the capacity of the transportation system to handle the enlarged volume of traffic per unit of time. Most of these fields are capital intensive with no direct or with delayed productive effects. In effect the economies in the volume of investment may not be as great as they appear at first glance. The plan includes a special investment programme which is geared to the task of increasing the number of shifts in various enterprises and eliminating bottlenecks throughout the economy.[43]

Other measures include attempts to reduce the gestation period of investment, more economical use of materials and power, and investments in scientific research. They were all expected to play a very important role in the Second and Third Five Year Plans and in the original draft of the plan for 1971-75. Again, there is no guarantee that the governments will have more success with them now.

The only important change seems to be in the field of the development strategy and it may easily become the crucial element of the whole plan. The priority of heavy industry is going to be reduced. It has been accepted that, as a Polish economist has stated, "a point has been reached beyond which the continuation of this policy is impossible, as it was clearly demonstrated at the end of 1970 and the beginning of 1971."[44] For this reason, within the first three years there will be a significant shift in priorities towards the production of consumption goods and services in order to provide commodities which are needed to meet the increasing purchasing power in the hands of the population.[45] The essential question is, of course, what will happen afterwards.

---

[42] *Ibid.*, p. 8.
[43] *Ibid.*
[44] Karpiński, "Strategia rozwoju gospodarczego Polski w ujęciu perspektywicznym," p. 394.
[45] Secomski, "Five Year Plan 1971-75," p. 12.

Unlike the measures which were introduced in 1971 as an immediate reaction to the riots, the revised plan for the period up to 1975 is more than just an attempt "to remove, in a short period of time, the accumulated results of the past neglects, but an effort to prepare such structural changes which would allow the country to achieve simultaneously a high degree of the satisfaction of social needs and the dynamic pace of the development of the economy."[46] It seems, therefore, that this time the change in the strategy is regarded as a more permanent modification than the policies of the consolidation and "slow-down" period which followed the excessive pace of industrialization in the early 1950's and the collapse of the Six Year Plan.

The essential part of the modified strategy is the role which is assigned to international trade in the process of development. Trade is expected to make a significant contribution to the supply of consumption goods for the domestic market and to provide machines and equipment for the reconstruction, modernization and expansion of productive capacities throughout the economy. The plan envisages the use of foreign credits from the non-socialist countries to supplement the limited foreign exchange earning power of the export sector.[47] It has been recognized that the realization of the programme of the socio-economic development of the country, which was accepted by the VI Party Congress, requires a new approach to international trade. As Gierek himself pointed out at the Congress, international trade must become an integral part of the economic life of the country and an effective engine of growth.[48] Instead of being simply a measure for removing shortages or reducing surpluses it will be allowed "to influence the directions and the structure, the level and the organization of production, as well as to reduce the social cost of production."[49]

This is a crucial point. It may decide whether the increase in the use of imports, financed by foreign credits, will subsequently be replaced by a forced return to the old policies with strong autarkic tendencies, or

---

[46] S. Chłestowski, "Ofensywa w roku 1972," *Życie gospodarcze*, No. 49 (1971).
[47] "Podstawowe założenia rozwoju gospodarczego Polski w latach 1971-1975," *Gospodarka planowa*, No. 2 (1972), p. 71; H. Kosk, "Handel zagraniczny w planie pięcioletnim," *Życie gospodarcze*, No. 13 (1972).
[48] "Kierunki rozwoju handlu zagranicznego w świetle uchwał VI Zjazdu PZPR," *Handel zagraniczny*, No. 1 (1972), p. 4.
[49] *Ibid.*

whether a new industrial structure will emerge which is well adjusted to the requirements of international specialization and trade.[50]

The appeals for support for the new policy, the references to social needs and the well understood real self-interest can give results in the short run. Credits from the non-socialist countries for the modernization and reconstruction of the industrial structure cannot be obtained in unlimited quantities and sooner or later must be repaid. In trade with the developed non-socialist countries Poland is still mainly the exporter of food and raw materials. The forced expansion in the export of machines and equipment, the products of the priority branches of industry, have encountered considerable obstacles outside the CEMA region. In trade with the advanced countries exports were hampered by an inadequate technological level, the lack of proper marketing, advertising and servicing facilities, and sometimes also by delays in delivery and shortages of spare parts. In trade with the developing countries the main difficulty was the inability to grant sufficiently large credits or unwillingness to expand imports in the face of serious balances of payment difficulties and still strongly entrenched autarkic tendencies. At the same time the traditional markets for the export of consumption goods were lost and the potential of that sector of the economy neglected.[51]

In this situation it is extremely important for Poland to develop the production of some high quality and/or low cost products which could penetrate the markets of the advanced countries. This task would be facilitated by making it possible for Polish industrial enterprises to enter into various arrangements of cooperation, the field in which Poland is far behind other socialist countries, especially Hungary and Rumania.[52]

If export to the West cannot be expanded, the only alternative is further integration of Poland with the CEMA bloc. This would lead to the expansion of trade with other countries of the bloc which would, to a large extent, consist of the exchange of outdated and technologically

---

[50] Z. M. Fallenbuchl, "Growth Through Trade in the Socialist Economies," ed. W. D. G. Hunter, *Papers and Proceedings of the Conference on Current Problems of Socialist Economies* (McMaster University, Hamilton, 1970) (mimeographed).

[51] *Ibid.*

[52] "Sprawozdanie z ogólnopolskiej konferencji na temat: Problemy rozwoju i kierowania handlem zagranicznym," *Handel zagraniczny*, No. 1 (1972), p. 2.

poor machines and equipment. The present practice of obtaining a share of the export market by accepting, in return, imports up to the same total value, both exports and imports calculated at some artificial prices, would be maintained. The tendency to balance not only total trade but also individual groups of commodities on a bilateral basis would remain strong. In this situation statistics would still show high rates of growth of international trade, industrial production and national income. There would, however, be no improvement in the standard of living.[53]

In the long run the success of Gierek's manoeuvre will depend on how determined the present leaders are to introduce and to maintain the new development strategy, to effect the necessary changes in the industrial structure and, above all, how far they are prepared to go in reforming the system of management and planning. So far, although a special joint Party-government commission has been appointed to prepare economic reforms, no significant systemic changes are visible. However, without reforming the system it is doubtful whether the efficiency of the investment and production processes can be increased and whether the structural changes which are effected will be of the sort which will eventually result in significant improvements in the standard of living without reducing the rates of growth of the economy.

[53] Z. M. Fallenbuchl, "The Soviet Union and Eastern Europe: Development and Trade in 1971-75," a paper presented at the Conference "Canada and Eastern Europe" at Carleton University, Ottawa, March 1972.

Polish Foreign Trade: A Retrospective View

WITOLD TRZECIAKOWSKI

Foreign trade in a planned economy must be subordinated to the general strategy of development. In the early stages of Polish economic growth the choice of strategy was relatively simple. In the take-off period the average productivity of labour was low, the share of the industrial sector in total output was negligible, unemployment (together with disguised unemployment in the agricultural sector) was high and there existed a structural disequilibrium between labour resources and available capital. In those circumstances the general strategy called for accelerated industrialization and a high rate of investment. This required the creation of technical capacities for investment and an increase in social savings.

The creation of technical capacity for investment entailed dependence either on domestic production of capital equipment or on imports. The strategy of internal and complex industrialization was selected. Limited export possibilities and general insufficiency of raw materials resulted in channelling of investments to primary sectors (mining, heavy industry, etc.) which are highly capital intensive, where investment has a long gestation period and where new employment is created in the long run. On the other hand, increased social savings required the preparation of a scheme for drawing surplus labour into activity. Employment was raised by various means: by creating cheap new capacities, by increasing the number of shifts, by utilizing obsolete equipment, and by a programme of intensive education and training. All this led to a centralized system of planning and an inward-looking strategy of development. Also in foreign trade detailed and central decisions determined overwhelmingly the shape of foreign trade in those early stages of growth.

For a long time, foreign trade was mainly concerned with supplying the country with factors indispensable for accelerating production: machinery and equipment, industrial semi-products, raw materials and fuels not produced in Poland or produced in insufficient quantities. Foreign trade was regarded as a factor in eliminating "bottle-necks" in production appearing in the process of a quick economic growth. The possible role of foreign trade as a factor in a rational international specialization was not duly appreciated. Imports were restricted to "indispensable imports" only, and exports were conceived as an outlet for surpluses with which to pay for imports. That is why stronger emphasis was given to developing anti-import production than to producing goods for export, as a specialized activity. Consequently industrial production was excessively dispersed and, because of its small scale, its costs were high and its technical level relatively low.

The "inward-looking" character of the Polish strategy of development can be illustrated by Table 1, where the share of our foreign trade in world foreign trade is compared with the share of Polish industrial production in world industrial production in consecutive stages of development.

TABLE 1[1]

The share of main groups of countries and Poland's in world industrial output and world foreign trade in 1950, 1957, 1968, and 1970

Group of Countries	Share in World Industrial Output				Share in World Exports				Ratio of the Share in World Exports to the Share in World Industrial Output			
	1950	1957	1968	1970	1950	1957	1968	1970	1950	1957	1968	1970
Capitalist Developed	74.8	63.9	59.9	58.2	64.8	65.6	70.4	72.6	0.86	1.02	1.17	1.23
Common Market	12.4	13.3	12.7	13.1	17.4	21.2	27.1	28.6	1.40	1.59	2.13	2.18
CEMA	16.6	23.5	30.5	30.9	6.2	8.2	10.7	10.1	0.37	0.34	0.35	0.33
CEMA without USSR	4.9	6.8	8.5	8.6	4.0	4.9	6.2	6.0	0.81	0.72	0.72	0.71
Poland	1.0	1.8	2.3	2.3	1.0	1.0	1.2	1.1	1.0	0.55	0.52	0.50

In 1950 our share in the world trade amounted to 1 per cent, corresponding to our share in world industrial production. In the course of twenty years our industry reached considerable achievements and our

---

[1] Compiled by J. Soldaczuk, "Miejsce handlu zagranicznego w rozwoju gospodarki narodowej," in *Handel Zagraniczny*, 12 (1971).

share in world industrial production rose to 2.3 per cent. In the same period our share in world trade remained almost stagnant (+0.1 per cent). Consequently the ratio of our share in world trade to our share in world industrial production fell from 1 in 1950 to 0.50 in 1970. Also the comparison of the Polish index 0.50 with an analogous index of other People's Democracies places Poland in the last position (GDR 0.63; Czechoslovakia 0.75; Hungary 1.33; Rumania 0.60; Bulgaria 1.00).

The "inward-looking" character of the Polish development may be further illustrated by another index: foreign trade per capita in selected countries in 1970.

TABLE 2[2]

Countries	Foreign Trade Value per capita in $	
	Exports	Imports
Bulgaria	237	212
Czechoslovakia	261	262
G. D. R.	267	276
Hungary	230	229
Poland	109	111
Rumania	92	96
USSR	52	48
France	343	375
Italy	243	281
Federal Republic of Germany	577	499

It can be seen that the gap between Poland and comparable socialist countries as well as developed capitalist countries did not diminish to any significant extent in spite of a favourable rate of growth of industrial output.

With a constant development of the economy and with its growing diversification there occurred important changes in the patterns of growth. From the initial stage of speedy and extensive development of

---

[2] Compiled by the Foreign Trade Research Institute in *Polish Foreign Trade* (Warsaw: Polish Chamber of Commerce, 1972).

a highly autarkic economy Poland went over to a more mature stage of a diversified economy with constantly diminishing reserves of extensive factors of development. Hence the need arose for exploring intensive factors; this meant, first of all, an increase of the share of foreign trade in the national income. This general tendency is illustrated by the following table: first the drastic fall in the take-off period (1950-1967) and then a steady growth in the next decade.

TABLE 3[3]

Per cent ratio of imports and exports to gross national income
(measured in domestic prices)

	Imports	Exports
1950	14.0	15.5
1955-1957	10.0	10.2
1958-1963	17.1	15.4
1964-1968	20.0	18.9

The important change in the strategy of growth is clearly visible if one compares the average rates of growth of national income, industrial output and foreign trade in the consecutive ten-year periods, 1951-1960 and 1961-1970.

TABLE 4[4]

	1951-1960	1961-1970
	Average Annual Rate of Growth	
National Income	7.6	6.1
Industrial Output	13.0	8.5
Exports	5.9	10.4
Imports	8.6	9.5
	Relation of Average Ratio of Growth	
Exports to National Income	0.78	1.70
Exports to Industrial Output	0.45	1.22
Imports to National Income	1.13	1.56
Imports to Industrial Output	0.66	1.12

---

[3] P. Bożyk, B. Wojciechowski, *Handel Zagraniczny Polski 1945-1969* (Warsaw: PWE, 1971), p. 292.
[4] *Polish Foreign Trade* (Warsaw: Polish Chamber of Foreign Trade, 1972), pp. 10, 12, 13.

The growth of foreign trade and of its share in national income was accompanied by a parallel change of the commodity structure of exports and imports. This can be seen in the comparison of the commodity structures of exports and imports for 1957-1965-1970 in Table 5.

TABLE 5
(in %)

Commodity Groups	Share in Exports			Share in Imports		
	1957	1965	1970	1957	1965	1970
Machinery and Equipment	20.0	34.4	38.6	23.8	32.8	36.4
Fuels, Raw Materials, Materials	61.0	35.1	32.5	53.1	47.3	47.8
Agricultural Products	12.6	18.2	13.3	17.4	13.2	9.6
Manufactured Consumer Goods	6.4	12.3	15.6	5.7	6.7	6.2
	100.0	100.0	100.0	100.0	100.0	100.0

After a period of twenty-five years of all-round industrialization and a change in the economic structure from a raw-material-agricultural structure to an industrial-agricultural structure, Poland finds itself at the threshold of a new strategy of its development. In this strategy, the development of a rational, international division of labour based on branches specializing in exports assumes a special significance. To complete the overall view of the Polish foreign trade till 1970, one more cross-section may be needed — the geographical structure of turnovers.

TABLE 6

Group of Countries	Share in Exports			Share in Imports		
	1945-68	1969	1970	1945-68	1969	1970
Socialist	62.0	65.7	63.9	63.6	65.9	68.6
Developed Capitalist	31.3	26.8	28.4	30.3	27.8	25.8
Developing	6.7	7.5	7.7	6.1	6.3	5.6
	100.0	100.0	100.0	100.0	100.0	100.0

In general the geographical structure shows a remarkable stability over the past twenty-five years.

FOREIGN TRADE POLICY UNDER NEW LEADERSHIP

It is quite obvious that any new political and economic leadership cannot implement its new ideas at once. New economic policies have to be translated into long- medium- and short-term plans and changes of the management system must be carefully elaborated. All this requires time. Although it is definitely too early to evaluate the result of foreign trade policies of the new leadership, the following seem possible:

(1) to describe the starting point of the new policy, i.e., foreign trade in 1971;

(2) to discuss new elements in foreign trade policy and strategy;

(3) to present forecasts of foreign trade, actually constructed in Poland.

(1) Foreign Trade in 1971

The overall results in Polish foreign trade in 1971 compared with 1970 are shown in Table 7.

TABLE 7[5]

Groups of Countries	Value Million $		Growth in 1971 compared with 1970 in %
	1970	1971	
Total Exports	3,548	3,874	9.2
Socialist Countries	2,266	2,443	7.8
Capitalist Countries	1,282	1,431	11.6
Total Imports	3,608	4,036	11.9
Socialist Countries	2,473	2,717	9.9
Capitalist Countries	1,135	1,319	16.1

There was a faster growth in turnovers with capitalist than with socialist countries, both in exports and imports. Imports from capitalist countries increased at a rate exceeding more than twice the average annual index of 1966-1970. The share of foreign trade in national income increased. The value of trade exchanges per capita went up from 109 to 118 dollars in exports and from 111 to 123 in imports.

The most important group in Polish exports were goods manufactured by the eletcromechanical industry. The rate of growth in that group amounted to 11.4 per cent as compared with 1970. The share of electro-

---

[5] *Polish Foreign Trade, op. cit.*

mechanical industry products rose from 41.5 to 42.5 per cent. The highest dynamics in exports was characteristic of fuels and energy in 1971. As a result of an increase in the value of exported fuels and power by 22.1 per cent, the share of those commodities in exports came up from 12.5 in 1970 to 14.0 per cent in 1971. The export of agricultural products and foodstuffs decreased by 4.1 per cent below its 1970 level, and its share in total exports fell to 12.7 per cent. In 1971 chemical products achieved a growth rate of nearly 19.0 per cent in exports. Light industry exports increased by 17.6 per cent. The share of each of these exports reached about 9 per cent of total Polish exports.

In Poland's imports electromechanical industry products constituted the most important commodity group and amounted to 36.9 per cent of total imports. The share of metallurgical products amounted to 16.5 per cent; the share of agricultural products and foodstuffs attained 14.9 per cent; and the share of chemical products rose to 11.3 per cent of total imports.

Over 80 per cent of the value of Polish trade exchanges in 1971 went to thirteen main partners. The USSR was the most important trade partner with its share of over one third of Poland's total foreign trade. The other partners were GDR, Czechoslovakia, the F.R.G., Hungary, Great Britain, Italy, the U.S., Bulgaria, France, Yugoslavia, Rumania, and Austria.

(2) New Elements in Foreign Trade Policy and Strategy

The reordering of social and economic priorities, announced in the fall of 1970, had its impact on both the current foreign trade policy and long-term strategy.

The new leadership abandoned the former policy of over-centralization, hampering social initiative at executive levels and leading to a harmful rigidity of the whole functioning of the economy. The first reaction to administrative overcentralization has been a new re-ordering of authority; the administrative decision-making powers of the Central Committee of the Party and functional ministries have been delegated to branch ministries. In turn a portion of authority of branch ministries has been delegated to industrial associations. Also the decision-making power of directors of enterprises has been increased. This process of delegating authority from the centre to lower, mainly intermediary, decision-making levels has been administrative in character and therefore susceptible to later re-centralization tendencies, unless coupled with economic reforms. Hence the new leadership called into existence a mixed Party-government and expert commission for the improvement of the system of management including foreign trade. These problems will be dealt with in the last part of this article.

Foreign trade has played an important role in the implementation of the new policy of the government:

(i) Increased imports of consumer goods have helped in a decisive way in filling the gap between increased demand of the population and insufficient domestic supply. Several restrictions and limitations in imports have been abolished and a basic change of general priorities in favour of consumption has redirected foreign trade reserves available from investment to consumer goods. Thus foreign trade has played a decisive role in keeping the financial balance between incomes and expenditures of the population.

(ii) A new active credit policy, based on economic considerations, has brought an impressive growth in foreign trade with capitalist developed countries, abolishing the former policy of "clear mortgage."

(iii) All central limits for machinery imports from socialist countries have been abolished. Any enterprise can now freely substitute imported machinery for domestic machinery within the general disposable funds for investments.

(iv) Yearly budgetary limits for all the remaining imports have been liberalized: unused import limits from one year (1971) increase automatically the disposable import fund of the next year (1972). This measure leads to a more rational import policy of domestic buyers, avoiding budgetary spending for the sake of fulfilling the import fund of a given year.

(v) A new, much more elastic policy in the sphere of effectiveness control has been introduced. All purely administrative limits have disappeared and have been replaced by broader economic considerations.

(vi) A new "outward-looking" foreign trade policy has been broadly introduced. The so-called "anti-import" commissions, aiming at the replacement of all possible imports by domestic production, have been dissolved. A broad cooperation and specialization policy by all industrial sectors has been encouraged within the CEMA countries, as well as with capitalist developed and developing countries. Common investments with other CEMA countries have been undertaken.

Imports from capitalist countries in 1971 and especially in 1972 rose dynamically at an unprecedented rate surpassing all econometric forecasts and are still rising. This policy of import promotion is being strictly connected with an export promotion policy.

The general investment policy should aim not at the development of all branches (as it used to be in the past, when the "law of proportional development" was obligatory), but at a specialized development with special reference to export possibilities. Also new forms of "joint ventures" with capitalist developed and developing countries are being worked out. It has to be stressed that all these new developments are not only characteristic of the current foreign trade policy in 1971/72, but also for the new long-term strategy.

The rate of growth of foreign trade, and especially that of imports from capitalist countries, is assumed to be higher than that of the growth of industrial production. Assumptions of an outward-looking strategy have been incorporated into the preliminary directives for the long-term plan. However, the policy of export based on specialized development cannot be easily imposed by the central planner. It has to be implemented in conditions where broader decision-making powers have been delegated to industrial branches, being traditional recipients of investment funds. The success of the whole strategy of specialized development depends mainly on the extent to which central, and not partial, preferences will determine the allocation of investment funds. This remains to be seen.

The elaboration of the long-term plan is still underway and hence it is too early to discuss its final result. Nevertheless, for the sake of illustration, it might be useful to present the techniques and the preliminary results of foreign trade forecasts for 1971-75. (A similar forecast serves as a basis for the elaboration of a perspective plan for 1971-1990).

(3) Forecast of Polish Foreign Trade (1971-1975) [6]

The forecast has been prepared according to an econometric model made up of equations, where endogenous variables (dependent variables) are the turnover of Polish trade, i.e., exports in the particular commodity groups to, or imports from, particular groups of countries, and the determining quantities are the exogenous variables (concerning the economic development of Poland in the years 1971-1975) and the independent external variables (concerning the development of world trade in the years 1971-1975).

---

[6] Based on the econometric model by W. Piaszczyński and compiled by a programming team headed by P. Bożyk at the Foreign Trade Institute.

The general notation of equations adopted in the forecast is as follows:

$$y_i = a^1_{ij} x^1_{ij} + a^2_{ij} x^2_{ij} + b_{ij} \quad \begin{matrix} (i = 1 , \ldots \ldots , 8) \\ (j = 1 , \ldots \ldots , 3) \end{matrix}$$

where
y_{ij} = endogenous variable, i.e., exports or imports of i-Commodity Group to or from j-Group of Countries,
x^1_{ij} = exogenous variable (internal),
x^2_{ij} = exogenous variable (external),
a^1_{ij}, a^2_{ij}, b_{ij} = parameters of the model.

For the purpose of a statistical verification of the adopted assumptions, an estimation of sixty-eight functions was carried out on the basis of a fifteen-year time series, i.e., data for the years 1955-1969. An estimation through the method of the least squares was carried out for functions of type $y = ax_1 + bx_2 + c + u$, where y is an endogenous variable (Polish exports, imports), x_1, x_2 are the respective exogenous variables (independent internal variables — national income, output, etc., and world trade turnovers broken down by groups of countries and groups of commodities), a, b, c are parameters of the function, u - a random component.

The econometric forecast presented here is based on the assumption that exogenous internal and external factors will affect the volume of turnovers in the years 1971-1975 just in the same way as they did in the past. The way in which they will act depends on the general form of the equation and on the magnitude of the parameters. Since it has been assumed that the influence of internal and external factors in the future will remain unchanged as compared with the past, parameters a, b, and c for the period of the forecast remain unchanged.

It has been assumed that the volume of trade in 1971 and 1975 depends, on the one hand, on the form of the function expressing the dependence of turnovers on domestic and foreign values, and on the other, on the extent and rate of growth of domestic and foreign values.

Among the exogenous internal variables used in preparing the forecast the following magnitudes characterizing the economic development of Poland in the years 1971-1975 have been classified:
– gross national income
– industrial output including output of fuels and electric energy, of

the metallurgical, chemical and electromechanical industries, of the textiles and clothing industries, of agricultural products and foodstuffs, of the forestry and timber industry (except raw materials of animal and vegetable origin)
- gross investments
- consumption of foodstuffs and of articles other than foodstuffs.

The forecast of the magnitudes of independent internal variables for the years 1971-1975 has been based on an extrapolation of trends of their development in the years 1961-1970. The results of the forecast obtained by this method have been amended in a number of cases in accordance with the opinions of experts.

TABLE 8

Development of the Polish Economy — Forecast for 1971-1975

Exogenous Internal Variables	Average Annual Rate of Growth 1971-1975 percentage
Gross National Income	6.4
Industrial Output:	8.0
– Fuels and Electric Energy	7.2
– Metallurgy	8.8
– Chemical Industry	11.8
– Electromechanical Industry	11.2
– Textile and Clothing Industry	6.6
– Food Industry	3.1
– Forestry and Timber Industry, Agricultural Products (except Materials for the Food Industry)	2.9
– Remaining Branches of Industry	7.4
Gross Investments	10.7
Consumption:	
– Foodstuffs	3.3
– Manufactured Consumer Goods	7.2

The forecast foresees a 9.2 per cent average annual rate of growth of exports for 1971-1975 and a 9.0 per cent rate of growth of imports. The dynamics of turnovers for Commodity Group VIII is shown in Table 9.

TABLE 9

Polish Total Foreign Trade Econometric Forecast

Exports					Commodity Groups	Imports				
Average Annual Rate of Growth 1969/1965 percentage	Value Million Exchange Zlotys** 1970	1975	Average Annual Rate of Growth 1975/1971 percentage	1975/1971 (1971 = 100)		Average Annual Rate of Growth 1969/1965 percentage	Value Million Exchange Zlotys** 1970	1975	Average Annual Rate of Growth 1975/1971 percentage	1975/1971 (1971 = 100)
*	1,891.5	2,491.1	5.3	123	I. Foodstuffs	2.2	1,661.4	2,328.8	5.7	125
1.2	439.1	639.3	5.5	124	II. Raw materials of Animal and Vegetable Origin	4.0	1,216.8	1,567.1	3.1	113
2.4	1,763.0	2,253.3	4.9	121	III. Fuels	7.2	947.6	1,523.5	8.6	139
12.0	1,476.2	1,895.9	6.8	130	VI. Ores and Metals	11.1	2,832.9	4,005.3	9.4	143
20.1	1,033.6	1,653.4	7.0	131	V. Chemical Products	9.4	1,331.9	1,697.6	6.8	130
13.0	5,813.0	10,030.5	12.1	158	VI. Machinery and Transport Equipment	10.7	5,419.3	8,858.2	10.9	151
12.5	882.8	1,546.3	11.4	155	VII. Textiles	21.6	321.7	391.8	3.8	116
11.4	893.1	1,535.3	8.6	139	VIII. Other Manufactured Goods	1.2	694.7	1,392.3	17.5	191
9.0	14,192.4	22,045.1	9.2	142	Total	8.2	14,426.3	21,764.6	9.0	141

* The sign "·" means that the respective commodity group does not show any growth of exports (or imports) in this period

** 1 $ = 4 exchange złotys

The starting point in preparing a correct forecast of developments in the foreign trade were the statistical results of the econometric model. After a discussion by experts, and having taken into account the commercial agreements concluded (with socialist countries) and other commitments in trading with foreign countries — on the basis of the variants of the econometric forecast — the final forecast of Polish foreign trade for 1971-1975 was prepared. That forecast is close to the maximum variant of the econometric forecast. It was decided that:

- a possibly dynamic growth of Polish exports is indispensable not only to cover the "necessary imports" of raw materials, semi-products and fuels, as well as machinery and equipment, but also to make a wider use of imports of consumer goods, both agricultural and industrial, as a steady part of rational policies of supplying the home market, widening the range and the quantities of consumer goods in supply on the market, and of satisfying the demands of the community;

- a fast growth of exports is necessary also from the point of view of a long-term development of large scale production, more efficient and technologically sound, as well as to secure foreign currency reserves, which would enable to follow more rational commercial policies, free from excessive tensions, and to apply proper credit policies.

It was accepted in the course of discussions that it is possible to obtain results according to the forecast if:

- a re-orientation of the industry takes place and if production potential is shifted towards export production in those groups of commodities for which there is demand abroad and which already now have achieved a sufficient level of rentability. Substantial untapped reserves exist mainly in the machinery, chemical, and light industries;

- an extensive use of many forms of "imports for the sake of exports" takes place, i.e., imports of all sorts of raw materials and semi-products, imports for co-production, imports for the extension and modernization of manufacturing installations in the branches specializing in export goods, as well as imports of finished goods, which would enable furthering exports of Polish finished articles while satisfying to a greater degree the needs of the industry and of the home market;

- imports of grain and feeding stuff as a prerequisite of stepping up the growth of breeding to increase exports of goods of that origin, while supplying the home market with more meat products, is accepted as a permanent feature of our foreign trade plan and at the same time a wider use of the so-called "barter exchange" within certain ranges of articles is adopted.

Moreover, an essential assumption of the present forecast is a generally balanced level of exports and imports in exchanges with developed capitalist countries and with developing countries, and a deficit (debit balance) in our trade exchanges with socialist countries (because of a traditional surplus in the field of services).

It is assumed that the volume of imports adopted in the forecast could be larger if:

– export possibilities rose through a fuller use of existing industrial capacities, or through raising the effectiveness of industrial exports owing to improved quality of goods and higher prices, etc.;

– foreign credits allowed additional imports (among other things within the framework of the so-called "complex undertakings" of an export favouring character) with a view to stepping up the modernization of industrial installations of branches specializing in exports.

The final quantities forecast indicate that Polish exports and imports will probably grow at an average annual rate of about 9 per cent and 10 per cent respectively. In 1975 the level of exports per capita would thus amount to 158 dollars and the level of imports to 166 dollars.

But a comparison of those quantities with the data relating to exports and imports per capita in other countries indicates that the level of our trade exchanges and the extent of our participation in the international division of labour will still remain relatively low.

From a comparison of the volume of exports and imports as forecast with the forecast volume of world exports and imports it appears nevertheless that there is a certain possibility of a slight increase in the Polish share in total world trade exchanges. Thus, the share of Polish exports in world exports would rise from 1.2 per cent in 1969 to 1.3 per cent in 1975, and the share of our imports in world imports would rise from 1.2 per cent in 1969 to 1.4 in 1975.

The above growth rates of foreign trade cannot be considered satisfactory. The new role of foreign trade would require more ambitious targets and higher coefficients of elasticity of foreign trade. Practical results, already achieved in 1972 would support this point of view and

TABLE 10

Total Polish Foreign Trade Forecast for 1971-1975
(Corrected by Experts)

	Exports				Commodity Groups	Imports			
	Value Million Exchange Złotys*		Average Annual Rate of Growth 1975/1971 percentage	1975/1970 (1970=100)		Value Million Exchange Złotys*		Average Annual Rate of Growth 1975/1971 percentage	1975/1970 (1970=100)
	1970	1975				1970	1975		
	1,891.5	2,440	5.2	129.0	I. Foodstuffs	1,661.4	2,380	7.4	143.3
	439.1	640	7.9	145.8	II. Raw Materials of Agricultural Origin	1,216.8	1,570	5.2	129.0
	1,763.0	2,450	6.8	139.0	III. Fuels	946.7	1,869	14.5	197.4
	1,476.2	1,890	5.1	128.0	IV. Ores and Metals	2,832.9	3,820	6.2	134.8
	1,033.6	2,060	14.8	199.3	V. Chemical Products	1,331.9	1,780	6.0	133.6
	5,813.1	9,350	10.0	160.8	VI. Machinery and Transport Equipment	5,419.2	9,701	12.3	179.0
	882.8	1,495	11.0	169.3	VII. Textiles	321.7	557	11.6	173.1
	893.1	1,616	12.6	180.9	VIII. Other Manufactured Goods	694.7	1,510	16.8	217.3
	14,192.4	21,941	9.2	154.6	Total	14,426.3	23,187	10.0	160.7

* 1 US $ being equal to 4 złotys (before devaluation)

should lead to a further correction of the plan, based on higher rates of foreign trade growth.

FOREIGN TRADE MANAGEMENT

Foreign trade management, as all management systems, must be looked upon not as a static, but a dynamic system, changing in the course of the general development of the economy and of the diversification of its foreign trade structure.

The main stages of the evolution of foreign trade management were the following:

- In the early 1950's a fully centralized system of decision-making in foreign trade functioned with a complete disregard of efficiency requirements. Exports were looked upon as a means of procuring funds necessary for paying for indispensable imports. The costs of exports did not matter in essence.
- In the late 1950's — with the steady development of the economy and a growing diversification of foreign trade — first attempts were made to construct export efficiency indexes, aimed at an "export" assessment of decisions taken up by planners.
- In the early 1960's a complex system of effectiveness was elaborated on the basis of an overall model of optimization of short-run planning. The concepts of marginal foreign trade rates (shadow prices of currencies), calculative prices of materials and the profit maximization criterion were theoretically derived and introduced as obligatory analytical tools of effectiveness analysis of plan variants. A complex system of calculative prices was elaborated and applied parallelly to prices of the obligatory financial system.
- In 1966 a first indirect system of foreign trade management, based on the criterion of profit maximization was introduced in the form of a macro-economic incentive system in industries working for exports. The system was based on calculative prices, including scarcity rents and was a rational instrument of a correct allocation of resources.
- In 1967 a first attempt was made (within the s.c. "Polfa-experiment") to connect the incentive system not with calculative prices, but with obligatory prices, by reforming obligatory prices of the financial system into correct parameters of a rational allocation of resources (but only in a single association of the pharmaceutical industry).

– In 1970 a general reform of producers' prices was worked out and was introduced in 1971. Instead of a complete separation between domestic and world prices, a new system of domestic producers' prices, closely related to world prices, was introduced. This created new possibilities for a closer integration of the incentive system in foreign trade with the functioning of the domestic financial system. However, before this integration can take place, there are several difficult questions to be answered and problems to be solved.

Pricing exportable domestic raw materials, correct from the point of view of rational decision-making containing rents due to limitations and alternative uses, leads in an ultimate effect to a reduction in overall national outlays. Hence, correct pricing is not in general identical with the cost pricing which only indicates the cost of material without indicating its exportability. Informative function of prices in a decentralized system should indicate not merely "How much has this really cost us?" but also "What are the other realistic alternative uses?" Obviously, evaluation of those rents may prove a complicated technical task: easier in exports, but more difficult in domestic production, often calling for iterative procedures or operative calculations, and occasionally altogether technically unworkable. Wherever we are practically capable of determining these rents, i.e., when we can determine the parametric equilibrium prices, we may actually draw away from rationing and central directives. Where we cannot do this, directive forms of fixing tasks and allocations through rationing must be retained. This is the fundamental principle in selecting a management system, connected with the feasibility of determining equilibrium prices and their effective control.

The next problem is that of realistic price control. The matter at stake is the parametric character of prices for producers: price must not depend on cost manipulation. Wherever this proposition is impracticable, one should not introduce incentives depending on profits, because it will inevitably cause an uncontrollable tendency to overpricing. In factory price or any similarly operating cost price, profit is a normative category derived from costs. Price formula of this type implies the principle: the higher the costs, the higher the profit. Profit of this kind cannot be maximized. On the other hand, in parametric price, profit is a resulting category. Its maximization implies an improvement in the effects of economic management, and therefore may serve as a basis for remunerative incentives.

The next fundamental principle is the continuous bringing up to date of prices of domestic exportable and imported goods, and the widest possible application of transaction prices.[7] The technical bother caused by changing calculations should not carry sufficient weight to induce a departure from correct pricing. On the other hand, where we opt for fixed prices, we should fix permissible deviation zones. When these are exceeded, prices have to be brought up to date. At least a part of the effects of these changes in currency prices should reach producers.

Consequently, in cases where determining parametric equilibrium prices, their effective control and bringing up to date is doubtful,

- one should not depart from centralized allocation and directive limits;
- one should not combine the criterion of profit maximization with material incentives.

The above reservations mainly apply to effects in certain branches of domestic production which are difficult to measure. They do not apply to exports and imports where the effects are, as a rule, objectively measurable. Notwithstanding, these reservations are sufficiently important for integration or non-integration of export profits with domestic profits as a base for incentives.

In view of the above considerations, it appears that:

- full integration of both kinds of profits is desirable and possible where the effects of activity for the home market are measurable in parametric equilibrium prices, just as are the effects of activity for a foreign market;
- full integration of both profits is not desirable where determination of parametric equilibrium prices, their effective control, and continuous bringing up to date, are unrealistic or doubtful.

It seems that pilot policies introducing parametric indirect management methods should be primarily applied in fields where realistic and objective measurability of outlays and effects is possible, which as a rule applies in foreign trade. If, in a pilot combine we have on the output side parametric equilibrium prices in the form of transaction prices (in production for export and the home market), and on the input side raw material costs correctly assessed, the criterion of profit maximization must operate correctly for improved effects, raised utility

---

[7] World prices multiplied by the unified foreign trade rate.

value (i.e., transaction prices), improved structure of production (also transaction prices) and lastly, reduced operating costs.

If, on the other hand, we deal with unique production, difficult to measure, unexportable or very highly cooperated, then introduction of indirect active incentive management methods does not appear realistic. Hence the conclusion that "pilot producers" should be primarily sought in the field of production connected with foreign trade.

A parametric system of active indirect management liberates specific tendencies at executive levels. Fixing central parameters in the form of foreign trade rates, surcharges and charges, subsidies and tariffs as well as an active pricing policy, gives rise to potent consequences for enterprises and industrial associations. An information system on the basis of which central authorities determine parameters may become subject to sundry distortions. Changes in operating conditions require continuous watching of external price movements, market fluctuations, productivity, premium and taxation trends, etc. An absence of continuous reaction by central authorities to the behaviour of economic subordinates under changing external conditions, is unthinkable. This new function of central authorities requires utmost skill in an apparatus representing the central state interests in the face of economic units conscious of their own interests.

How these complex problems will be solved remains to be seen.

The Industrial Workers

ALEXANDER MATEJKO

The development of the industrial proletariat in Poland really began in the latter half of the nineteenth century. At that time urbanization and industrialization advanced quickly. In the period from 1860 to 1910 the urban population rose from 18 per cent to 29 per cent,[1] at the same time that the index of people employed in industry, in the present Polish territory, had grown from 12 to 43 per 1,000 population[2] — considerably less than in Western Europe, but still representing substantial economic progress. The textile industry amounted to one fifth of the whole industrial employment; power, machine building, minerals, and foodstuffs each employed from 12 to 16 per cent.

After the destruction caused by World War I the prewar level of production was not attained until 1929. Soon after, economic progress was impeded by the Great Depression. Combined with the rapidly growing population, this allowed an increase on the index of industrially employed people to only 50 per 1,000 population.[3] At that time, foreign capital amounted to one half of all industrial investments. World War II brought new destruction. In addition to the over six million people who perished, half of the energy equipment, one third of all industrial buildings, and 45 per cent of all technical equipment were destroyed. Industrial production in 1946 represented only 45 per cent of that in 1937.

The high rate of industrial growth in the following years changed the entire socio-economic structure of Polish society. The contribution of industry to the gross national income grew from one third in the late 1940's to three fifths in 1971. Simultaneously with the progress of industrialization, the working class developed rapidly. In 1971 over 50 per cent of the economically active people were employed in industry. At present, among the rural population, 43 per cent maintain themselves from non-agricultural sources, usually by commuting to the nearest

---

[1] Stanisław Misztal, "Industrializacja ziem polskich w okresie kapitalizmu," in Stanisław Leszczycki and Teofil Lijewski, editors, *Geografia przemysłu Polski* (Warsaw, 1972), p. 123.

[2] *Ibid.*, p. 120.

[3] *Ibid.*, p. 133.

industrial centres.[4] Although housing conditions still remain inadequate, migration to towns is very attractive, especially for the young people.[5] The urban areas gained in population at the expense of the rural areas: the percentage of the urban population grew from 32 per cent in 1946 to 52 per cent in 1970.

Today the workers represent 40 per cent of the total population. Six and a half million workers are employed in the nationalized economy, most of them in the state-owned nationalized industry and in the co-operative industry. Three hundred thousand workers are employed in the state-owned agricultural enterprises, and 127,000 in forestry. The number of workers in private, non-agricultural enterprises is only 164,000.

* * *

According to the official ideology the workers are the ruling class in Poland. The workers comprise two fifths of the membership in the ruling Polish United Workers' Party; in contrast, the peasants comprise only 11 per cent. The workers have benefited greatly from the progress in employment opportunities, health services, cultural development and especially education.

Educational opportunities have been considerably expanded for the working class. Compared with only two fifths in the early fifties, at present nine tenths of all 14 to 17-year-olds attend school. In 1970-71, first year higher education students of workers' origin comprised 33 per cent in all daily courses, 60 per cent in the evening courses and 48 per cent in the extension courses. (Corresponding figures for the students of peasant background were 15 per cent, 15 per cent and 30 per cent.) In 1969-70 the graduates of workers' origin amounted to 28 per cent in the daily courses, 57 per cent in the evening courses, and 48 per cent in the extension courses. (The corresponding figures for the graduates from the intelligentsia families were 23 per cent, 19 per cent and 50 per cent.)[6] The progress in education is evident in the improved qualifications of the workers.

---

[4] In industry in general one fourth of all employees commute to work daily from another locality. In some southern regions the commuters come close to half of all the employees. Even in Warsaw, 23 per cent of all industrial workers commute from the suburban areas. *Ibid.*, pp. 111-12.

[5] For a more detailed discussion of the migration from the villages to towns see Alexander Matejko, "From Peasant into Worker in Poland," *International Review of Sociology*, VII, No. 3 (December 1971).

[6] *Rocznik Statystyczny 1971* (Warsaw: The Central Statistical Office, 1971), p. 499.

The Growth of Educational Level of Workers in the
Nationalized Economy* (in per cent)

	Workers in General 1958	Workers in General 1968	Industrial Workers 1968	Construction Workers 1968
ELEMENTARY				
Uncompleted	43	24	20	24
Completed	46	56	56	58
Craft	8	17	20	17
SECONDARY				
Uncompleted	2	1	1	1
Completed or Higher	1	2	3	(0)
Total	100	100	100	100

* *Rocznik Statystyczny Pracy 1948-1968*, pp. 260-262.

The Polish economy continues to develop rapidly. Although it is still lagging behind the developed countries, its progress is evident. In many areas of industrial production Poland compares favourably with other countries of similar size.

Comparative Position of Poland in Production of Selected
Industrial Products (in kg per capita in 1971)*

	Poland 1960	Poland 1971	Czechoslovakia	East Germany	West Germany	Sweden	Canada	Yugoslavia
Electric power (in kwh)	987	2,134	3,257	3,870	4,393	8,200	10,050	1,431
Coal	3,516	4,443	1,987	50	1,824	3	668	34
Crude steel	225	389	832	290	681	648	507	119
Sulphuric acid	23	69	80	60	71	88	121	39
Cement	222	399	549	472	661	472	390	289
Cellulose	10	14	32	24	14	833	484	19
Paper	22	29	59	62	92	542	528	29
Sugar	46	47	67	35	34	27	5	19

* *Rocznik Statystyczny 1972*, p. 651.

The growth of the Polish economy is, however, somewhat of a mixed blessing for the workers. First of all this class does not diminish numerically as fast as in some developed countries. In the years 1960-1971 the number of manual workers in the non-agricultural nationalized economy diminished from 67 per cent to 65 per cent; in industry the drop was from 84.5 per cent to 82 per cent, in construction from 78 per cent to 73 per cent; in transport and communication it remained at the same level of 70 per cent.[7]

Furthermore, this type of economy, overburdened as it is by heavy investments, does not provide enough room for a Western style consumerism. The expansion of social, cultural and recreational facilities, generously subsidized by the state, does not offer a sufficient substitute for a higher standard of living. In a way, this is even more true of the workers than the intelligentsia.

In 1971, out of his monthly gross income of 2,778 złotys, the average worker in a nationalized industry paid 270 złotys in taxes, leaving him with a net income of 2,508 złotys. What could he buy with it? Food in Poland is relatively inexpensive. For his monthly wages the worker could get 657 kilos of bread, or 929 litres of milk, or 239 kilos of sugar, or 45 kilos of pork loin or 40 kilos of butter. Clothing, however, is very expensive. For the same amount of money one could buy only 9 pairs of mediocre shoes, or 1.3 woolen suits, or 12 cheap shirts. Various industrial articles are even more costly. In terms of the above mentioned monthly wages, the cost of a refrigerator, depending on quality, would amount to from 1.2 to 2.7 incomes, a motorcycle — 3.8 incomes, and the cheapest Polish car — 30 incomes.

There is a considerable diversity of incomes among the workers employed in the different industries. The wages per month are over 4,000 złotys in mining, over 3,000 złotys in steel mills, and close to 3,000 złotys in construction and power industries. At the same time, only a little over 2,000 złotys are earned in many other branches of industry such as textile, foodstuffs, leather, clothing, etc. In the state-owned agricultural enterprises the workers earn even less (1,800 złotys in 1970/71), but they have some additional income from their private plots.

---

[7] *Rocznik Statystyczny 1972* (Warsaw: The Central Statistical Office, 1972), p. 112.

The Distribution of Industrial Workers and Their Monthly
Gross Incomes (1971)*

	Number	Average Monthly Income in złotys	Per Cent of the Average Income
Textiles	364,000	2,192	82
Foods	345,000	2,270	85
Coal	295,000	4,471	168
Transport equipment	284,000	2,856	107
Machinery and structural metal products	272,000	2,727	102
Chemicals	223,000	2,422	91
Metals	199,000	2,450	92
All others	1,250,000	(.)	(.)

* *Rocznik Statystyczny 1972*, pp. 183, 191-192.

The study of household budgets done in 1971 by the Central Statistical Office shows that in that year for workers' families food constituted 45 per cent of expenditures (as compared with 39 per cent in the intelligentsia families), clothing and shoes — 15 per cent, housing — 9.5 per cent, culture and leisure — 7 per cent.[8] Almost all the workers' families now have radios, TV sets, and washing machines. Refrigerators and sewing machines are owned by half of them.

The Polish workers, and especially those in the lower paid industries, show evident dissatisfaction with the current standard of living. Even if the food supply is satisfactory, their diet still consists of too many potatoes and cereals, and the consumption of meat is below the level of developed countries. Their buying power of other consumers' goods is generally very low.

In the decade between 1960 and 1970, the major interests of the population changed from goods for direct consumption to more luxurious goods and services. Taking the purchases in 1960 as 100, the index for 1970 was only 126 for foodstuffs, but 303 for electrotechnical gadgets, 223 for goods and services in the fields of culture, education, tourism and sport, 194 for housing equipment, and 187 for transport

[9] *Ibid.*, p. 549.

and communication.[9] From 1950 to 1970 the consumption of potatoes diminished from 595 lbs. to 434 lbs. per person, and the consumption of cereals from 366 lbs. to 291 lbs., while the consumption of sugar almost doubled, the consumption of wine grew six times, and that of tea eight times. The purchases of shoes and silks almost doubled.

Polish society still suffers to a large extent from poor housing, unsatisfactory communications systems (especially the poor telephone services), a severe shortage of private cars, and general shortcomings in several important social services. At the same time the exposure of the population to higher social and cultural needs leads to a constant growth of its aspirations. People who read many good books, watch TV programmes (generally more sophisticated than the commercialized television in the West),[10] and communicate with their numerous relatives who live abroad, are not easily satisfied. They compare their own situation with that prevailing in other countries, seek a better life and are increasingly critical of the ineptitude of the Polish ruling elite. The pressure of growing expectations and unfulfilled desires creates tensions in the country and may spell serious troubles for its political rulers, as it did in 1970.

* * *

According to leading sociologists the contemporary Polish society is basically egalitarian. Professor Jan Szczepański claims that, in comparison with the interwar years, the emerging new order is indeed more egalitarian and closer to the ideal Marxian image of a classless society.[11] Professor Włodzimierz Wesołowski relates egalitarianism to the variety of stratification criteria in a Communist society.[12] It is true that egalitarian aspirations are widespread in today's Poland, particularly among

---

[9] *Rocznik Statystyczny 1971*, p. 569.

[10] Among the urban inhabitants reading books is a common form of recreation; among the manual workers from one fourth to one third; and one half or more of the intelligentsia read books regularly. Theatres and operas are regularly attended by 6 to 12 per cent of manual workers and 20 to 30 per cent of the intelligentsia. Marcin Czerwiński, *The Dissemination of Culture in Poland* (Warsaw, 1967), p. 51. (Data from the survey done by Anna Pawełczyńska.)

[11] Jan Szczepański, *Polish Society* (New York, 1970), pp. 145-6. See also the critical review of this book by A. Matejko in *American Sociological Review*, 36, No. 5 (October 1971).

[12] According to Wesołowski, in today's Poland "if any group is overpaid, it is the less-skilled group." Włodzimierz Wesołowski, "Strata and Strata Interest in Socialist Society," in Celia S. Heller, ed., *Structured Social Inequality* (London, 1969), p. 474.

the workers. A large number of them made their social and educational advancement under the Communist system, moving from the poor villages to the towns, to industrial establishments, and even into positions of influence. A good many officials, executives, and even a large portion of the intelligentsia are of worker origin.[13]

Yet, the presence of egalitarian aspirations does not mean that the people are satisfied with the *status quo*. On the contrary, the existence of formal equal rights and privileges makes even more unbearable anything which contradicts this model. As a result, the egalitarian aspirations are even stronger in the lower social strata than among the intelligentsia.[14] Unskilled workers and people with less education in general, feel that they are deprived of status. The sense of real improvement in life seems to be much stronger at the higher social levels than at the bottom. According to data collected by Professor Stefan Nowak, the feeling that their present social status is higher than that of their fathers at the same age, was prevalent among 46 per cent of the intellectuals but only 23 per cent of unskilled workers.

Another significant observation by Professor Nowak is that the higher the social position of the people, "the more rarely are they convinced that certain social differences create divisions among the people in Poland. [Moreover, the higher their] position the greater the tendency to see the animosity as coming from the bottom. The lower the position, the greater is the tendency to see it as coming from the top."[15]

Egalitarian postulates are definitely stronger among the workers than among the relatively privileged strata of Party officials, managers, specialists, and intellectuals. The workers' main grievance is not the economic difference between them and the intelligentsia which has diminished considerably over the past twenty years. The ratio of the gross monthly incomes of manual workers in comparison with the non-manual professions changed as follows: *

	1950	1960	1965	1970	1971
Manual workers	100	100	100	100	100
Engineers and technicians	180	160	164	153	151
Administrators and clerks	124	104	107	101	101

* *Rocznik Statystyczny, 1972*, p. 190.

[13] See Alexander Matejko, "The Executive in Present Day Poland," *The Polish Review*, XVI, No. 3 (Summer 1971).

[14] See Stefan Nowak, "Changes of Social Structure in Social Consciousness" in Heller, *op. cit.*, pp. 235-47.

[15] *Ibid.*, p. 246.

The main issue for the Polish workers is their dependence on an autocratic and highly impersonalized bureaucracy. The workers have to depend on the decisions of somebody at the top, quite distant and often out of touch with their own problems. In the centralized system there is very little scope, not only for individual, but even for group initiative. Worse than that, there exist within the system various deeply entrenched groups which have vested interests in its perpetuation.

Common sense tells blue collar workers that the highly bureaucratized Communist economic system does not function effectively enough. There is too much waste, contradiction, parochialism, and ossification in the current managerial system. According to the available sociological data, the workers blame the current organizational and managerial set-up for the existing low efficiency and inadequate wages resulting from it. The fact that an average industrial worker wastes one quarter of his working time, is not due to his laziness but to the inherently chaotic state of a centrally planned and managed economy. The young generation of workers is increasingly aware that without introducing some basic economic reforms any successful modernization is simply impossible.

The use of shifts, for example, illustrates the unnecessary waste and rigidity prevailing in the industrial enterprises. The second and third shifts are not adequately utilized. From all the working time of industrial workers employed directly in production in 1971, 62 per cent was spent on the morning shift, 27 per cent on the afternoon shift, and only 11 per cent on the night shift. Only in a few industries (coal, ferrous and non-ferrous metallurgy, textile) was a little more than half of the working time spent on the second or third shifts. It should be possible to hire more people to utilize all the shifts fully[16] without raising costs too much, but the rigid bureaucratic setup stands in the way. Another example of the rigidity of the existing system is the use of the traditional Communist work brigades (in 1968 there were 44,000 of them with 407,000 members) to stimulate competition and rationalization in production. Yet, they are largely ineffective in accomplishing these goals and should be replaced with some new organizational forms which would provide a more effective outlet for the workers' own initiatives.

---

[16] At the end of 1971 there were 12,000 qualified workers and 52,000 unqualified workers who were looking for employment. *Rocznik Statystyczny 1972*, p. 117.

The rigid structure of management is further aggravated by the existence of many individuals who enjoy at least temporary support at the centre, as members of informal cliques which penetrate the whole industrial organization from the top to the bottom. Furthermore, these individuals are vitally interested in developing their own sub-cliques. The exchange of mutual favours between the various cliques influences to a very large extent the circulation of funds, goods, and services in the entire economy.[17]

The main issue, then, is to introduce a new organizational structure in industry which would bring the working people closer to the immediate economic goals. As a senior Polish economist, Professor Edward Lipiński, defined it: "It is a real problem of the socialist economy to motivate staff and management to formulate and achieve realistic social needs for their enterprise. The experience of years has proved that this can be achieved neither by directives nor by intensifying central control. If 'self-control' or an automatic interior mechanism, which continually corrects any deviations from the 'balance' with 'social' does not act, then no outside control can do it."[18]

Most of the Polish industrial enterprises are of such a small size that it should be easy for them to achieve some meaningful social cohesion. Fifty-two per cent of the state enterprises employ from 201 to 1,000 people, and 17 per cent from 1,001 to 2,000 people.[19] The establishment of some effective form of workers' self-government should stimulate loyalty, stability of employment, better utilization of work hours, and the development of some kind of a collective management.

* * *

The working class in Poland is becoming more and more aware not only of its problems but also of its own strength. Its social consciousness is not able to crystallize to the full extent without establishing autonomous class institutions. At present neither trade unions nor workers' councils perform this role. There is also still too much pressure from both the Party and the intelligentsia. The workers used to live for years under the shadow of these forces — the first political and the second cultural. Yet, as the events in the coastal cities in December 1970 dra-

---

[17] See George R. Feiwel, *The Economics of a Socialist Enterprise: A Case Study of the Polish Firm* (New York, 1965).
[18] Edward Lipiński, "The Theory of Socialist Enterprise" in Michael Kaser, ed., *Economic Development for Eastern Europe* (London, 1968), p. 293.
[19] *Rocznik Statystyczny 1972*, p. 193.

matically demonstrated, there are growing aspirations among the Polish workers to assume a more independent role — to exert their political strength and to exploit the existing socio-political opportunities.[20]

In the past the Polish workers lacked both economic security and the democratic experience to stand up for their rights. The socio-political involvement of Polish workers before World War II was considerably limited by the severely restricted labour market, the relatively low level of education, and the unfavourable political conditions under the Piłsudski regime. The socialist parties and even the underground Communist Party were largely dominated by the intelligentsia.

During the entire period of the Stalinist regime until 1956, the working class steadily grew in size. The opportunities of employment, education and promotion were widely utilized by people from the lower social strata. Yet the whole institutional framework of the Communist Party and the Communist-dominated trade unions was imposed on the working class without asking its consent. There was no opportunity for people in Poland, and particularly for the workers, to evolve any institutions, if not independent, at least autonomous of the Party. The attempt to establish autonomous workers' councils in 1956 was soon stultified by the Gomułka regime.

Since then, the situation of the workers has largely improved. Not only is the working class numerically very strong, but a high level of social mobility in People's Poland has considerably expanded the scope of social contacts and influences available to the workers. They now have friends and relatives almost everywhere. At the same time, the mechanism of political indoctrination among the working class has functioned much less effectively than among the intelligentsia, which has often been motivated by self-interest in adapting to the new political system. The workers' attitude towards the Communist regime was always based on common sense; they were less exposed to the illusions and disillusions so characteristic of the post-war Polish intelligentsia.[21] The socio-economic modernization, promoted by the Communist regime, was welcomed by the workers because it meant a very substantial im-

---

[20] On the political image of the Polish working class see a critical article by Ewa Wacowska, "Polska klasa robotnicza," *Kultura* (Paris, 1972), pp. 7-8.

[21] On the role of the intelligentsia in post-war Poland see Alexander Gella, "The Life and Death of the Old Polish Intelligentsia," *Slavic Review*, 30, No. 1 (March 1971) and Alexander Matejko, "Status Incongruence in the Polish Intelligentsia," *Social Research*, 33, No. 4 (1966).

provement in their life opportunities. Nevertheless, in their attitude towards the Communist ideology they have remained lukewarm.

The present Party leadership, in contrast to the Gomułka regime, is fully aware how ineffectively the existing socio-economic system works. Yet, to change it would mean above all to permit the working class to formulate its own social identity, largely independent of the Polish United Workers' Party. For ideological reasons, domestic as well as external, this does seem to be possible. It is probably for this reason that the reforms in the field of management have been constantly postponed and that no meaningful reforms have been introduced in the workers' self-government. The VII Congress of the Trade Unions held on 13-15 November 1972 did not produce anything strikingly new.

However, the government remains under constant pressure from the workers. Changes within the existing system are urgently needed and support by the working class is absolutely necessary if any substantial socio-economic progress is to be made. The question before the ruling elite, then, is how to gain the support of the workers without at the same time losing control over them. In the long run some kind of compromise must be found. Eventually, some new socio-political alliances are bound to develop. These alliances and the power play based on them may change the nature of the entire system in Poland.

Changes in Agriculture

WITOLD LIPSKI

Since World War II fundamental structural change has taken place in People's Poland. The nation has been transformed from an agricultural and raw-material producing country into an industrial and agricultural one. Despite this, agriculture remains a very important branch of the national economy, providing employment for approximately six million people, or about 36 per cent of the total actively employed population. According to the preliminary data from the 1970 census, the number of people in our country who derive their livelihood from agriculture was 9.6 million, that is, 29.5 per cent of the total population.

Agriculture and the agricultural food industry account for approximately one third of the national income. The importance of agriculture is further underlined by the fact that agricultural products account for more than half of the national consumption fund. Also, during the past twelve years exports of agricultural origin have been a significant source of foreign currency.

Many factors, and above all the demographic situation, are responsible for the fact that small-scale agricultural production remains the dominant sector in Poland. In 1971 the small farms represented 83 per cent of the cultivated area, the State Farms 15.1 per cent, cooperative farms 1.3 per cent, and the Agricultural Circles 0.6 per cent. However, the socialized sector's share of the cultivated area, and the total value of its production, is slowly but systematically increasing.

The State Farms' significance is greater than is indicated by their share in the surface of cultivated land. They play an important role in the intensification of agricultural production, supplying agriculture with high-yield grain, fodder crop seeds, seedlings, and pedigree stock. Their role in this regard is constantly increasing.

Despite the fact that small-scale farms are the principal sector in agriculture, the state has at its disposal a number of effective means to influence the development and direction of the entire agricultural production. It should be noted that Polish agriculture exists within the overall framework of a socialist economy. Individual farming is subordinated to the socialist system in a variety of ways and at different levels.

The state, besides directly administering the State Farms, also exerts indirect but effective influence on individual farms by providing various economic incentives, and above all by determining prices of agricultural goods as well as the industrial equipment needed by agriculture. The state is also largely responsible for the agricultural market. Its purchases account for almost 90 per cent of the marketable produce for agriculture. A very important instrument in planning the development of agriculture is the contract system for purchase of sixty-one categories of farm produce.

In the individual farms' sector there has been a constant expansion of the socialistic ownership of the means of production. Between 1965 and 1970 the number of tractors owned by the Agricultural Circles doubled, amounting at present to 92,000. The value of the machinery and equipment owned by the Agricultural Circles in 1970 corresponded to about 30 per cent of the total value of the machinery and implements of individual farmers. The technical services, the system of contracting the purchases of farm produce, the industrial processing of agricultural raw materials, as well as their distribution, all exert a socialist influence on the private agricultural sector.

The present system of agriculture has stemmed from the agricultural policy adopted in 1956. This policy was a reaction to the attempted forcible reshaping of the agrarian system during the years 1950-54. The main principle of the new policy was harmonizing the possibilities for the rapid development of agricultural production in all existing sectors of ownership (state, cooperative, and private), with a simultaneously gradual socialist transformation of agriculture. While it was flexible in its implementation, it categorically rejected the possibility of a capitalist development in Polish agriculture. The achievements of Polish agriculture in the period 1955-1970 indicated that in those areas where this policy remained faithful to its underlying principles, positive results were obtained, with regard to both the increase in production and the advance of social transformation in the countryside.

Unfortunately, in the late 1960's many negative features appeared in the implementation of the agrarian policy. The most important among them were the following: methods were adopted which disturbed the process of commodity exchange between agriculture and industry, such as the quota deliveries; the principle of profitability of agricultural production was neglected; and overly complicated means of influencing agricultural production were used. At the same time, a dogmatic approach to some economic problems, such as the restrictions on the import of grain, was revealed. Administration suffered from excessive red tape.

As a result, during the Five Year Plan (1966-1970), the real incomes of the peasants remained unchanged. The unfavourable relation between the prices of fodder and meat resulted in decreasing pig chattel. In general, ignoring consumption inevitably led to a serious neglect of agriculture.

* * *

The new political leadership which came to power in December 1970 had to adopt energetic measures to improve the situation in agriculture. At their joint session on 14 April 1971, the Political Bureau of the Polish United Workers' Party and the Presidium of the Supreme Committee of the United Peasant Party examined the goals of agriculture for 1971-1975, and reviewed the possibilities of increasing agricultural production and of accelerating the pace of social transformation in the rural areas. It was stressed at the meeting that the principle of profitability of agricultural production should be observed. Moved by concern to satisfy the needs of the society, the leadership of the two parties came out with the following directives:

(1) To abolish quota deliveries of slaughter animals, cereals and potatoes as of 1 January 1972 and to expand the contract cultivation system as the basic form of purchases by the cooperative and state organizations.

(2) To maintain the Agricultural Development Fund as the main source of investments in peasant agriculture, provided that the fund be accumulated in cash and within the framework of an adequately collected land tax.

(3) To prepare, in the course of 1971, a reform of the land tax, including contributions to the Fund. The excessive tax progressions were to be reduced, providing tax relief for the farmers cultivating poorer land.

(4) To ensure adequate agriculture supplies for the intensification of agricultural production, the expansion of breeding and, also, for the mechanization and electrification of agriculture. Special attention was to be given to supplies of agricultural implements, building materials, fuels, and means of transportation.

(5) To improve the efficiency of purchases and processing of agricultural produce so as to eliminate losses in perishable produce, reduce to a minimum the time spent by farmers in selling their produce, and to allocate indispensable means for an expansion of the agricultural and foodstuffs industry.

(6) To improve the working and living conditions of agricultural

labourers, and to introduce, on the basis of social insurance, health services for the agricultural population.

It was emphasized that the implementation of a new agricultural policy should be limited to an expansion of the system of agricultural self-government in the rural areas. The growth of self-government should reflect an expression of civic attitudes and the participation of the rural population in the management of the state and the national economy.

The joint decisions by the PUWP and the UPP were implemented by the *Sejm* and the government during 1971 and 1972. They met the postulates of the peasants by creating conditions more conducive to the growth of agricultural production and social progress in the rural areas. The decisions were also in the interest of the working class and indeed of society as a whole, because they sought to provide a more ample supply of foodstuffs for the entire population.

At the VI Congress of the Polish United Workers' Party the development of agriculture was given high priority. This was due to the close connection existing between the efforts to raise the real income of the population and the expansion of agricultural production. It is expected that in the years 1971-1975 average real wages will increase by 17-18 per cent, and the overall growth of consumption by 38-39 per cent. Since food represents 40 per cent of the average family budget, a real improvement in the standard of living of the population can take place only when agricultural production is developed. Only then will the increased income be matched by a supply of different food products to meet the demand. This is precisely why, in the current Five Year Plan, an 18-21 per cent increase in agricultural production is anticipated.

The concern of the present agricultural policy is to harmoniously combine immediate tasks and the objectives of today with long-range goals — not an easy task. The foundation of our state structure is the workers-peasants alliance, based on cooperation between the Polish United Workers' Party, the leading political force in the country, and the United Peasant Party which represents the interests of the peasants. The primary objective of this cooperation is to achieve an all-round harmonious development of a modern, socialist economy, and to secure a rise in the living standard of the people.

Conditions in Poland make it possible to achieve a higher level of intensity in farming through an increase in industrial supplies and a greater capital outlay for agriculture. The supply of better equipment, greater profitability of agricultural production and the perfection of the organizational methods — these are the three fundamental conditions which would enable agriculture to carry out its difficult tasks in the coming years. We are also going to be faced with the necessity of expanding the agricultural food industry. This will require industrial investment outlays to cope with the increased agricultural produce and efforts to improve the functioning of the distribution system.

* * *

The entire set of decisions taken in 1971 regarding agriculture satisfied the most important demands which had been voiced for years by the rural population. They have already produced several positive results.

The marked improvement of material conditions was advantageous for the rural population. Its income, derived from agricultural production, yet used for consumption and investments not related to agriculture, grew by some 7 per cent in 1971. The increased profitability of agricultural production also made it possible to augment the outlays on production investments in the peasants' holdings and cooperative farms by 15.5 per cent, of which the purchases of agricultural machines represent 45 per cent. Moreover, it also enabled replenishment of the farmers' reserve funds, which were badly strained in 1969-1970, and which are indispensable for a further growth of agricultural production.

The increase of agricultural production in 1971 and in the first half of 1972 demonstrates that the new agrarian policy has been effective. According to official estimates, overall agricultural production in 1971 and 1972 surpassed the level of 1970 by 10-11 per cent. The growth of market production was still greater, with best results obtained in animal production. Cattle production was 6.5 per cent higher in mid-1972 than in 1970. At the same time, the number of pigs reached the record level of 3.9 million, that is, 29.1 per cent higher than in 1970. Under the new conditions, the cash income received by agriculture from the sale of its produce was 15 per cent higher in 1971 than in 1970.

The present land legislation is also better adapted to specific needs in the development of the peasants' economy. The law on the protection of arable land and forests should provide for a more rational use of land resources. The new law on affranchisement has improved the legal and economic position of some two million farmer-owners. Finally, amendments to some of the provisions of the Civil Code, regarding land turnover, are expected to bring about positive changes in the agrarian structure. All of these measures should increase the trend towards specialization on privately owned farms.

Another important achievement, and benefit to the individual farmer, was the introduction on 1 January 1972 of socialized health services in the countryside. This represents a step forward in the creation of equal social working conditions in industry and agriculture, and should make work in the country more attractive.

It must be emphasized that improvements in the agricultural policy carried out since December 1970 have not been aimed at solving the problems in the peasant sector of agriculture alone. The state will also extend more help to all peasant associations and collective farms. The activities of the Agricultural Circles will be given greater attention. Many impractical, bureaucratic regulations, which had hampered their activities have already been removed. Simultaneously, greater concern has been shown for the development of cooperative farms, especially those which combine agricultural production with processing. Cooperative farms set up on a voluntary basis will enjoy all-round state assistance. Finally, various measures have been undertaken to create better conditions for further development of the State Farms.

*   *   *

In spite of all the achievements, it must be admitted that in comparison with agriculture in the developed Western countries, as well as in some of the socialist countries, Polish agriculture remains poorly developed and in some respects even backward. The facts tell us the brutal truth: a continuing high level of employment in agriculture, deplorable living standards in some of the rural areas, poor labour and land productivity, a still negligible degree of mechanization, widespread use of horses, etc., etc. Estimates of the expenditures which would have to be made to resolve the problems of insufficient water supply in the rural areas, the land amelioration, and the mechanization of farms, indicate clearly that a tremendous amount of work still remains to be done in Polish agriculture. To this list should be added another important problem, namely, the archaic land structure. This is illustrated by the existence of 3.5 million farms and some 10 million land plots.

In agriculture we are also faced with a kind of "vicious circle": the low standard of farming methods results in insufficient incomes, yet low incomes perpetuate the low standards of farming. Regions, districts and individual farms (either socialized or private) which obtain results comparable with those of the more developed countries, are examples that clearly testify to the possibilities inherent in our agriculture and to its potential reserves. At the same time they serve as a reminder that our national average, which itself is not very high, is still not attained in many districts or even in entire provinces. It is obvious that unless we abolish the backwardness of our rural areas, the present favourable tendencies in agriculture will soon run up against insuperable barriers.

A crucial problem for the future of Polish agriculture is in modernization, designed to achieve better production results. This, of course, will require tremendous investments in this branch of the national economy. Above all, it will involve an extensive mechanization, motorization and further electrification in order to ensure the growth of labour productivity. The reduction of employment and the transfer of a considerable part of the labour force to more productive sectors would improve living standards in the rural areas. The long-term objective must be to attain a productive efficiency in agriculture which will enable those employed in it to enjoy all of the highly valued social benefits already enjoyed by those employed in industry.

The entire logic of the development points to a specific target pattern for agriculture in Poland; in essence, to attain a level of organization and equipment of labour in agriculture high enough to ensure that its productivity is similar to that obtained in industry. This is the only basis on which identical living and working conditions in these two sectors can be achieved. The ultimate objective, then, is to realize the fundamental principle of socialism, which so far as the agrarian is concerned, could be reduced to the simple formula of equalizing the working and living conditions in the urban and the rural areas.

Reform of Rural Administration

SUSANNE S. LOTARSKI

Reform of rural administration in Poland has been one of the important policies initiated under the political leadership of Edward Gierek.
The nature of this reform offers some insight into the style, motivations
and priorities of this leadership.

The need for reforming rural administration was signaled in the
guidelines prepared for the VI Congress of the Polish United Workers
Party (PUWP)* and was prominently mentioned in the speeches of
both the First Secretary and Premier Jaroszewicz at the December 1971
Congress. During 1972, several Politbureau meetings considered the
subject and principles for the reform were announced at the 20 June
meeting. The project received the approval of the entire Central Committee at its VI Plenum on 27 September, and the government's draft
was presented to the *Sejm* on 19 October. Even before the Plenum,
however, concrete steps for implementing the reforms as of 1 January
1973, were already being taken. New boundaries for the countryside
were being drawn and personnel to head the new units was being selected
and trained.

Impetus for the reforms can be found in the importance which the
Gierek leadership attaches to improved agricultural productivity. Agriculture is seen as a key to the success of the Party's efforts to solve
existing economic problems and to fulfill its promises for an improved
standard of living. "The development of agriculture," Premier Jaroszewicz told the VI Central Committee Plenum, "is one of the decisive
requisites for achieving a highly dynamic development of the whole
economy and an increase in living standards."[1] The most significant
economic reforms undertaken since Gierek came to power have con-

---

* The proceedings of the VI PUWP Congress of December 1971 are printed in
Nowe Drogi, No. 1 (1972). Speeches from the VI Central Committee Plenum
are to be found in *Trybuna Ludu*, 28 September 1972. Extensive discussion of
the reform appeared in the weekly periodical devoted to the people's councils,
Rada Narodowa, throughout the second half of 1972. Results of the extensive
empirical research on the pre-reform commune are to be found in *Problemy
Rad Narodowych*, Nos. 17-22 (1970-1972).

[1] *Trybuna Ludu*, 28 September 1972, p. 4.

cerned agriculture. The proposed reform in administrative units and their organization is intended to complement and facilitate the economic actions in support of agricultural development.

The decision to introduce major reforms stemmed from a conviction that many problems result not only from inadequate resources, but also from poor administration and mismanagement of existing resources and improper utilization of personnel. Both Gierek and Jaroszewicz referred to this in speeches at Party gatherings. "One of the most important factors determining the effectiveness of social and state action is and will be efficiency in the organization and direction of work. This applies to all areas of life and all levels. An inadequate, and often low level of organization is our weakness," Gierek told the VI Party Congress.[2] Premier Jaroszewicz similarly told the VI Plenum that human potential and material wealth were "poorly administered and utilized."[3] Proper management is one of the foremost concerns of the current Polish leadership.

The rural areas of Poland are administered through the system of people's councils, a uniform framework that encompasses the entire country, both urban and rural. The system consists of three tiers: provinces (*województwa*), counties (*powiaty*), and primary units in the form of towns, settlements and communes. The people's councils at all levels are similarly organized. There is in each people's council an elective council and its committees, an executive-administrative body of three or four full-time and three part-time members called the presidium, and several departments. In the commune there is, instead of departments, a bureau which includes various offices servicing rural needs. The entire system is linked by a series of vertical lines of subordination. Organs of the communal people's council are subordinated to their correspondent organs on the county level, counties to provinces, and provinces in turn to the central authorities. The organization of the system and the powers of each of the units are regulated by a Statute adopted in 1958 and revised in 1963 and 1972.

Over the last decade various reforms concerning the people's councils have been suggested. It is not without significance that a leadership concerned with efficient management should begin reforming the system first at the communal level. The communes have generally been ack-

---

[2] *Nowe Drogi*, No. 1 (1972), p. 92.
[3] *Trybuna Ludu*, 28 September 1972, p. 4.

nowledged to be the worst functioning units in the entire system. Reform of the communal councils is also consistent with the importance given to agriculture since the communes are the basic units in the countryside.

As the primary units of government for all the agricultural areas, the communal councils, under the 1958 Statute, were charged with initiating activities aimed at the development of agricultural production; coordinating the activities of agricultural circles, of agricultural production cooperatives and of other local institutions and organizations; coordinating the advance purchases of agricultural produce by the state; cooperating with the workers' self-government on the state farms; protecting forests; cooperating with the supply and marketing cooperatives providing the countryside with industrial and consumer goods; running small production plants, mills and service units; ensuring communal services and maintaining unsurfaced local roads; ensuring proper accommodation and service for the primary schools, agricultural vocational schools, and other social, cultural and health facilities. As branches of the state administration, they also collected taxes and other dues, and kept the registry office. Nearly one half of the country's population lives within the jurisdiction of the communes.

The weaknesses of the communes as constituted had been manifest for some time. The communes had neither the authority nor the resources to provide for the basic needs of the population. There was a great gap between what they should have been doing and what they actually could do. They were almost totally dependent on the counties for their resources, and all important decisions for the life of the communes were made at the county level. The communes had no autonomy over their budgets and economic plans. In effect, the communes were branch offices of the county administration. Even in this they were of limited value, as a majority of matters were handled by the counties. In most of their dealings with the state, rural residents had to go to the county. There were many such matters, resulting in interminable delays, red tape, added costs and loss of precious time.

Community services in the villages also suffered from the communes' lack of power and resources. The communal people's councils were charged with coordinating the activities of the various economic institutions serving their area. They were supposed to assure that such institutions as the village cooperatives, milk collectives, savings and loan associations, agricultural circles, farm machine stations, fertilizer and fodder warehouses, grain mills, and various repair shops serviced the commune adequately and properly. In many cases, however, this was impossible because the territory under their jurisdiction did not coincide with that of these institutions. The communes were too small to be efficient economic units able to serve as a base of operation for the institutions. Their branches normally encompassed several communes. Prior to the reforms there were, for instance, 4,313 communes, but only 2,125 consumer cooperatives. Because the organization of these vital service institutions was supra-communal, the commune had little influence over their actions within the commune and the quality of services they provided. Even where organizational boundaries coincided, the communes had few means to enforce their decisions upon these institutions. Their powers were solely in coordinating.

The quality of administration in the communes was also low. Both the competence and use of personnel was responsible for this situation. Over 60 per cent of the personnel in communal bureaus had not completed secondary education. Those that did have secondary or higher education moved quickly to other institutions offering more responsibility, prestige and pay. Salaries in the communes were notoriously low, office equipment was scare and primitive, means of communication and transportation were inadequate. High turnover prevented the creation of an experienced, cohesive cadre. Those who did stay were often those least qualified. Many of the higher trained personnel, such as agronomists and veterinarians, were swamped with paper work and unable to provide their expertise and services to the population. The performance of the communal authorities was in general abysmally low. The population was dissatisfied with them, as were the communal councillors, chairmen and secretaries themselves. So, too, apparently was the national leadership.

*   *   *

Various changes have been introduced to deal with these problems. The size of the commune has been doubled in area and population. Instead of 4,313 there are now just under 2,400 communes. Their average size has increased from 56 to 129 sq. km., with an average population of 7,000 residents instead of only 3,500. It is hoped that in this way the commune will be a more efficient economic unit, able by itself to support the various necessary economic institutions. The goal is to achieve a parallel structure between the units of state administration (communes) and those of the economic agencies. The new commune, in fact, has been projected as a socio-economic microregion containing eventually all the economic, social, educational and cultural facilities expected in a modern society. Such facilities are seen as necessary for increasing agricultural productivity, and for retaining and attracting young people to the countryside. It is hoped that consolidation will lead to more efficient utilization of existing resources and a more dynamic and rational development of additional facilities.

The reform has also embraced the small towns and settlements which were frequently the centre of communal life but administered separately. Under the reform, the 300 towns of less than 5,000 population have been incorporated into the communes through a joint town-communal people's council. The fifty-four settlements of a mixed urban-rural nature have been transformed into communes, except for a few larger ones which acquired town status in a town-commune complex. It is hoped that these changes, by erasing the artificial barrier between the towns and the communes which they service, will contribute to the accelerated development of these towns and provide better service for the residents of the communes.

The internal organization of the new communal people's councils has also been altered. The major change is the introduction of one-man communal managers (*naczelnicy*) appointed by the chairmen of the provincial presidiums. Under the old system, the communal executive had been a collegial body (the presidium), whose chairman coordinated the work of the various bodies and exercised certain additional administrative functions. In theory the presidium was elected by the council and responsible to it, but in practice the members of the presidium were selected by the county. The presidium performed a dual function. On the one hand it served as the executive committee of the elected council, planning and coordinating its work. On the other hand, it was an executive-administrative body with independent responsibilities, charged also with directing the local departments. For many years there were suggestions that these functions be separated and entrusted to two different bodies. It was argued that this would strengthen both the council and the administration. With the creation of the communal manager, these suggestions have been implemented, but only at the communal level.

In acquiring new boundaries and a new executive, the communes have also acquired a new name, or rather reverted to an old one. Throughout the inter-war period and until 1954, the commune was known as *gmina*. In the 1954 reform of rural administration which brought the countryside into line with the rest of the system of people's councils, the 2,500 *gminy* were divided into 8,000 *gromady*. Their appointed executive, the *wójt*, was replaced by the supposedly elected collegial presidium. The return to the name *gmina* emphasizes the similarities of the new communes with those of pre-1954 — which in the opinion of many were more effective and powerful. The historic and very Polish title of *wójt*, however, was not accorded the new manager.

The vesting of authority in a single person rather than a collegial body is intended to clarify the question of responsibility and introduce strong leadership into the communes. Among the many weaknesses of the old system had been the difficulty of holding decision-makers accountable for their performance, which led to a situation referred to as "anonymous responsibility." With the appointment of a communal manager, such responsibility should be more clearly defined. The new communal manager (*naczelnik*) has been granted substantial executive powers. He has the duty to control the parish agricultural service, prepare the drafts of the economic plans, assure that the citizens fulfill their obligations to the state, coordinate the work of the various economic and social institutions operating within the commune, and ensure public order. The manager has also been made responsible for the local administration and given extensive authority in individual matters concerning agricultural production, residential and economic construction, licenses for handicraft and service workshops, health and social insurance. Most of these matters were previously handled by the county authorities. The creation of a strong chief executive, together with the high educational and professional requirements being set for the holders of this office, is expected to improve the efficiency of local administration.

*   *   *

The redrawing of communal boundaries and the appointment of communal managers were the first and easiest aspects of the reform to implement. Even these, however, encountered problems. Consolidation of communes had been going on for several years. The latest prior to the present reforms had taken place in January 1972 and had eliminated 352 communes. This still meant reducing the number of communes by almost one half. The redistricting involved conflicting demands concerning boundaries and the location of the communal seats. Villages preferred to be incorporated into other than assigned communes because of ease in communication, better economic services, or traditional ties.

114

Dissatisfaction was also expressed by villages which were being demoted from the rank of a communal seat and from those which found the selected site inconvenient for easy transaction of business.[4]

Problems on the personnel front likewise arose. One of the postulates of the reform had been that the communal executives and also the communal secretaries would be persons with a higher education in either agriculture or economics, or in exceptional cases, with at least secondary education and five years of experience. It was expected that all the other personnel of the communal bureau (six to twelve persons) would also have at least a secondary education and three years of experience, and that the personnel of the communal agricultural service (four to eight persons) would have higher or technical secondary education. The educational and experience requirements were seen as a way of ensuring competent administration.

Even before the reforms were formally adopted, it became a foregone conclusion that these standards would not be met immediately. The reserve of persons qualified and willing to fill these positions was inadequate to the demand. Only a small proportion of the current communal chairmen and secretaries met these standards and could take office in the new communes. Some of the managers and secretaries for the new communes were drafted from the ranks of the county and provincial personnel. All in all, however, less than half of the new managers and secretaries boast diplomas from institutions of higher education.

The stress on education introduced various actual and potential cadre problems. Many of those selected had not previously worked in the state administration and had come from the agricultural service or various other economic institutions. (Not only may the communes suffer from their lack of experience, but other institutions are being deprived of trained personnel.) Others had worked in state administration but in branches unrelated to agriculture and had no experience with the problems of agriculture. For some the position involved a move from larger cities to small towns or villages and was accepted primarily as an opportunity for quick advancement. Thus the endemic problem of high turnover and instability among administrative personnel is likely to be exacerbated. The inability to fill a larger proportion of the communal posi-

[4] A delegate from the Kielce province reported to the VI CC Plenum that over 60 petitions had been received in the province concerning these questions, over half asking that the site of the seat remain as of old. *Trybuna Ludu*, 28 September 1972, p. 7.

tions with more highly educated person may, in fact, stem from an unwillingness of many such persons to accept transfers to the countryside.

The consolidation of communes and the recruitment policies also forced the laying off of a large proportion of communal personnel. Not only former chairmen and secretaries were affected by the changes, but also accountants, section heads, chiefs of registry offices and secretarial personnel. Some of these could return to their private farms and others were guaranteed the right to return to former employers. Those who had tenure in the commune or state service were assured new positions elsewhere. For some, of course, especially those with least education and experience, the changes meant job-hunting in a market already suffering from high unemployment. At the very least, the changes mean a loss of prestige for many rural functionaries. Here lies another source of dissatisfaction.

Consolidation of communes and creation of a communal manager would not alone, however, solve the problems of administration and development in the countryside. If the communes were to become centres in which all business with the government could be settled locally and if they were to serve as the driving force of local development, they had to be outfitted with many additional powers and resources, and given jurisdiction in matters heretofore resting with the counties. These aspects of the reform are more difficult to implement and present a complex set of problems which cannot be solved entirely by the adoption of appropriate statutes.

Readjustment of the relationship between the communes and the counties is essential for the success of the reforms and requires changing not only laws but also long established customs. One of the intentions of the reform is to shorten the distance which the farmer must travel to government authority, both literally and psychologically, and to decrease the amount of red tape and time involved in settling his business. Earlier, the number of certificates, affidavits and verifications which had to accompany each request was drastically reduced. To further facilitate transactions, the reform has foreseen the transfer of authority in many matters from the county to the smaller and less distant communal councils.

The other major objective of the reform is to improve the supply of goods and services, especially those related to agricultural production, both by improving the availability and use of existing facilities and by introducing greater energy and rationality in the development of new ones. This goal is also being pursued by transferring authority from the counties to the communes. Success thus hinges on readjustment of the relationship between the counties and the communes, a readjustment which is fraught with difficulties.

The first step in this readjustment was revision of the Constitution and the Statute on People's Councils. Learning from past experience, the reformers declared that the transfer of authority from counties to communes would be made mandatory rather than relying on the willingness of the counties to do so voluntarily.[6] Revision of the Statute on People's Councils, however, covers only a minute portion of the county-commune relationship, and this only generally. In addition to the Statute, the respective spheres of authority of each level are regulated by thousands of laws and orders in specific matters. One estimate was that there were over 15,000 laws which had to be revised to carry out the reform.[7] Such a massive project cannot be carried out in a day. Yet this administrative aspect of the reforms, the transfer of authority in specific matters, is easier to accomplish than the strengthening of the communes as managers of their areas.

If the communes are to be the driving force in rural economic development, they must likewise be given actual control over the necessary resources. Heretofore the communes disposed of very little independent revenue and even the use of this was restricted by the county. The communes served primarily as tax collecting agents for the county. They then received an appropriation from the county to meet expenses for services imposed on them by the county and which the communal revenues could not cover. Under the reform, the communes have been given an independent permanent revenue. This will come from the land tax and other village obligations, a share in taxes paid by rural cooperatives, the fees of handicraft workshops in the villages, and the funds which the state grants for promoting projects in which the local population volunteers its services. In some cases, however, a share will have to be turned over to the counties for their expenses. The reform has also postulated greater autonomy for the communes in the drafting of their

---

[6] "The transfer by the counties of appropriate authority to the communes . . . will be mandatory," Premier Jaroszewicz told the VI Plenum. "The possibility which has existed since 1956 for voluntary transfer of some rights from higher to lower councils was inadequately utilized." *Trybuna Ludu*, 28 September 1972, p. 4.

[7] Michal Szpringer, "Małe miasta — centra dużych gmin," *Tygodnik Demokratyczny*, 13 August 1972.

budgets and economic plans. Heretofore they have had no say in these decisions. As long as the present centralistic system of economic planning is maintained, however, such autonomy will continue to be greatly restricted.

Adoption of appropriate laws and the transfer of authority in various matters from the county to the commune does not automatically readjust the relationship between the communes and counties. The counties continue to retain their rights to supervise and control the communes in the vertical line of subordination. Through the controls which county departments carry out in the communal agencies and through the directives they issue, the counties can, as in the past, interfere in communal matters and usurp both the authority of the commune and the communal manager. The provinces and counties have always also exerted considerable informal influence on the communes, influence resulting from personal ties, powers of appointment and promotion, the authority of their chairman's office and his ties to the Party, etc., rather than statutory powers. There is nothing in the reform which will lessen these pressures. The manager of the new commune, as that of the old, will have to compete with the county and provincial authorities for control of the local administration. He will also have to compete with the superiors of the local economic institutions of influence on their activities.

Given these various problems, the immediate impact of the reforms on administration is unlikely to be spectacular. Transfer of real authority, readjustment of the relations between the communes and the counties and economic institutions, improvement in quality of personnel, and institutionalization of the position of the communal manager can be achieved only gradually. The farmer may have to wait a while before all his business can be transacted in the commune and even longer for it to be settled properly and efficiently.

The reform, likewise, does not immediately solve the problems of goods and services where these are lacking. With expanded authority and more efficient administration, the enlarged commune may contribute to a consolidation, better distribution and more rational utilization of existing facilities. The new commune, however, cannot offer services and facilities where they are non-existent or inadequate. If the communes are really to become socio-economic microregions, large amounts of capital will have to be allocated for these purposes. Investment is the only solution for many of the problems of the countryside. Better organization and management can only ameliorate these problems. To the extent they do so, they can give the leadership a grace period in which to attack the more difficult problems.

* * *

The instituted reform of rural administration is essentially an attempt to decentralize. It thus continues a policy first initiated at the beginning of the Gomułka era. One of the first steps of the Gomułka regime, as that of its successor, was the reform of the people's councils. Decentralization was among the most important avowed purposes of the reform which went into effect in January 1958. The amount of actual decentralization achieved over the next decade, however, was very limited. It became common to speak of decentralization having stopped at the provincial level. Some power devolved from the central government to the provinces, but went no further. Later attempts to make the county the keystone of the entire system were likewise unsuccessful and served merely to sap the effectiveness of the communes.

The approach of the Gierek leadership to decentralization differs from that of earlier attempts. It tackles only a part rather than the entire system of sub-national government, and more importantly, begins the process from the bottom of the pyramid rather than from the top. It also begins with the unit which can have greatest impact on production. The services which the communes can provide to agriculture are much more important for its expansion than are the services of cities or even counties and provinces for industrial development. This may provide for more sustained interest at the top in seeing that its reforms are carried out at the bottom. Many of the same forces which hindered earlier decentralization, however, continue to operate. The reluctance of higher levels to delegate authority downward has not disappeared, nor have their various formal and informal influences over the commune. More importantly, the highly centralized system of planning remains intact. Reform of administration and reform of the planning system are complementary. One without the other is incomplete. If the reforms in rural administration are successful, they will provide a suitable base for any decentralization in economic management which may follow. Without such economic reforms, however, the administrative reform can be only partially effective.

One weakness which the reforms do not attack is the imbalance in strength between the elected council and the administration. In the theoretical model of the people's councils, it is the elected council which is supposed to manage the local area by deciding the most important policies and directing and controlling the administration. In practice, however, it has been the administration which has directed the council and done the decision-making. Control by the councils of the administration was shallow and sporadic. With the creation of the office of a communal manager, the presidium of the council has been transformed into a body charged solely with planning and coordinating the work of the council. Its members will come from among the councillors, will serve without pay, and will have no additional administrative functions as did the old presidium. The acquisition of a truly executive committee may go some way in strengthening the position of the council *vis-à-vis* the administration. The problem is that while the position of the council has been strengthened a little bit, that of the administration has been strengthened far more.

In presenting the draft of the reform to the *Sejm,* Premier Jaroszewicz tried to reassure its members that the proposed changes would not weaken the council. "Here I would like to state that creating a strong executive organ in the commune does not and cannot mean reducing the role of communal self-government. . . . On the contrary, it will in fact strengthen the communal council. . . ."[8] A journalist who remembered his own enthusiastic reception of earlier reforms and his subsequent disenchantment was not as certain. "At the last plenum [VI] Comrade Gierek said that socialist democracy can advance only through the fusion of two factors: an ever more efficient, highly skilled executive apparatus and an ever more perfect representative organ able to initiate and control. I see quite clearly the road to improving the executive authority, but am uneasy about the position of the representatives. How can one assure for them an authentic exercise of power? How can one protect them against domination by people appointed by the province and equipped with a diploma?"[9] The reforms provide no insurance against such domination, and in fact increase its likelihood.

The reform is a vast and complex undertaking which involves considerable upheaval in the countryside. Not only the state administration, but also all other institutions are affected by it. The Polish United Workers' Party, for one, has had to restructure its organization and consolidate Party units so that they would correspond to the new communes. Such consolidation strengthens the Party organizations by con-

---

[8] *Trybuna Ludu,* 20 October 1972, p. 3.
[9] Bijak, *Polityka,* 14 October 1972, p. 3.

centrating their resources. At the same time that communal managers and secretaries were being selected for the communes, Party leaders were also being chosen for the reduced number of positions in the new Party units.

Party influence on communal affairs had never been as strong as it was in the cities or the counties and provinces, and in fact was not as necessary, given the power of the counties over the communes. With the introduction of an appointed manager and expansion of communal authority, Party interest would seem to call for expanded influence of the local Party leadership in communal affairs. If the qualifications of Party leaders do not match those of the communal officials, it might be difficult for the Party leadership to exert such influence. If in the same situation, it does try to exert substantial influence, the administrative goals of the reform and the benefits of expertise in administration could be undermined. In either case, overly great differences in the education and qualifications of the two groups of local leaders might create political problems.

Although the reform is at present limited to the communes, its impact and implications for other levels are quite clear. The position of the next link in the chain, the counties, is obviously already being modified, a surplus of personnel is being created, and the need for certain county units is being questioned. An eventual restructuring of the entire system from the cities up to the provinces is inevitable. Already at the September 1972 Plenum of the Central Committee voices were heard advocating early introduction of such changes. In a unified system of multiple links such as exists in the Polish people's councils, one element cannot for long be out of step with the rest without the rise of serious tensions.

The reform of rural administration, affecting as it does the two most important local institutions, offers an opportunity for large-scale personnel shake-ups. In light of the membership verification campaigns which are being conducted in the Party, it would seem that this is not an unimportant aspect of the reform. Changes in the top echelons of both Party and state leadership were achieved by the end of the VI Party Congress in December 1971. The process of reforming rural administration provides an occasion for doing so at lower levels. The reform could thus contribute to consolidating the hold of the Gierek forces over the Party.

Reforming rural administration obviously does not solve all the problems involved in increasing agriculture productivity and improving administration. In many ways, however, it is a low-risk policy. Politically the reform holds few dangers. The principles of the reform involve no major controversies, and in fact implement many long-standing suggestions. Its implementation, because of the prior state of affairs, cannot have a really negative effect either on administrative efficiency or on agricultural production, in the latter case especially because the transition was timed to coincide with seasonally reduced activity. At the same time, the reform has the potential for considerable long-term benefits. If successful, it will provide a more effective organizational structure for modernizing the countryside. It can also serve as a catalyst in the necessary rationalization and improvement of administration.

Reforms and readjustments of the complex administrative mechanisms are not new in Poland. They were undertaken previously on a larger or smaller scale in 1950, 1954, 1958 and 1963. The reforms of 1972-73 are being greeted more cautiously than were their predecessors. After more than two decades of programs which promised more than they delivered, a certain amount of scepticism is inevitable. Edward Gierek and the team he heads are noted above all else as experienced administrators attuned to the importance of managerial factors. The reform of rural administration is at heart a managerial approach to the problems of the countryside. It will prove an important test of the leadership's ability to initiate and sustain a managerial revolution throughout the system.

The Role of the Intellectuals

GEORGES H. MOND

An attempt at an evaluation of the role of intellectuals in Poland goes beyond a mere sociological and political study. The question is bound up with various historical peculiarities deeply ingrained in the Polish national and social consciousness. It becomes even more complicated when viewed within the context of the situation in the 1970's — full of hope, but also of anxiety and doubt. Looking at the reality of contemporary Poland, it is impossible to dissociate past from present, or to ignore the fact that the intellectuals of today are the products of preceding periods which have left profound marks upon their minds and consciousness.

Even the exact definition of intellectuals poses some problems. The American sociologist, S. J. Ravin, observed that "the core of the Polish intelligentsia consists of 'the creative intelligentsia,' comprising writers, journalists, film-makers, architects, composers, artists, etc."[1] In the present study, the term "intellectuals" is more or less synonymous with that of "the creative intelligentsia." Its scope, however, is broadened to include scholars, some young academics and high school teachers, some lawyers and judges, the lay Catholic intellectuals and some priests, as well as a few of the ideologues of the Communist Party. This corresponds roughly to the definition offered by *Polityka*, singling out intellectuals as the most important group among the intelligentsia, and adding that this group is even more distinct among the intelligentsia, than the intelligentsia is among the general public.[2]

There are, in fact, several criteria for belonging to the socio-professional and cultural stratum known as the intellectuals. First there is *education,* perhaps the most significant distinguishing characteristic of an intellectual; then there is the *profession* which he performs; and finally there is the *socio-cultural and socio-political role* which he plays in the society. To these quasi-traditional criteria must be added *moral and socio-political behaviour and attitudes.* Indeed, in this respect, the traditional definition of the intelligentsia, included in the Concise Oxford Dic-

---

[1] S. J. Ravin, "The Polish Intelligentsia and the Socialist Elements of Ideological Compatibility," *Political Science Quarterly*, No. 83 (September 1968), pp. 353.

[2] *Polityka,* 7 August 1965.

tonary and cited with approval by the prominent Polish sociologist Professor Jan Szczepański, applies to today's intellectuals. Intelligentsia, it says, is "that part of a nation that aspires to independent thinking."[3] In Poland this last criterion has been extremely important in the past as well as at present. The Polish intellectuals and especially the writers, journalists, and men of letters in general, have a great tradition of nonconformity; they have long been "the conscience of the nation." This is still true in the 1970's.

The social profile of the Polish intellectuals is probably largely responsible for their continued regard of themselves as "the conscience of the nation." This social group represents a unique intellectual, spiritual and politico-cultural blending of outstanding personalities from different social strata, and from different ideological as well as spiritual backgrounds. There are among them Kotarbiński, Iwaszkiewicz, Wańkowicz, Łubieński, Małachowski, Mikke-Korwin — all descendants of the Polish nobility. There are Kwiatkowski, Ossowski, Słonimski, Korotyński, Strzelecki and Piasecki, all descendants of the traditional old intelligentsia, itself often of minor nobility origin. There are also Bandys, Hertz, Wolanowski, Kostrzewski, Natanson, and Lipinski, all of upper or lower middle class, often of foreign extraction but assimilated two or three generations ago. Finally, there is a growing number of intellectuals of first, or at the most second, generation of peasant or worker origin: Kafel, Burda, Rakowski, Czeszko and Roskowski, who often make an exceptional effort to integrate into the older intellectual elite. As Louis Bodin correctly noted: "The problem that now seems most acute to the Polish intelligentsia is that of harmony between the old-style intellectuals (those who have always formed a separate milieu, jealously maintaining its distinctive qualities *vis-à-vis* the rest of society) and the new-style intellectuals, emerging from the ranks of the proletariat, or produced by accelerated educational programmes."[4]

It is not unusual that the newcomers envy their colleagues. The descendants of the old intelligentsia have considerable advantages — they received their educational training early in childhood; one might say they have been scholars for generations. Yet, the people of worker or peasant origin, even though they try hard to integrate with the traditional intellectuals, still introduce some new aspects into this group.

---

[3] Jan Szczepański, *Odmiany czasu teraźniejszego* (Warsaw, 1971), p. 92.
[4] Louis Bodin, *Les intellectuels* (Paris, 1964), p. 51.

Indeed, many of them have assumed influential positions in the socio-cultural and moral life of the nation. In doing so they have often been backed by the Communist power. Even so, the problem is that in intellectual endeavours official support is not enough. In order to gain access to the intellectual milieu it is also necessary to be talented and to be a real scholar. As a result, unique traits of the Polish intellectuals include their good grasp of world affairs, the knowledge (especially among the 50-70 age group) of Polish history, and of the past as well as present Polish culture.

To sum up: a Polish intellectual is a person who has received higher education, whose profession is in the field of culture, science, or com-munications, who has deep roots in the national tradition, who is marked by an independence of intellect, and often by non-conformist behaviour in the exercise of his profession, as well as his style of life. The non-conformist behaviour, of course, does not constitute a *condicio sine qua non* of belonging to this group, since there have been many intellectuals who have had a long record of collaboration with the Communist power. Yet even the conformist intellectuals, as the events in the mid-1950's, early 1960's and again since 1970 demonstrated, are capable of quickly modifying their attitudes, and thus still come within the broad scope of the definition.

* * *

How many intellectuals are there in the present Polish population of 33 million? The following statistical table was drawn from various available sources:

	Members of the "Creative" Union or other organizations	Others	Total
Writers [5]	1,130	30	1,160
Journalists [6]	5,000	1,000	6,000
Scholars/Scientists [7]	40,000	—	40,000
High School Teachers [8]	32,000	—	32,000
Architects [9]	5,000	1,000	6,000
Painters, Sculptors [10]	4,200	2,000	6,200
Film and Theatre Actors, Directors [11]	2,600	200	2,800
Composers [12]	3,400	100	3,500
Others [13]	10,000	500	11,500
Total	103,330	4,830	108,160

---

[5] *Cf.* Stefan Koźnicki, "Mały atlas anatomiczny pisarza polskiego," 1-5 *Kultura* (Warsaw), 4 July - 26 September 1971; see also *Time*, 21 February 1972, p. 18.

In terms of social origin there is a striking contrast between the intelligentsia and the intellectuals. During World War II, 35 per cent of the pre-war Polish intelligentsia perished, and in the next twenty-five years their numbers dwindled even more. Thus, in 1971-72, more than 90 per cent of the people who could be classed as belonging to this social strata have studied in People's Poland. A majority of them (more than 55 per cent) are of worker or peasant background. Their number can be estimated today at about 3,000,000. In contrast, among the intellectuals, even though the process of integration into their ranks of the newcomers has been going on at a steady pace, the majority still are not of worker or peasant origin.

The social origin of the intellectuals is probably one reason for their restricted participation in the political life of the country. Among twenty-seven writers and journalists elected to the *Sejm* in 1972, twelve belonged to the PUWP, three to the Democratic Party, two to the United Peasant Party, two were members of "Pax" (progressive Catholics who support the Communist Party), four belonged to the Catholic group "Znak," and four were independents.

An even smaller number of intellectuals are members of the highest Communist Party bodies — the Politbureau and the Central Committee. Their number, however, has increased since 1971. For example, in 1969 there were only twelve writers and journalists in the Party exe-

---

6 *Cf. Prasa Polska* for the years 1970-72, *Neue Deutsche Press,* 13 (1972), p. 8, and *Novinar,* 7/8 (August 1972), p. 8. Among the 1,000 "others" there are younger people who are not as yet full-fledged members of the Union of Journalists and others who no longer belong to it, usually because they have not paid their subscriptions.

7 *Cf. Rocznik Statystyczny 1971* (Warsaw), pp. 473, 488, 508 and 509. Note that between the two categories (scholars/scientists and teachers) there is a certain amount of "statistical osmosis."

8 *Życie Warszawy,* 7-8 December 1969; among the 1,000 "others" are included about 400 who are working temporarily abroad (of whom 200 are in Paris) and approximately 600 who do not belong to the Union.

9 These figures are not up to date; they are taken from the book by Jan Szczepański (Warsaw, 1971), *op. cit.* p. 107; the figure of 2,000 refers to painters, sculptors and graphic artists who are not Union members.

10 A. Wallis, *Artyści plastycy, zawód i środowisko* (Warsaw, 1964); also Szczepański, *op. cit.,* p. 108.

11 *Ibid.*

12 *Ibid.*

13 Jerzy H. Mond, ed., *6 lat temu* (Paris, 1962), p. 195. For the text in French see Georges Mond, *La Presse Polonaise et celle des autres Democraties Populaires* (Doctoral thesis presented at the Sorbonne on 18 June 1963), p. 422.

cutive, while at present there are eighteen. Even so, the fact remains that among the intellectuals of any stature, even among those who are members of the Communist Party, only a very few have any real political influence.

Another reason for the gap between the ruling elite and the intellectuals has been the traditional tendency on the part of the intellectuals toward non-conformist thinking. The relations between the ruling Party and the intellectuals in post-war Poland have been characterized by mutual suspicion. The two sides have been caught up in a vicious circle. The political leaders suspect the intellectuals of independent thinking, a factor that negatively affects their attitudes towards the intellectual elite; in turn, the intellectuals often display an equal degree of mistrust of those in power. In particular the political leaders resent the role of the intellectual as "the conscience of the nation." This was demonstrated by the attacks of Gomułka and other political leaders against the eminent figures in Polish culture and science. At the meeting with the journalists on 5 October 1957 Gomułka said: "You claim that the writers are the conscience of the nation and they must convey what they see in the nation. . . . Comrades, the conscience of the nation is the Party, the Communists. We are also the conscience of the nation, although we are not writers."[14]

*   *   *

The controversy over what should be the role of the intellectuals in contemporary Poland — should they be the critics of the existing system or troubadours at the service of the ruling Party — was well illustrated by the dilemma which faced the journalists in reporting on the ferment among the workers in the coastal cities which culminated in the rebellion of December 1970. In two articles which appeared in the organ of the Polish Union of Journalists, *Prasa Polska*, published in the spring of 1971, the newsmen's problems were depicted with an unusual frankness.

A reporter from Gdańsk, Józef Królikowski, described the difficulties in reporting the evident signs of growing dissatisfaction among the workers in the shipyards of that city:

It was pointed out to us, the journalists, especially those of us who are Party members, that we are the militants of the "ideological front"; that the

---

[14] Józef Królikowski, "Kilka refleksji nie tylko o prasie," *Prasa polska*, 4 (April 1971), pp. 5-7.

mass media should support the Party . . . to advance its policies and stimulate the masses in their productive efforts.

At the same time it was made impossible for us to carry out these tasks because of the restrictions on our activities, through the multiplication of the subjects and questions which were declared as "taboo." This was done by refusing the right to publish any critical remarks and to articulate the worries which were gnawing at the workers, which stemmed from the economic decisions made in recent years.

It was, therefore, understandable that in such a situation the role of critic which the press was supposed to play was minimized. Such very anaemic criticism as did occasionally appear in the press was not effective and found no response, since the attitude taken by the representatives of the Party and the administration in general, was to ignore criticism on the part of the press.

All the failures and shortcomings of the administration, the poor organization of work, the irregularities in the distribution of rewards, prizes, and other material benefits were, alas! outside of the sphere of press criticism.[15]

A reporter of the Szczecin daily, Adam Kilnar, described in some detail the reaction of journalists to the workers' rebellion and its bloody suppression by the police. He admitted that even though the newsmen's sympathies were on the side of the workers, they did not dare defy the Communist Party:

When, on the morning of 18 December 1970, after the tragic Thursday in Szczecin, our editorial board gathered in the printing shop, we thought about what we were going to write, and how we could assess the events which had happened in the streets during the preceding day.

We could not condemn the workers' protests, not only because that would have produced a renewal of the demonstrations in the streets, but, above all, because we were convinced that the protest of the shipyard workers, and of those from other industries, was justified.

The journalistic circles of Szczecin and of Gdańsk, thus, found themselves in a particularly delicate situation. . . . We were aware of the justice of the workers' protests, yet we could not openly say it because that would have implied that we rejected the assessment by the Party and would have been a violation of Party discipline.

In spite of this anguish, and in spite of the great psychological pressure, there was probably not one journalist on the Baltic Coast who would present the "information for the masses" in a fashion independent of the Party

[15] Adam Kilnar, *Prasa polska*, 3 (March 1971), pp. 6, 7.

line, let alone opposed to the Party line. We all believed that the Party would find enough strength to overcome the crisis. All the efforts of the journalists were concentrated on hastening that process and on calming down public opinion.[16]

Kilnar, however, drew the right conclusions from his experience in December 1970. He acknowledged that the journalists failed to perform their functions in the society and in this way they contributed to the tragedy in the coastal cities:

Those memorable days were a good lesson for every journalist. We realized the import of each written word, and the weight of our responsibility. The responsibility was that much greater because we were all convinced that we were partly responsible for everything that had happened on the Baltic Coast — for the policies as well as tragic events. . . .

In fact the people told us: "We prefer the most bitter truths to a dolled-up version of the facts. We want factual information transmitted in two directions, from us to the authorities and vice versa."[17]

Since 1971 the Polish press has been freer, more diversified and openly critical of those in power. Many outspoken articles by writers and scholars have appeared in the papers. There has also been an effort on the part of the government to supply more information to the press. A special spokesman, with the rank of Under Secretary of State, was appointed in March 1971 to keep the press regularly informed about the activities of the government as well as of the top Party organs.

* * *

With the freer atmosphere in the country the old question of the role of the intellectuals has once again been revived. The preference given by the Communist authorities to political loyalty over intellectual and moral qualifications has come under heavy fire. A well-known jurist and sociologist, Andrzej Piekara, writing in *Prawo i Życie*, minced no words in suggesting that a proletarian social background and membership in the Party should not be the only criteria for placing people in positions of influence: "Even the most advantageous social background, together with a Party member's card, cannot eradicate such characteristics as laziness, lack of moral scruples, careerism and social egotism, as well as a desire for an easy life that has not been deserved and earned

---

[16] *Ibid.*
[17] *Prasa polska,* 4 (April 1971), p. 4.

through honest work. . . . Before putting someone in a position of public trust, what is as important as his class origin is his general behaviour. How does he live and work? . . . What sound contributions has he made?"[18]

Professor Jerzy Bukowski of the Warsaw Politechnic, argued along similar lines in the Warsaw daily, *Zycie Warszawy*: "Bourgeois attitudes show up as frequently among Party members as among non-Party members; sincere social radicalism and a responsible attitude can also be found among non-Party members. . . . This may seem to be obvious, but needs to be reiterated because of the all-too-common tendency to set the intelligentsia apart from the rest of society."[19]

Similar opinions were voiced among the university students. In the fall of 1971 their paper, *Student*, came out with a critical analysis of the past, and expressed the hope that the intellectuals who had been harassed after March 1968 would be rehabilitated. It also suggested that henceforth a more important role should be given to the intellectuals: "In March 1968, Poland found itself faced with the same problems as in December 1970, a loss of the people's confidence in those in power, a loss of contact between the Party and the masses, the concentration of power through centralization of the State, violation of democracy, complete incompetence in economics. The fact that in 1968 the conflict was between the Party and the creative intelligentsia and the students, while in 1970 it was a clash between the Party and the workers, only proved that during the three years the crisis spread and went deeper." The conclusion of the students' paper was not much different from that of the intellectuals of the older generation: "Our country is in such a situation that we can no longer keep any human resources in isolation just because of their political dissension. We must dispute their opinions, but we should not pretend they do not exist."[20]

In March 1972 a memorandum signed by some leading Polish scholars (among whom were the noted philosopher, Professor Tadeusz Kotarbiński and the senior-economist, Professor Edward Lipiński) was addressed to Gierek, calling his attention to the critical situation of Polish science and Polish universities. The authors of the memorandum also

[18] Andrzej Piekar, "Partia liczy na uczciwych," *Prawo i Życie* (19 September 1971), p. 1.
[19] Jerzy Bukowski, *Życie Warszawy* (14/15 February 1971), p. 3.
[20] Stanisław Dziechciaruk, *Student* (1-14 November 1971).

pleaded that the social origin of the scholars and their political commitment should not be the criteria for their evaluation by the political authorities, and that the scientists who had been repressed under Gomułka be rehabilitated. It seems that at least a few of these recommendations have been implemented, but their total impact is still difficult to evaluate.

Professor Kotarbiński, in an interview for the Warsaw weekly, *Kultura*, emphasized even more strongly the need for teaching and research free from interference by the political authorities: "A good teacher and lecturer should be factual and convinced of the accuracy of what he teaches and, for that, he must be able to draw on fundamental sources of truth. In a climate of half-truths or misleading evidence, the teaching profession cannot function. A light that is limited in scope becomes a laser; it can cut but it can no longer help us to see."[21]

The conclusion reached by this esteemed scholar is almost a classic example of the critical views among the intellectuals towards those who exercise political power. This must have been obvious to every ordinary reader in Poland. No doubt it has also been evident to the censor. The very fact that such remarks have been published is, therefore, a reassuring sign of the situation in Poland after 1970.

The Polish intellectuals have thus assumed the role of a pressure group. They try, in one way or another, to influence those in power and to participate in decision-making in the socio-cultural, and even political matters. Those aspirations were clearly articulated in an article published in *Życie Warszawy* by a well-known sociologist, Jan Strzelecki. He argued that in order to mobilize all the social energies necessary for a scientific and technological revolution in Poland needed for its progress and prosperity, it is necessary for the country to evolve in the direction of democracy. He recommended that those in power strive to make life in the country more consonant with the democratic customs and traditions. Strzelecki closed his article quite firmly: "I emphasize," he wrote, "that I consider such an attitude on the part of those in power the most important condition for the realization of all the tasks that are before us."[22]

Yet, not all of the articles in the press equally anticipated an increased

---

[21] Jerzy Mikke-Korwin, "Ideolog człowieczeństwa," *Kultura* (6 August 1972).
[22] Jan Strzelecki, "Partnerstwo i dialog," *Życie Warszawy* (21/22 November 1971).

role of the intellectuals. There were some negative opinions as well. Writing in *Prawo i Życie*, Wiesław Mysłek took a different stand; indeed, he anticipated possible ominous consequences of such a development: "The campaign to reinforce the role of the intelligentsia has had a precedent. It reminds one of what happened in Czechoslovakia only a few years ago. We know what its results were."[23]

The Communist daily, *Trybuna Ludu*, reproached the intellectuals, and especially the writers, for their "universalism" and their "European penchant," which is attributed to the social make-up of the literary milieu. This is why the writers "evade the major problems and only deal with marginal concerns." "Polish culture," concluded the Party organ, "cannot fulfill the role which is incumbent upon it, if it is dominated by a mania for blindly imitating models which correspond neither to our ideology nor to our national genius, whilst the European complex which is still evident in certain quarters, aims at the blind dissemination of fashions and attitudes formed on the basis of regimes that are alien to us. . . . We can find many examples of such tendencies."

* * *

There are several schools of thought and several *Weltanschaungen* among the contemporary Polish intellectuals. It is possible to distinguish several Catholic groups: the pro-Communist "Pax"; the realist group of "Znak," linked in some ways to the ecclesiastical hierarchy; and the Catholic conservative intellectuals, laymen as well as clergy — Cardinal Wyszyński being himself a noteworthy intellectual.

Among the Marxists there is still a fairly large group of neo-Stalinists: the liberal-modernists (although the word liberal in the Polish context has other connotations than in the West); the technocrats-pragmatists, who are concerned above all with the effectiveness of the new economic and social policies; and the anti-Stalinist intellectuals, who are neither liberals nor technocrats.

Finally, there are quite a few independent intellectuals who belong neither to the Marxist nor to the Catholic groups. Professor Tadeusz Kotarbiński and Stefan Kisielewski (the well-known columnist of the Catholic weekly *Tygodnik Powszechny*, who declares he is not a member of any Catholic group) are the best examples of these.

---

[23] Wiesław Mysłek, "Tropienie socializmu," *Prawo i Życie* (26 December 1971), p. 3.

The Polish intellectuals cover a wide spectrum of political positions: complete conformity, positive commitment, opportunism, apathy, nonconformity, and occasionally even open opposition. Thus, it is extremely difficult to arrive at any generalization concerning the political views of the intellectuals. They do not have many illusions about the West, if only because of Poland's geo-political location and the existing international realities. Nevertheless, it would seem correct to state that the great majority of them are not bound to orthodox Marxism. The legacies of the past make the official ideology very difficult for the minds of the intellectuals to accept. Not only are they well informed about what goes on in the world, but the internal dissemination of the news among them is also quite considerable. This again contributes to their ideological caution.

In many respects the intellectuals continue to play the role of the "conscience of the nation." Their attitudes certainly affect the broad strata of the Polish intelligentsia, and through them the entire society. Despite the intensive programme of ideological indoctrination, backed by all the means at the disposal of the state, especially its control over the mass media, it is openly admitted that the socialist consciousness of the nation has yet to be moulded. It is noted by inside as well as outside observers of the Polish scene that the old aristocratic and bourgeois traditions are still alive in Polish society, especially among the intelligentsia.[24]

Raymond Aron's analysis of the role of intellectuals in the West applies to some extent also to Poland: "Intellectuals realize their inability to change the course of events, but they are unaware of their influence. In the long run, the politicians are the disciples of professors and writers. . . . The theory taught in universities will become, in some years hence, the guide to action by the administrators and the ministers."[25]

Yet, in the present political atmosphere there are also signs that the Polish intellectuals see for themselves opportunities to play a more direct role in the public affairs of the country. It is rather significant that since 1970 the emigration of intellectuals from Poland, which was fairly wide-

---

[24] See for instance, Jan Szczepański, *Polish Society* (New York, 1969), pp. 174-78; and Adam Bromke, "A Pole Views His Country," *Problems of Communism*, XX (July-August 1970), pp. 75-76.

[25] Raymond Aron, *L'opium des intellectuels* (Paris, 1955), p. 258.

spread in the late 1960's, has practically ceased. Also, some of the major figures of the March 1968 movement, Antoni Słonimski, Stefan Kisielewski, Jerzy Andrzejewski and others, have accepted some *modus vivendi* with the Communist Party.

The final note in this study is neither optimistic nor pessimistic. The cultural, moral and even socio-political influence of the intellectuals in Polish society is undeniable, and those presently in power seem to be aware of it. Thus, if the promises of 1971 are kept, in spite of all the reservations and the still very narrow limits for their activities, there is a chance that the intellectuals may be given an opportunity to use their talents and knowledge in the service of the country.

Social Sciences and the Reform of the Education System

JAN SZCZEPAŃSKI

For the social sciences in Poland, 1971 marked an important turning point in relations with the political authorities in the People's Republic. Prior to that year, representatives of the social sciences had on numerous occasions presented various proposals regarding the practical exploitation of their studies as a basis for the shaping of the state's policies in specific fields of action. These proposals were treated with polite scepticism. The political authorities' interest had been focussed on the ideological function of these sciences, their influence on the social consciousness of the nation, and therefore only on their ideological content and their conformity with the ideological line of pure Marxism-Leninism.

A major change in this sphere was brought about by the events which took place at the end of 1970, which the Party recognized as having been rooted in the inappropriate economic and social policies. The plenary meetings of the Central Committee of the PUWP at the end of December 1970 and in January 1971 accepted the need for changes and for basing the policy on rational foundations. Several committees of experts were set up to conduct scientific studies of the various aspects of community life, and to formulate principles for the adoption of the best possible policies in these various spheres. The areas under consideration were mainly the economy, and the methods of planning and directing it; public administration, and its most effective functioning; the elaboration of guidelines for an improved educational policy, and an improved model of the educational system; a social policy which would better satisfy the citizens' needs, etc. All of these are no longer concerned with the ideological usefulness of the social sciences. The basis of evaluation has become their engineering value, their ability to produce improved techniques for the shaping of society and for directing its development, and their ability to formulate principles for the nation's policy concerning its structure, organization, and functioning. It is precisely in this sense that the social sciences are at present undergoing a political test.

*   *   *

Are the social sciences ready and able to carry out such tasks and to meet such a test? This question is no longer really valid. It could have been posed in this way when the practical application of the social sciences was still contained in a "make-believe" context, but not when they are requested to cope with the concrete tasks. Until recently, only the economic sciences have been in a different position, the planning and management of the socialist economy having been based on the political economy of socialism and on particular economic theory. Even there the situation was not clear since it was difficult to recognize to what extent the shortcomings and errors of the planned economy were the fault of the economists and to what extent that of the politicians, who, according to the economists, were not listening to their advice. Now, however, the role of the economists has been made clear, and they, too, are included in the various commissions working on the preparation of a new economic policy, and the various aspects of the economic model.

Of particular interest here, however, is the role of sociology. It could be said that it was the sociologists who were most vigorous in advancing their various proposals and who were most actively involved in practical work in the community. On the one hand, the applied sociologist has emerged as a professional figure, engaged in industry, in health services, in education, in cultural institutions, etc.; a sociologist whose role is, to a large extent, that of an expert working under a specific supervisor. On the other hand, sociologists have often voiced wider ambitions. This writer did it himself in various articles written since 1948: in "Sociology, Ideology and Social Technique," published in 1948 in *Przegląd Socjologiczny*; in "The Social Sciences and Politics," published in 1957; in "Sociological Basis for Planning the Expansion of Cultural Goods and Services," published in 1959, and in others. In recent years, the proposal most vigorously promoted was that of "sociotechnique," conceived by Podgórecki as an independent science falling somewhere between sociology and practical social work in the various spheres of communal life. The work of Adam Podgórecki and his colleagues is contained in three volumes: A. Podgórecki: *The Foundations of Sociotechnique* (Wiedza Powszechna, 1966); *Sociotechnique: The Practical Applications of Sociology* (Książka i Wiedza, 1968); and *Sociotechnique: How to Influence Effectively* (Książka i Wiedza, 1970), as well as in various articles found in numerous journals. These are the first systematic attempts at the elaboration of a technique to apply sociology and social research in the various areas of practice with a view to provide scientific solutions to practical problems.

Sociotechnique is not, however, the only such attempt on the part of the sociologists. One could also mention the papers and articles written by various groups proposing the establishment of institutes for applied research; in particular, the activities which led to the setting-up of the Centre for Public Opinion Evaluation affiliated with the Polish Radio; the proposals submitted to the Committee for Research and Forecasting, "Poland in 2000," of the Polish Academy of Sciences, etc. Lawyers, brought together in the Academy of Science's Institute of Legal Studies, conducted research into administration and other spheres of social life, in the hope that the results of their studies would make it possible to improve the legislative process and to make law a more effective tool in determining social developments. Pedagogy is another social science which has been prominent in the process of improving practice; the results of various studies in this field should lead directly to improvements in the school system. Psychology also plays its part as an applied science in many fields, from industry to education, supplying techniques in personnel selection, in motivation, in conflict resolution.

Since they have been putting forward proposals of this sort for a long time, it seems that the representatives of the social sciences have felt confident that they have at their disposal a sufficient body of knowledge to be of use in improving the political mechanisms of the functioning of society. Of course, some academics and social scientists may have felt that the interest of politicians in their work would enable them to obtain the resources necessary for the conduct of research and the training of the scientific cadre. They felt that their studies would eventually bring about practical results. Such proposals were often based more on the desire to develop the discipline, rather than to improve current practice. The putting forward of practical proposals was often used as "bait" — a method of capturing the imagination of the politicians, who, not understanding the theoretical problems of the various sciences, were not open to any other approaches.

All this is now more or less a thing of the past. At present, the work of the various groups of experts and financing in the various disciplines is directly linked to applied research; the academics are presented with concrete, practical problems to solve, and for this purpose they are provided with considerable resources, permitting the expansion of research facilities.

* * *

The expert at work in the evaluation of the worth and social effectiveness of the school system, encounters a number of questions which lie outside the routine and everyday practice of the social sciences. These are, above all, questions about the criteria to be used in the evaluation of both the existing state of affairs and the desirable changes to bring about improvements. It is astonishing to see how varied and at times even ill-thought-out are the criteria of evaluation used by the different representatives of the school system and the people involved in its activities. It is obvious that the criteria of evaluation used by teachers and pupils must be, and are, divergent. But the criteria applied by the administration and management of individual schools, by the organs of the Supreme Chamber of Control, by the trade unions, and by the teachers are either completely incompatible or, at least, very different. As a result, for example, the evaluations of the existing system of vocational training in Poland made by representatives of industry, by the departments directing these schools, by the state organs of control, by the teachers working in these schools, by the Ministry of Education, and finally by the parents of the pupils of these schools, amount to a veritable mosaic of widely divergent views.

Nevertheless, in order to carry out an expert appraisal, one needs an evaluation of the effectiveness of the pedagogical, economic, social, and political activities of the secondary school system, as well as the higher elementary and specialized schools. There is a need here for clearly defined criteria for the degree of effectiveness with which all of these schools fulfill their functions. This leads us to the first set of questions: What criteria for the evaluation of the pedagogical effectiveness of the present school system can the teaching profession offer? What criteria can the sociology of education offer, when the social effectiveness of the system is considered? With what criteria does social policy evaluate the functioning of the school system? Have the economists developed some criteria for the measurement of economic effectiveness of the school system and for the evaluation of its possible variants? What does psychology have to say about the value of the programmes and of the scope and content of teaching, in relation to the capacity and the functioning of the brain?

The question of criteria is one of outstanding importance in the scientific solution of the educational problems. In the past, the development of school programmes, the organization of the school system, the decisions concerning the amount of material the pupils must memorize, etc., have been guided by poorly quantified experiments, and by the reactions and intuitions of the practitioners, rather than by precise analysis. There arises, however, the question of whether such precise analysis is possible. Can expert appraisals be based on any system of scientifically tested criteria? The answer to the question will be given by the specialists called in to prepare a scientific appraisal of education. The results of their work will thus represent the test about which we spoke at the beginning of this article.

* * *

It would be an interesting exercise to explore all of the tacit assumptions underlying thinking about models of the educational system. Often, when we talk about a model of education, we have in mind a certain structure and organization of the school system, marshalling the flow of young people through that system (according to their ability, the desire for study, their aims in life and the existing socio-economic opportunities) into particular channels of education, and placing the graduates in specific occupations. We thus see the school system as a relatively rigid organizational structure, which corresponds to the needs of society (of economy, of culture, of administration, etc.) and which satisfies the aspirations of the young generation. Such a scheme, once accepted, can last for several years or even decades, and changes in it are acomplished by ceremonial acts and undertakings known as reforms.

The model undergoes minor corrections on the basis of legal acts. Changes within the model — addition or elimination of some constituent elements, such as the setting-up of particular programmes; revisions of the programmes; changes in grades or in the style of teaching; emphasizing or de-emphasizing specialization; the creation of new regulations; changes in the duration of instruction or of studies, etc. — are at times also called reforms; but in fact this is a purely ceremonial step, which attempts to enhance the importance of a minor change by giving it a more impressive name.

It is clear that the structure of the school system should correspond to the current situation and to trends in the development of society. It is up to the sociologists concerned with education to determine the general relationship between the structure and development of the society and the structure and development of the school system. This interrelationship is founded on many principles, a few of which may be pointed out here: the school system prepares the citizens for full participation in all forms of community life; it gives each citizen the opportunity to make decisions regarding the goals of his life within the society;

it offers specialized training according to the differentiations within the society; and it prepares the citizens for the perpetuation and development of the nation's cultural heritage. The school system also trains cadres for management and for leadership; that is, it provides the training which makes possible the emergence of people well prepared for decision-making leadership at all levels and in all spheres of society. To fulfill these functions, the school system must in some fields be ahead of the general level of development in the society, while in others it must serve its need for continuity and stability.

The question then arises, how to evolve a model for an educational system which at the same time would satisfy the current needs of society and the future needs arising from its development. It seems that thinking about a model for the school system of the future must be based on several principles. In the first place, one must do away with ideas about a lasting and rigid framework of levels of training, numbers of grades, areas of specialization, etc. The time has passed when one could plan a model of the system which, once brought into being, could last several years or decades without change. The school does, however, by the nature of its activities and of its characteristics, belong to the type of institution which changes exceedingly slowly. This can be observed in many countries. The phenomenon of the school development lagging behind that of society as a whole has often appeared in history. In planning the school of the future, which should be an element contributing to the dynamic development of society as a whole, we must plan the school system according to a model that would keep up with, and even run ahead of, the rate of change in society. It follows that such a school system must be a *self-adapting system*.

Yet the capability to adapt itself, built into the school system, will still not resolve all the problems connected with its social functions. It is also necessary to build into the school system the capability for *self-improvement*; that is, performing in such a way that, in the course of adapting to the changes in society, the level of the school's work and especially the level of its effectiveness would be enhanced.

So the school system of the future must be a flexible one; rigidity must be abandoned. In times of rapid change in the substance of education, the changing needs of society for qualified cadres, and the changing attitudes of the citizens who want to participate optimally in society and quickly to achieve widely divergent goals in life, it is inconceivable that the school system could remain unchanged for more than a decade.

It is necessary that the new model of the school system be sufficiently flexible, at all levels and in all fields of teaching, so as to be able to adapt itself to the social changes; and simultaneously to perfect itself, in accordance with the dynamic development of society as a whole.

*   *   *

The above statement is not particularly novel; similar ideas have often been advanced in the past. Yet, a whole series of questions must be raised: How can we avoid the poorly planned and hasty changes which have been the nightmare of the school system during the last decade, and assure the rationality of future changes? What mechanisms would have to be built into the school system in order to give it the new desirable qualities? What institutional elements would provide for such a flexibility in the school system that it would be able to continually adapt itself at all levels, from the ministries supervising it at the top, all the way down to the individual school classes?

The solutions to these problems, regardless of their scope or level, must be submitted to a dual test. The first of these is the *test of necessity,* which consists in ascertaining whether the change in question is really needed, or whether it can be avoided. The second is the *test of effectiveness* which consists of an examination of the means and methods of the proposed changes, to determine whether they will really bring about the desired effect in the performance of the school system.

It follows, then, that to each proposal for a new model of the educational system there must be added an appendix elaborating how it is going to meet those two tests. This should stem the tide of ill-conceived and hasty changes, brought in without proper preparation and without accurate predictions of their effects. Any change produces a certain measure of unforeseen and undesirable consequences, so an effort must be made from the outset to keep them to a minimum.

The second problem is no less complex: How can we build mechanisms into the school system for self-adaptation and self-improvement? It would require the abandonment of many principles of the supervision and administration of schools, which are at present regarded as sacred. Is it possible to maintain the central supervision of the school system, to ensure that the training of students in a certain type of school is similar or even identical throughout the entire country? Can we preserve the central direction of teaching programmes at all levels, and at the same time develop the self-adaptability of the school? What must be the scope and the initiative of the individual teacher, the school director, the inspector and curator, departmental director or minister, if we build into the school system the capability for self-adaptation and self-improvement? These questions will have to be answered before the operational principles of a new school system model of the future can be adopted.

It seems that the mechanisms of self-adaptation and self-improvement should be based on organized research and on observations of the results of the school's operations. The mechanism for this should be as follows: Each level of management from the school director to the minister should have access, independent of the administration, to a body of observation and analysis of the operations results of its own particular segment of the organization. This should be based on research into the performance of the pupils, the trends of developments in the particular occupational areas for which they are trained, as well as the changes in society at large, and finally into the aspirations of the individuals within the changing social context. In turn, each level of management would supply necessary information to the schools, to ensure that they did not fall behind and become disfunctional in relation to the development of society.

The adoption of such a system would require not only the development of research facilities and institutes, but also the expansion of the scientific cadre to carry out the observations. At the same time it would require from the administrators at all levels an ability to take advantage of these studies and use them to introduce corrections into the system. Finally, it would require the improvement of managerial methods throughout the school system, so as to preserve its internal cohesion. The limit of change to be allowed at each individual level of management would have to be very precisely defined.

The planning of a new model of the educational system, then, is not a task that can be accomplished in the course of one or two years. It is a task for the future, requiring many efforts and, above all, the basic transformation of the old ways of thinking about education.

*   *   *

In my essay, "Sociology - Sociotechnique - Law - Administration" (*Państwo i Prawo*, 3-4 [1971]), I tried, by tracing a path back from sociology through sociotechnique to the prescriptions of law and their effects on the functioning of the administration, to show the great distance between theoretical knowledge and the applied techniques which could be used in the actual management of social life. In light of the above discussion on the role of the experts in preparing reforms, this problem must be placed in a broader perspective. Diagnoses and changes should not be sporadic phenomena, appearing only at times of crises and tensions, but should be a "normal" component of the day-to-day functioning of the economy and the administration.

I have postulated the "building-in" of science into the economy and in other spheres of public affairs. This postulate may seem obvious, especially when one is concerned with, for example, industrial production. It is natural that a very large industrial complex or plant should have its own research organization to control the pace of technological development and carry out an on-going appraisal. Its scientists should be members of the management team and take part in the decision-making process. However, such an organization should not include only technologists, mathematicians, and representatives of the natural sciences, but also economists, sociologists, psychologists, doctors and so on.

By analogy, one can envisage each people's council — at the level of a large city, a province, or the national administration (the central organs of the political authorities) — as having groups of scientists "built in" as a "normal" part of the team. The scientists would take part in elaborating the principles of general policy in the various spheres, would participate as equals in the decision-making process, and would examine the implementation of decisions to ensure that the organs responsible for policy formulation and decision-making received the feedback necessary for the correction of policy.

Can the social sciences supply the people capable of performing such a role? Must there always remain between the "ruler" and the "expert" a difference in the perspective of reality due to the prisms of their different professional interests? To put it another way, the politician always tends to approach the solution of problems not solely on the basis of their merits, but from the point of view of exercising power, safeguarding his own position, and perpetuating himself in power. In contrast, the expert tends to view issues solely from the point of view of methodology and substance. It seems that in our political system, where the party in power is not seriously threatened by an organized opposition, it is possible to overcome this divergence in attitudes; moreover, the very nature of the power is conducive for the politicians to come to an understanding with the experts, and to perceive their point of view.

If the politicians are able (and we think that they are) to pass the test of science, then the question arises, whether the social sciences are ready for a political test. The present work of the groups of experts is to some extent their initiation into such a test. If, in their reports, they prove themselves to be useful in the planning and formulating of economic, social, housing, educational, and other policies, the first great dialogue will have been successful. One can then begin to think of the second stage, the permanent inclusion of scientific workers in the economy, in the administration and in other spheres of public life.

*   *   *

Are the social sciences, their research institutes, their academic societies, their faculties of higher studies, aware of this test, which could have such profound effects on their future activities and development? Of course, it will always be possible to engage in these sciences, as heretofore, on an *ad hoc* basis with limited resources, working in small research groups, and solving fragmentary problems. The involvement in expert appraisals and in the study of problems related to the national plan opens up possibilities for the organization of large research facilities and the bringing together of large interdisciplinary teams. It also presents the opportunity for social science studies to come into the mainstream of life by solving key problems directly related to the national policy and to the basic social problems. If this opportunity is not exploited, and the social sciences do not succeed in passing the test; if they prove incapable of making a real contribution to the implementation of effective reforms; if they are not able to satisfactorily answer the call of practice; their worth will once again be evaluated solely by ideological criteria, in terms of the assistance which they can render in shaping the social consciousness.

The choice between pure and applied research is a difficult one to make. Involvement in the tackling of key problems provides a powerful stimulus to the pursuit of pure research. It opens up greater opportunities than in the past, when research was conducted by small groups or by individuals. This is because pure research in the social sciences also requires extensive facilities, with a widespread network of researchers, and a good supply of mechanical equipment. At the same time, in the solution of problems relating to national policy the need for sound theoretical knowledge will no doubt continue to be extremely important.

Contemporary Theatre

BENEDYKT HEYDENKORN

Even in its most abstract forms, art is never divorced from life. It never comes to fruition suddenly, but has its roots in the past. Regardless of its universalistic values, art also has specific national characteristics. These are often easier to detect in one field than in another, but they are always there. Even when some artistic trends spread over wide areas in the creativity of the artists from different countries, one still may observe their unique national contributions in substance, form, and style.

Contemporary art in Poland is deeply rooted in national tradition. This does not mean that what one witnesses in that country represents a continued evolutionary process — that each next stage in artistic activity is a logical sequence of the preceding one. On the contrary, some trends have been interrupted, at times for decades, by other fashions whose origins could be traced to an entirely different epoch. Nevertheless, the country's cultural heritage is by now rich enough that even during dramatic breaks with the past there is a tendency to revert to some old Polish patterns. Thus at each stage of development, regardless of the artistic field and expression, some uniquely national characteristics are always present.

This essay will confine its attention exclusively to one field of art in today's Poland, namely, the theatre. The theatre is undoubtedly one of the most effective artistic means of influencing the masses. It could be argued that the film is an even more effective instrument for reaching large audiences. This is true, but not all films are artistic creations, as their objective might be entertainment, education, or even political propaganda. Some films, of course, do have high artistic value. From the late 1950's to the mid-1960's, Polish films aroused a good deal of interest abroad and scored many international successes. There is an excellent Higher Film School in Łódź which students from many countries attend.

Although Polish films are more easily understood by foreigners, the Polish theatre enjoys an even greater renown throughout the world. This is amazing not only because of the language barrier, but also because of its uniquely Polish character. The theatre in Poland is spectacular, but not ornamental; it is romantic, but not sentimental. Above all, it is extremely rich.

The contemporary Polish theatre still remains under the influence of the two great pre-war producers, both of whom were still active in the immediate post-war years: Leon Schiller and Juliusz Osterwa. Each represented a different approach. Unlike Osterwa, Schiller was not an actor, yet he was clearly a paramount figure in the Polish theatre. Schiller combined great literary and musical talents. He produced drama as well as musicals, comedies, operas, and even miracle plays. He not only adapted the texts, but supplemented them with his own songs and ballads. He was the master of spectacular shows, and could get the best out of leading actors while at the same time remaining in full control of large supporting casts. Schiller also was a founder of the National Theatre Institute in Warsaw. As a professor in the Institute he taught several contemporary producers, all of whom have continued his traditions, although none have taken Schiller's place. His heritage was so rich that it has been divided among his successors, with each developing a particular aspect of it.

The best known of Schiller's successors is Erwin Axer (b. 1917), the most conservative and the most classical of the contemporary Polish producers. His shows are extremely compact and elaborate in every detail. He has produced many plays, Polish as well as foreign. His repertoire has been basically contemporary; even when doing older plays, he has managed to give them a modern character.

Also among Schiller's disciples, and very different from Axer, is Kazimierz Dejmek (b. 1924). Fascinated by spectacular and more poetic shows, Dejmek has reproduced some of Schiller's plays, but in a new form; for example, Mickiewicz's "Forefathers," and "The History of the Splendid Resurrection of Nicolas of Wilkowieck." Djemek had a great success in Łódź where he presented a fine production of "Henry VI on the Hunt," based on an opera by Karol Karpiński, first produced in Warsaw in 1811. The manuscript of this opera was discovered recently in Dresden. Dejmek, however, reworked the music in cooperation with the outstanding composer Jerzy Dobrzański, and a writer of popular songs, Wojciech Młynarski.

Other well-known Schiller disciples are the Warsaw producers Ludwik René (b. 1914), Aleksander Bardini (b. 1913), Jerzy Kreczmar (b. 1902), and Lidia Zamkow (b. 1914). It would be a mistake, however, to confine one's attention exclusively to Warsaw. In Poland there are at present some eighty theatres, as well as several opera houses. Some very able producers are working in various provincial cities: Krystyna Skuszanka, Jerzy Krasowski, Konrad Swinarski, Zygmunt Hübner, Jerzy Jarocki, and Marek Okopiński. In recent years the younger generation has increasingly been making its own contribution. The most outstanding younger people are Bolesław Prus, Jerzy Grzegorzewski, Roman Kordziński, Giovanni Pampiglione, Piotr Piaskowski, Helmut Kajzer, Izabella Cywińska and Jan Skotnicki.

*   *   *

A quite separate theatrical category is represented by Adam Hanuszkiewicz, producer and director of the National Theatre in Warsaw; Jerzy Grotowski, founder and director of the Experimental Theatre in Wrocław; and Henryk Tomaszewski, founder and director of the Pantomime Theatre in Wrocław.

Hanuszkiewicz (b. 1924) is probably the only actor and producer without roots in any of the traditional theatrical schools. His is a great, and completely original talent. He started his career as a director of television theatre, where he gained a reputation for presenting bold productions. Later on he revealed the same talent in the theatre, and became the most revolutionary producer, in the sense of departing from traditional presentations of classical plays. He succeeded in captivating, and in some ways even shocking his audiences. This was especially true of his modernized versions of Krasiński's "Undivine Comedy," Słowacki's "Kordian," and a highly original production of Shakespeare's "Hamlet." He did not hesitate to supplement the classical texts with new lines, or to introduce modern music and dances into the performances.

Grotowski (b. 1933) has completely departed from the accepted theatrical norms. His "poor theatre" has not only a highly original repertoire, but also an entirely novel approach to the concept of acting. In Grotowski's theatre the audience participates in the performance. There is no stage and little paraphernalia. The actors convey their messages simply by their gestures and the modulation of their voices: they must "live" their roles. In a way, Grotowski's plays resemble medieval mystery plays. Grotowski undoubtedly has been influenced by the tradition of the great Russian producer Stanislavsky, to which he was exposed during his studies in Moscow. From Stanislavsky he borrowed realism and the psychological approach, but then drastically adapted these to fit his own conceptions. The results are completely different from the classical realism found in the Russian theatre.

Grotowski started his career in a small theatre, "13 Rows," in Opole. His first performances were received by the public with curiosity but without great enthusiasm. The drama critics were even less friendly. To what extent his determination to overcome these initial obstacles contributed to his ultimate success, is difficult to judge. By consciously eliminating all stage settings he undoubtedly made great demands on the skills of the actors. Grotowski also abandoned any single author's text and instead produced a composite play made up of fragments by various writers. An example is the famous "Apocalipsis cum figuris," which consists of excerpts from the Bible, Dostoyevsky, T. S. Eliot, and Simone Weil. Grotowski's experimental work is one of the greatest inovations in contemporary theatre and has been highly acclaimed in Western Europe and in the United States.

Tomaszewski (b. 1924) began his artistic career as a dancer, and the ballet plays an important part in his pantomimes. He now directs the only pantomime theatre in Poland, one of the best of its kind in the world. Like Grotowski, he is solely responsible for the training of his actors. In contrast to Grotowski, however, Tomaszewski won immediate acclaim, and his successes abroad helped strengthen his reputation at home. Tomaszewski personally authors (if such an expression is appropriate for the pantomime) and directs most of the performances by his group. Each role is carefully designed and executed. The message is also conveyed by the costumes and by the music.

One other producer should be mentioned: Andrzej Wajda (b. 1926), who acquired international fame as one of the founders of the "Polish film" school. Recently he has directed some theatre plays and has been praised for his highly original production of Dostoyevsky's "The Possessed."

* * *

The theatres in Poland offer a wide variety of Polish as well as foreign plays. As an illustration, during one month in 1972 plays by the following Polish authors were performed: Jan Kochanowski, Aleksander Fredro, Władysław Broniewski, Idelfons Gałczyński, Maria Kownacka, Ernest Bryll, Ludomir Legut, Agnieszka Osiecka, Michał Bałucki, Leon Pawlik, and Jasrosław Abramow. During that same month many foreign playwrights were represented: Henrik Ibsen, Jean Giraudoux, Marc Camolett, Pablo Neruda, Carlo Goldoni, Jean Genet, Fyodor Dostoyevsky, Peter Whitbread, Anton Chekhov, Brendan

Behan, Vladimir Mayakovsky, G. K. Chesterton, Luigi Pirandello, Claire-Lise Charbonnier, and J. B. Moliere.

The large number of theatres and the wide variety of their repertoire provides work for many actors. From the pre-war generation only a few are alive and still active. At present the largest group of actors is comprised of people who began their stage career in the immediate post-war years. However, some young actors, born after 1945, have already made it to the top. Each year, the theatrical prizes bring a few new names to the public's attention.

Over the years relatively few actors have remained at the very top. This situation is not necessarily an expression of the conservative taste of the Polish public; rather, it stems from the fact that in any group great talent is scarce. The great actors, who are also producers, have already been mentioned: Dejmek, Skuszanka, Axer, Swinarski, Hanusz-kiewicz, and Grotowski. The most famous Polish actors and actresses are Gustaw Holubek, Jan Świderski, Czesław Wołłejko, Wojciech Siemion, Tadeusz Łomnicki, Irena Eichler, Elżbieta Barszczewska, Halina Mikołajska, Barbara Krafftówna, Zofia Kucówna, Marta Lipińska and Aleksandra Śląska.

. Famous set designers have also contributed to the success of the Polish theatre. If foreigners are impressed by the originality of the Polish theatre, it is due in no small measure to the achievements of these artists. Stage settings are innovative, modern, and often startling. Set designers too have their areas of specialization: some prefer spectaculars, while others prefer comedy, satire, or even the grotesque. Often the settings and costumes give a unique twist to the play. The best known set designers are Andrzej Stopka, Zenobiusz Strzelecki, Jan Kosiński, Jozef Szajna, Otto Axer, Jan Szancer, Ewa Starowieyska, Teresa Roszkowska, Lech Zachorski, Krystyna Zachwatowicz, Fran-ciszek Starowieyski, Krzysztof Pankiewicz, Marian Stańczak, and Andrzej Sadowski.

A word should be said about another field of artistic endeavour, which in a way supplements that of the theatre. This is the theatre poster, usually the work of a graphic artist. The foremost artist of this type is Henryk Tomaszewski, professor at the Academy of Fine Arts in Warsaw. Fascinating posters have also been produced by Tadeusz Grabowski, Jan Lenica, Eryk Lidiński, Roman Cieślewicz, Adam Hoffman, Waldemar Siwierzy, and many others.

The theatre in Poland is extremely popular, and receives generous support from the government. Many plays are profitable, but others, especially the more spectacular and the more experimental, often produce deficits. Theoretically, each theatre is an independent financial unit, yet it is clear that, without government assistance, development of the theatrical arts would have been impossible.

*   *   *

The Polish theatre is an inseparable part of the national culture, and is closely linked with the country's everyday life in all its manifestations. This does not mean that all shows necessarily reflect contemporary problems. Often they deal with Poland's theatrical tradition, which dates back to the sixteenth century, and even with earlier folk tales and songs. Yet, by giving these plays a modern twist, the artists link them to contemporary problems. Symbolism and satire in the Polish theatre frequently provide an outlet for the expression of sentiments which could not otherwise be articulated.

Adam Hanuszkiewicz, in presenting his highly unorthodox version of Krasiński's "Undivine Comedy," defined the role of the theatre in the following words:

The theatre does not simply consist of a literary script and the reenactment of the roles prescribed by it. The theatre is a creature of many different, mutually interdependent elements — all linked to an organic whole. Theatrical art is not confined to the producer and the actor; it also includes the set designer, the composer, the musician, the architect, and finally the spectator.

The theatre production is above all an act of courage. It is a constant synthesis of the maximum risk with the maximum responsibility. The risk involves presenting one's own vision of the world. The responsibility consists of the awareness of the theatre's social function and its role in the development of the national culture. And our great, bold, and often controversial national literature does not make the producer's life any easier. Its message cannot be conveyed on the stage in a soothing play devoid of any conflict without distorting it.[1]

Even the conservative producer, Otto Axler, defined the role of contemporary Polish theatre in a somewhat similar fashion: "The theatre which is not solely regarded as a handicraft, but which is guided by concern for the aesthetic values . . . cannot be static. [Purely tradi-

---

[1] Nota od reżysera, "Nieboska komedia," Program Teatru Narodowego.

tional theatre] could provide an object of admiration and controversy for the professional critics, but it would never attract the interest of the broad masses."[2]

Jerzy Grotowski, leader of the experimental school, in responding to a question concerning his attitude towards the Polish theatrical tradition, identified himself with it in no uncertain terms. He wrote: "I am a product of this tradition. And my collaborators are products of this tradition. . . . We need not consciously search for it. The [Polish] tradition is there like the air which one breathes — one does not think about it. If one must look for it and emphasize it in an ostentatious fashion, this means that the tradition is not there. There is no sense in pretending, for it is not true. . . ."[3]

In response to a similar question at the Polish-French meeting at Royanmont in October 1972, Grotowski defined his position in an even more precise way: "I have never tried to consciously produce anything which is universalistic, global, or whatever term one would use. At the same time in working with my colleagues I have never thought how to be a Pole — for I am one. And so are they. Thus in our relations, in our work, in our perceptions — without any conscious effort on our part — we have been affected by our own conditions of life. In our case it is the Polish life. And also, in a broader sense, simply human life. . . ."[4]

Contemporary Polish theatre combines national and humanistic values. This is its main achievement. This is also the primary reason for its appeal, both at home and abroad.

---

[2] *Dialog* (June 1972), p. 129.
[3] *Dialog* (October 1972), p. 118.
[4] *Kultura,* 24 December 1972.

The Changing Catholicism in Poland*

JERZY TUROWICZ

When I say in the title that Catholicism is changing in Poland, I am fully aware that the essence of the Catholic faith and the basic structure of the Catholic church cannot be changed and are not changing. But the expression of this faith, the Catholic thought, the Catholic attitudes and mentality, a language in which the Gospel is announced, can change according to changing conditions, and are changing. This is true throughout the world. The church has a mission, a role to fulfill and must make its presence effectively meaningful for the world, and consequently it must adjust to concrete changing conditions. This is the meaning of the *aggriornamento* proclaimed by Pope John.

What is changing in Poland? First, it is necessary to present some basic information about the situation of Catholicism in Poland. Poland has been a Catholic country for over one thousand years. The Catholic church has played an enormous role in Polish history, shaping its culture, customs, social and political attitudes. Political developments in the eighteenth and nineteenth centuries have strengthened ties between religious and patriotic feelings, with all the advantages and disadvantages of this situation. The average Pole has a deep sense of attachment and fidelity to his faith and his church, characterized by traditionalism and sentimentalism. Unfortunately, we have failed to develop a more rational approach to our faith. With few exceptions we have never had in Poland — in the past or in more recent times — great theologians. Neither have we produced heretics.

Since 1944 we have been confronted in Poland with quite a new, and in some ways, an unexpected situation. As a result of the political developments at the end of World War II, Poland joined the Eastern European bloc of socialist countries. An encounter of Catholicism and materialistic-atheistic Marxism inevitably resulted in a conflict. In fact, it was a double conflict: ideological — between the two incompatible doctrines; and political — between the Communist state striving to attain a monopoly of ideological influence upon its citizens on the one

---

* This paper was first presented as an Adam Mickiewicz Memorial Lecture at Carleton University, 27 October 1971.

side, and the church, whose pure existence as an institution with a large following is a political factor, on the other. But life is stronger than theory, and the Catholic church has remained very dynamic in Poland. Indeed, any government with a more or less pragmatic attitude towards reality must take this fact into account.

Poland with its population of thirty-three million, is today confessionally a more homogenous country than it was before the war. Around 90 per cent of Poles are members of the Catholic church. This does not mean that all of them are churchgoers or deep believers, but the percentage of religious practice today is high, certainly higher than, for instance, in Western Europe. On Sundays Polish churches are crowded, with even standing room at a premium. In all of the thirty Polish dioceses there are diocesan seminaries, most of which are full. Some of the seminaries must refuse applicants, since they outnumber the available places. All religious orders, masculine and feminine, active in Poland before the war, are active today, even if their field of activity is in some way restricted, and many of them continue to have a good number of novitiates. There are few evident signs of the so-called "priest's identity crisis." Some people say that priests are so busy, and have so much to do, that they do not have time to think about their identity.

There are only about ten Catholic private high schools, but even before the war they were not numerous. Although religious instruction has been eliminated from public schools, the church has succeeded in developing, outside the scholastic system, a network of courses on religion for the children and young people. The attendance at such courses is relatively high. We have a Catholic university in Lublin — the only one between Berlin and Shanghai. There is also a state-founded graduate Academy of Catholic Theology in Warsaw. During the past few years, several hundred laymen (including women) have studied theology at this Academy, with no intention of ever becoming priests. The Catholic press, although reduced in the number of titles, and subject to some difficulties and limitations, contributes to the development of the thinking Catholic elite and plays a substantial role in Polish cultural life.

All this does not mean that everything is in order, and that the situation is idyllic. On the contrary, the permanent tension in church-state relations in Poland produces numerous daily difficulties. Outside Catholic activity is seriously restricted. With few exceptions, there are no

Catholic organizations. Catholic activity among the youth or the workers is difficult, and the church has no access to important mass media, such as radio, television or film. There are serious limitations on building the new churches we so badly need in Poland. The church is also heavily taxed. The post-war period was one of real hardship: Cardinal Wyszyński, Primate of Poland, was interned from 1953 to 1956; the weekly paper, *Tygodnik Powszechny*, which had been published by a group of Catholic laymen, was suppressed.

But this period belongs to the past. The new political leadership which came to power in December 1970, as a result of the workers' riots on the Polish coast, has announced the intention of normalizing relations between the church and the state, and talks between the two sides are underway. They are progressing slowly and not without difficulties. Evidently there is a gap between what the church is asking for and what the state is willing to concede. Nevertheless, several problems have been solved.

A year ago Pope Paul beatified a Polish Franciscan brother, Maximilian Kolbe. During World War II Father Kolbe was a prisoner in a Nazi concentration camp in Auschwitz. He offered his life for the life of a co-prisoner, personally unknown to him, condemned to death by the Germans. The Nazis accepted his offer and Father Kolbe died. He was beatified as a *confessor fidei*. When the beatification took place in Rome, Polish authorities gave three thousand Polish pilgrims permission to attend these celebrations. Polish airlines organized an aerial bridge between Warsaw and Rome to assist their transportation, and a member of the Polish government was present in St. Peter's Basilica — as an official representative of a Communist administration at the beatification ceremony of a Catholic priest. Such a development could hardly have been foreseen even shortly before it happened.

One must add that for more than a year there were direct talks between the Holy See and the Polish government. Perhaps as a result of these talks some kind of diplomatic ties between Warsaw and the Vatican could be established in the future. A step in this direction has been made recently. After the ratification by the West German Parliament of the Bonn-Warsaw treaty, the Holy See proceeded to establish a regular church administration in the Polish western, post-German territories. The newly created dioceses have been organically incorporated into the traditional structure of the Polish church. Regular residential bishops have been appointed. Those decisions have been interpreted in

Poland as a final recognition by the Holy See of the present Polish western boundaries.

Summing up all of these developments I think we can hope to achieve a more peaceful co-existence between the church and the state. And I do not need to add that such a development would be badly needed in Poland given the fact that Polish Catholics are not rejecting the reality existing in our country. On the contrary, they are accepting and supporting positive achievements of socialist Poland, especially in the social and economic spheres, which they have helped to build, even though they still dissent in some other fields.

*　　*　　*

We now return to our initial question: How is Polish Catholicism changing, or is it in fact changing at all? As seen from the outside, the Polish church may appear to be one of the most pre-conciliar churches. Of course, it is only natural that given the external conditions created by the precarious status of a religious institution placed in the framework of an atheistic state, the members of this institution should adopt a kind of defensive attitude. Such an attitude stresses the feeling of monolithic solidarity, hampers change, and develops a kind of a ghetto mentality. Paradoxically, it is a ghetto for even though it includes ninety per cent of the population, in public life it is still given the status of a minority.

But at the same time the necessity of change is being felt as more and more urgent by the growing number of conscientious laymen involved in Catholic activities. The same attitude is taken by an ever increasing number of the clergy, especially the younger ones, and particularly by members of religious orders. This feeling of necessity for change is based upon the growing consciousness of the new sociological situation being created in Poland. It is not due to the impact of the Marxist, materialistic and atheistic ideology — propagated in Poland, but without much efficiency. Nor is it due to the changing social structures — rapid industrialization and urbanization. It is due to the impact of the mass media and the cultural progress of the lower classes. A new mentality is being created; new moral problems arise in the areas of personal and family ethics, the relationship of men to society, professional ethics, and in the ethics of labour relations.

Poland's traditional religiosity was the religiosity of the rural community, of the gentry, and of the urban middle class. Now all those social patterns are being shaken. It does not mean that this traditional religiosity should be uprooted. It has its value as long as it works, but there is a necessity to give some new content to traditional forms of expression. This is happening and such a change is underway.

Every summer great numbers of people make a pilgrimage on foot to the sanctuary of the Holy Virgin in Częstochowa. This summer ten thousand pilgrims marched from Warsaw to Częstochowa. Eighty per cent of those pilgrims were young people. They were behaving in a new way: they sang their kind of songs, played guitars, recited prayers written by themselves. Their new look was well received by the older pilgrims, simple people, who said: "Well, they are different. They depart from our customs, but it is good that the young are with us — that we are together."

What is evident is that one cannot give old answers to the new problems. They must be answered in a new language and by new categories. Of course the answer to this need of change was given by the Second Vatican Council. The Vatican II decrees began to be implemented in Poland. We now have, of course, the liturgy in the Polish language, and one should stress that it was generally received well and without resistance. But many lay people and a growing part of the clergy are complaining that the implementation of the Council directives is rather superficial and formal, a kind of lip service paid to the Council, and the spirit of the Council should permeate deeper into the life of the Polish church whose structure is still very authoritarian.

The attitude of the Polish people towards the church is changing. There is a slow, but constantly declining interest in church activities. As Poland ideologically becomes a more and more pluralistic society, we need a more open attitude in the church. We have to change the image of the church viewed as a beleaguered fortress, defending its rights. A strange kind of fortress, by the way, easier to leave than to join. What is needed now is a church seen rather as a stimulant by which human society is being reshaped from inside, a church more concerned about man's rights than about its own.

Because of the fact that the need for such a kind of change is not yet generally felt (partly as a result of a certain form of superficial optimism in evaluating the present situation and the future prospects of Polish Catholicism), we are experiencing a serious tension between the more open and progressive groups of Polish lay Catholics and clergy on the one side and the more conservative and traditional groups on the other. But this tension does not degenerate into open conflict, into radical polarization of attitudes, or into a breakdown in communications. We have in Poland no open crisis in the church, neither have we an open "contestation." Even such issues as birth control or celibacy have not resulted in sharp controversies. Institutional structures of the church, and church teaching have not been questioned.

What people are asking for is a renewal of the language in the church teaching and preaching; more participation by the "People of God," lay and clerical, in the process of decision-making; more sharing of responsibility. They would like some old forms of the church's membership to be replaced by a more responsible life in the faith, which presupposes personal involvement.

I am deeply convinced that the Polish Catholic experience in a socialist country may have more universal meaning and validity, particularly in the field of church-state relations. Vatican II did not say much on this subject, but the new relations between the church and the world as defined by its documents provides some new guidelines. As we know, the Catholic church withdrew from some past forms of interference in politics. One example of such interference was mentioned: in some past Italian elections the bishops directed the faithful to vote for the Christian Democratic Party. At the same time as it is abandoning the obsolete forms of political interference, conscious that those attitudes are a direct consequence of the Gospel's teaching, the church is becoming involved, more than ever, in the problems of peace and war, in social justice both on the national and international level, and in the development of the Third World. This new approach changes in some way the traditional attitude of the church towards Marxism and communism.

It is evident that the old patterns of church involvement in politics could not be operational in socialist or Communist countries. They would unavoidably lead to political confrontation, and result in a political conflict the church could not win, because in the strictly political sphere, the state, with its administrative means, would always be stronger. It might even be able to make the fulfillment of the church's mission nearly impossible. In contrast, if the church abstains from direct interference in politics and concentrates on its essential mission of shaping people's consciousness and transforming the human society into the community of authentic brotherhood based on love, its impact on public life, even in a Communist country, could be much stronger.

As paradoxical as it may seem, one should not exclude the possibility that to a certain extent a Communist state might benefit from the growth of authentically Christian values. The Communist authorities, while becoming more and more pragmatic, are often worried by the declining morals in family life, by the corruption of youth, spread of alcoholism, and poor ethics of labour. The so-called secular ethics often prove to be not effective enough. Thus, the Communists are also becoming conscious of the possible help they can get from Christians in the field of public and social morality. At the same time, it is becoming more evident that Western pragmatic materialism, the growth of consumerism and the affluent society constitute a much greater danger to the church and its spiritual values than the Marxist dialectic materialism.

Moreover, it is not the church's purpose to shape or change political regimes, but it is its duty to be present in every political situation. The great part of the world lives and probably will continue to live under Communist governments. If the Polish situation provides some patterns for the way in which the church should fulfill its mission in such conditions, this experience could prove meaningful also beyond Polish boundaries.

Another field in which Polish experience may have universal validity is the internal life of the church at a time of crisis, which we are actually witnessing in many places. A conscious and believing Catholic will consider those crises with optimism, as an unavoidable symptom of growth. From such crises the church should emerge stronger — purified and more relevant to the contemporary world. In the Western world we can hardly see for the moment the ways or means to overcome the present difficulties. By trying to find some new solutions under difficult circumstances and without shaking up the ecclesiastical structures, the Catholics of Poland may contribute to the universal search for the authentic renewal of the church. For under all circumstances it becomes evident that the return to old patterns and attitudes is no longer possible in the rapidly changing world.

I am fully aware that those perspectives impose very heavy responsibilities upon us. I understand that we are yet not equal to such responsibilities. Rather unexpectedly we found ourselves in a new situation for which we were not prepared; after all, nobody was. But we realize more and more that we will not find the solutions to the problems in our own country, if we do not start to think in a more universal, global, planetary way. I cannot say that we in Poland will be able to find the right answers. All I can say is that we shall try to do so.

The State and the Church

STANISŁAW STAROŃ

It was not necessary to wait long for conclusions to be drawn from the post-mortem examination of the tragic December 1970 events in Poland. The new First Secretary at once proclaimed that the villain of the piece was the former leadership because "it failed to communicate with the workers and intelligentsia and to follow the democratic procedures within the Party itself."[1] Echoing this verdict, a Warsaw mass circulation daily promptly declared that "the Polish community has long been waiting for the credibility gap between the nation and the Party to be overcome."[2]

The subsequent pronouncements of Gierek and other notables went a long way to make clear the *sine qua non* of redemption. It was now stressed that the task of successful socialist construction in Poland required the mobilization of Party and non-Party members of the body politic, of workers and intelligentsia, of town and country dwellers, of old and young citizens, and of believers as well as non-believers. On 23 December the new premier, Piotr Jaroszewicz announced at the special meeting of the *Sejm* that "the Government would now try to bring about a full normalization of relations with the Catholic church."[3]

While the term normalization is rather vague (and has since been subjected to criticism on that score), its use in the above context clearly conceded that state-church relations in the Polish People's Republic fell short of what was desirable and should be improved. How did the Catholic church fare during the three decades of Marxist regimen? It seems appropriate to examine the record briefly.[4]

It has been frequently asserted by Western observers that one of the features which makes Poland stand out among the socialist countries

---

[1] *Trybuna Ludu*, 21 December 1970.
[2] *Życie Warsawy*, 22 December 1970.
[3] *Trybuna Ludu*, 24 December 1970.
[4] For a discussion of state-church relations in the Polish People's Republic see: Adam Bromke *Poland's Politics: Idealism vs. Realism* (Cambridge, Mass., 1967) pp. 213-251; Stanisław Markiewicz, *Państwo i Kościół w okresie dwudziestolecia Polski Ludowej* (Warsaw, 1965); Hansjakob Stehle, *The Independent Satellite: Society and Politics in Poland Since 1945* (New York, 1965) pp. 60-119; Stanisław Staroń, "State-Church Relations in Poland: An Examination of Power Configuration in a Noncompetitive Political System," *World Politics* (July 1969) pp. 575-601.

is the strength and viability of the church. In a similar vein (and as if to explain this) Polish officialdom has been repeatedly presenting its policies toward organized religion as tolerant, fair, accommodating, and even generous. At the same time, although naturally with much less visibility because of censorship, the Episcopate has complained of ill treatment, abuse, and worse at the hands of the authorities. Where lies the truth? When the collective *dramatis personae* are locked in a confrontation it is difficult to assess their respective claims, especially when one antagonist is in full control of the mass media and the other's pronouncements are muffled. What is the truth?

Rather than becoming involved in a philosophical discussion of the foundations of Christian faith and of Marxism, we will view the state-church relations in Poland as a power contest of sorts where each side acts rationally to maximize its subjectively perceived objectives. This confrontation is influenced at all times by the basic beliefs of the contestants, which may set limits to what is negotiable and what is not. By and large, however, it is the existential and pragmatic considerations, the bargaining power, or indeed the brute power, that determines the outcome of these disputes. Where, as in Poland, the political culture has been fragmented and loyalties divided, where the church has enjoyed the support of large segments of the population, and where, on the other hand, the narrowly based ruling elite has been doggedly engaged in a most ambitious scheme of political and economic development (an elite

---

[5] For instance, in 1961, the Public Opinion Institute of the Polish Radio, in a survey of 3,000 urban dwellers found that 60.2 per cent of respondents with higher education, 66 per cent of "all intelligentsia" in the sample, 75 per cent of skilled workers and 82 per cent of unskilled workers declared themselves as believers. The Polish Academy of Sciences similarly disclosed that during 1964 the Sunday mass attendance in an unspecified number of churches ranged from 28 per cent to 40 per cent in the "old" urban areas inhabited by the long-established workers, from 40 per cent to 55 per cent in the new urban areas where the majority of workers is of recent peasant origin, and from 60 per cent to 84 per cent in the "randomly selected" rural areas. In Tadeuz Jaroszewski, "Dynamika praktyk religijnych i postaw światopoglądowych w Polsce w świetle badań socjologicznych," *Kultura i Społeczeństwo* (March 1966) pp. 133-149. The ecclesiastical data and estimates for religious self-identification and church attendance run expectedly higher. The table below points to the growth of the organizational cadres of the Catholic Church.

	1937*	1965**	1967**
Priests	11,348	17,333	17,986
Lay brothers	2,426	3,522	3,275
Nuns	16,820	28,190	27,975

* *Mały rocznik statystyczny 1939* (Warsaw, 1939).
** *Rocznik statystyczny 1968* (Warsaw, 1968).

hitherto divided by internal dissension at that) — in such a situation some manner of coexistent policy toward organized religion rather than a policy of open suppression or outright eradication clearly commends itself as a reasonable choice.

*   *   *

The *modus vivendi* between the Communist government and the Catholic church in Poland has been for the most part very precarious indeed. Coexistence it was, but essentially a coexistence in utter mutual isolation of the two ostensibly antagonistic social forces, each unhappily aware that it is doomed to suffer the other. Officially, the Party, following an oft quoted Lenin dictum that "religion is a private matter of the citizens," has always maintained that the state respects these beliefs of the citizens. This view found its institutional expression in the constitution which specifically provides for religious freedom and for the separation of church and state.[6] Not unexpectedly, however, as often happens in these matters (and not only in the Communist countries), these constitutional principles did little to resolve the conflicting secular and religious interests. To reiterate, then, the history of state-church relations in socialist Poland has not run a smooth course; on the contrary, it is a history of suspicion, recrimination, frustration, hostility, and discord.

Governmental policies toward the Catholic church generally tended to reflect the major changes in the Party line. Thus during the early period of "transition" (1944-47) the church was largely left in peace to enjoy relative comfort and security in the midst of frantic political manoeuvring and grievous economic deprivations. In the course of the subsequent phase of Stalinization, and in spite of and contrary to the 1950 state-church accord, severe administrative pressures were applied, culminating in the arrest and detention of the Primate himself. With the October 1956 transformation came a marked liberalization of the government's stance — but not for long. A tougher line was soon in force, its highlights being the relegation of religious instruction from schools to catechetic centres and the massive many-sided anti-Episcopate campaign during the millenial year. Toward the very last years of Gomułka's ascendancy, with the growing discord in the inner circle of Party leadership came a noticeable relaxation of tensions. Thus state-church rela-

---

[6] *The Constitution of the Polish People's Republic*, Article 70.

tions on the eve of the December 1970 events were certainly not at their historical worst.

It should be borne in mind, however, that in all of these ups-and-downs in the official treatment of the Catholic church there were some pervasive and enduring common practices. Special pains were always taken to avoid even the appearance of a direct attack on religion and the institutions of the church. In this respect much use was made of "jurisdictional" arguments. New restrictive regulations were presented as pertaining to activities which were not properly speaking religious but economic, political, social, educational and thus rightfully within the scope of governmental control. Furthermore, when a direct attack was deemed appropriate on some specific church policy, it was pointed out that it was some minority segment that was at fault and not the mass of the believers. Thus the Episcopate was pitted against the rest of the clergy and the laity, the clergy against the rest of the believers, one segment of the believers against the majority, and so on.[7] Much use was made of censorship. The occasionally embarrassing incidents of confrontation, especially at the grass roots level, never saw the light of day. However, when it was felt that the mass media approach was in order, the government's argument was given full airing, while the church was accorded only marginal or no publicity.

Even more important were the incomparably more substantial parallel efforts of the official policy makers and executors devoted to the task of general secularization, to the de-mythologization, as it were, of the masses. This has consistently been done in the name of science and, in the process, all the agents of socialization have been put to use. But the typical mode used in this ambitious undertaking clearly suggests the intent of avoiding attacks on specific religions even if they be the opiate of the people and a figment of the imagination. What has been constantly emphasized in these suasions is the validity of objective and certain knowledge based on empirical verifiability and, not infrequently, the scientific nature of Marxism-Leninism and the utterly unscientific character of all manner of myths, cults, superstitions and similar beliefs. Only the marginal Atheists' and Freethinkers' Association engaged from

---

[7] Staroń, pp. 592-596.

time to time in a frontal and direct attack on religion and organized churches as such.[8]

Throughout the decades of coexistence and confrontation, the political leaders continued to complain that the Catholic hierarchy did not declare itself unequivocally on the side of socialism and its program of justice and plenty, which goals, it was added, all men of good will should endorse. There is no question whatsoever that this recrimination was true. While on occasion the pronouncements of the Episcopate appealed to the believers to take an active part in rebuilding Poland and promoting social justice, the appeal was always on broad moral and patriotic grounds and always very carefully worded lest it be misconstrued as any kind of endorsement of Communist ideology or practice.

On this point Cardinal Wyszyński, firmly in the primatic saddle and fully in control of the public utterances of the Episcopate (as little is known about ecclesiastical decision making as about the Politbureau get-togethers), has never wavered. In general, over a period of years the Episcopate proved to be a formidable contestant. Its own policy *vis-à-vis* the civil authorities was well summed up in this statement of 1968: "The Episcopate takes a public stand only in the indispensable defense of religious life, Catholic education, Catholic culture, and the right of the Catholic institutions to develop to meet the demands of the believers."[9]

A closer look at the above undoubtedly most carefully worded pronouncement, by anyone familiar with its social context, will reveal that these demands, from the viewpoint of Communist practice (not to mention Communist ideology) are far less modest than their tone would suggest. Although shrouded in generality (with an eye on the censor, perhaps?) these claims have a quite specific meaning but only to the more sophisticated Poles interested in these matters. The "defense of religious life" clause refers to complete freedom from governmental interferences for all religious practices and observances. In this respect, government policy and practice have been quite permissive, though not

---

[8] To the contrary, the Episcopate has been repeatedly and vigorously protesting that the governmental secularization policy was nothing else but thinly disguised atheistic propaganda.

[9] *Słowo Powszechne*, 11 January 1968.

without some jarring incidents to the contrary.[10] Whenever these occurred, the hierarchy protested most vocally both from the pulpit and in formal complaints to the authorities, and generally not in vain.

In the matter of religious education of children conducted on a voluntary basis on church property, the Episcopate has similarly insisted on complete immunity from control. In fact, government regulations established in 1961 provided for the registration of the catechetic centres, submission of the lists of students, and periodic inspection by the authorities (to ensure that religion and nothing else was taught). It is interesting to note that in the face of wide-spread non-compliance by the parishes, the actual enforcement of these regulations was far from uniform. While there are no official statistics on this, hearsay has it that a large number of unregistered and unregulated catechetic centres remained in operation in 1970.

The Episcopate's claim of "the right of the Catholic institutions to develop to meet the demands of the believers" means, first of all, the right to build more churches. Between 1945 and 1970 about 500 new churches were built. Of these more than half were constructed during the first six years after the war. In the last years of Gomułka's leadership church construction slowed to a snail's pace. (At the end of 1969 there were 13,291 churches and chapels in Poland.)[11] At the same time the population increased from just under twenty-four million in 1945 to just under thirty-three million in 1970. Furthermore, there was a very pronounced shift from rural to urban areas, increasing the percentage of urban population from 31.8 percent in 1945 to 50.3 percent in 1967.[12]

---

[10] For instance, in 1966, when the state-church relations reached their lowest ebb since the Stalinization period, the government frequently resorted to all kinds of disruptive tactics to hinder the success of the religious observances of the millennial year. These tactics included petty administrative and police interference with religious processions.

[11] The actual figures for new church construction were: 1966 — four, 1967 — six, 1968 — three, 1969 — fourteen. At the end of 1969 there were 13,291 churches and chapels in Poland, *Rocznik statyczny 1970*. The whole issue of church building is a good deal more complex than these strictures would suggest. Obtaining the construction permit is only the first step in accomplishing the purpose. Since allocation of building materials is also in the hands of public authorities the continued good will of the secular planners is needed for the prompt completion of sacral structures. Moreover, as these allocation decisions are made by the local functionaries, situations may arise where church construction is delayed for years by many a minor satrap, even in the face of central authorities' directives to the contrary. (One suspects a certain understandable hesitancy of the top Party leaders to make such directives crystal-clear; that is, to assign to church building a definite priority over all other construction, including housing.)

[12] *Rocznik statystyczny 1968*, p. 23.

This latter trend was of special importance to the church since rural dwellers have always been its most devout and devoted members and because some of the newly built industrial centres were located nowhere near the existing churches. How to account for the government's most restrictive policy in granting permits for new church construction? It appears as if the winning to Marxism of these brand new members of the industrial proletariat was deemed worthy of the highest priority, even at the risk of breeding tension and outraging the believers. As a result, many a new industrial city had to do without a place of worship, even though the vast majority of its inhabitants pleaded and on occasion clamorously demonstrated for a permit.[13]

Similarly, the Episcopate felt that governmental interference with the training of priests, hindering the growth and even maintenance of the clerical cadres, was totally unwarranted. In the late 1960's many of the lower seminaries were actually closed. The Episcopate also asserted that, as a matter of principle, the clerics should be exempted from compulsory military service.

Next on the long list of grievances was a financial one. While churches in Poland, together with other nonprofit, religious, educational, charitable, cultural, and athletic organizations enjoy basic tax immunity, this privilege is severely circumscribed. Thus certain parts of church revenue are taxable. "To facilitate the assessment of income subject to turnover tax" the 1962 law required that the parishes maintain at all times detailed inventories of all their property, real and movable, for government inspection, and that they submit detailed reports on revenue and expenditure.[14] In practice, the state tax demands were quite burdensome but not equally so for all parishes, since assessment was in the hand of the local officials and the very nature of the whole process permitted much discretion on the part of the authorities. Sometimes the taxes were increased from the original assessment on the grounds that the parishes were underreporting their revenue. Under these circumstances, it was also possible for the local officials to use their fiscal power as a threat to pressure the clergy on other matters. All things considered, however, this taxation, while often cumbersome and aggravating, was rarely confiscatory, leaving the church establishment with enough resources to

---

[13] See, for instance, Stehle, pp. 84-90.
[14] These regulations applied even to the liturgical objects such as vessels and vestments.

carry on its work with a modicum of comfort. Of all tax regulations, the requirement to maintain detailed inventories for government inspection was the source of greatest resentment and irritation. The clergy were indignant at the very fact of having to account to an antagonistic authority for property, some of which had been in the hands of the church for centuries. Accurate, detailed inventories laid bare the true financial situation of the parish, making it so much easier for the authorities to apply the fiscal screws.

Also causing much bitterness toward the government was the matter of ownership of the church buildings in the western and northern territories. From 1945, these formerly German ecclesiastical holdings were considered state property (as other spoils of war) and were rented to the parishes. Involved in this were 4,700 churches and chapels, 2,200 other buildings, and small parcels of land adjoining the parish houses amounting to about 2,000 acres. To many Polish believers the inconceivable had happened: the parishes were now the tenants of an avowedly godless landlord. Not that the generally moderate rents were always paid or that eviction followed non-payment. It is significant that the rent collectors were less than zealous, allowing large rent arrears to mount.[15]

Finally, there was the Episcopate's claim "to speak on Catholic culture." What was being asserted — in spite of the obvious understatement and generality — was no less than the church's right to be a moral as well as a social critic and, as a prerequisite to exercising that right, the freedom and ability to make such criticism heard. It should be clear that this ecclesiastical demand represented a category of its own. The other church grievances and assertions, it could be argued in a Marxist manner, belonged to a class of religious, ergo negotiable matters; this one, to the contrary, amounted to openly challenging the foundations of Marxism and the monopolistic authority of the Party state.

Parenthetically, it must also be rememebered that the phrase "Catholic culture," repugnant to any Marxian ear, is in Poland no less than provocative. It brings back the often glorious memories of a thousand years of the Catholic past, of close cooperation of church and state, and particularly a memory of Poland being for centuries the "bulwark of Christendom," defending Europe against the might of Islam. While

---

[15] According to *The New York Times*, 23 June 1971, these properties were to be handed over to the Catholic Church without payment and "rent arrears would be cancelled and payments would be returned to the church" (*sic.*).

these sentiments are no more than nostalgic hankerings, admittedly far removed from contemporary social reality, their power to irritate should not be overlooked.

In actual practice the church hierarchy, without ever conceding its right to social criticism, exercised this right only with the greatest restraint. Only the Primate, a few bishops in their sermons, and the Episcopate collectively in pastoral letters, engaged in such criticism. Governmental policies which became targets of these challenges were most typically those which directly contravened some specific church rule, as in the case of governmental regulation of divorce and abortion. Yet the issue was not purely academic. The indirect and veiled critical allusions that were made from time to time, though limited to utterances inside the churches, were undermining the public image of the government and its program. The government, for its part, resented this ecclesiastic posture more than any other, branding it, time and again, as unwarranted and impermissible meddling in politics.[16] It was this issue of the right and the ability of the church to influence 'the institutions as well as the mores of society that became the centre of the state-church debate after December 1970.

* * *

The new leadership's pronouncement of the policy of "normalization" of relations with the Catholic church, while naturally welcome to the masses of believers and the clergy, was too general not to leave many interested Catholics with serious questions as to the specific intentions and plans of the government. For one thing, it was clear that much depended on the attitude of the church hierarchy itself. And if the public image of the Primate was correct, it was unlikely that any accommodation would be forthcoming from the Episcopate.

Cardinal Wyszyński, as it happened, was to deliver the Christmas Eve sermon barely twenty-four hours after Premier Jaroszewicz's normalization statement. He did not choose to respond directly, but the substance

---

[16] The most extreme example of such complaining occurred in response to the well-known 1965 Polish Bishops' Letter to the German Episcopate. On that occasion a lengthy and concerned media campaign was mounted replete with charges of Episcopal meddling in politics.

and the tenor of his remarks were conciliatory.[17] The New Year's message of the Executive Council of the Episcopate (read in all the churches), on the other hand, was hardly propitiatory. It even included a veritable bill of rights: "(1) The right to freedom of conscience and freedom of religious life together with full normalization of relations between the church and the state; (2) the right of freely shaping the culture of one's own nation, according to the spirit of the Christian principles of coexistence of people; (3) the right to social justice expressed in fulfilling just demands: (4) the right to truth in social life, to information according with the truth, and to free expression of one's views and demands; (5) the right to material conditions which ensure decent existence of the family, and of each individual citizen; (6) the right to such an attitude toward the citizens that they are not insulted, harmed, and persecuted in anything."[18] This far-reaching declaration was indeed startling if it were meant as an opening statement for the forthcoming state-church negotiations. Compared with the just discussed 1969 Episcopal statement, it went much farther in asserting the church's role as a social critic and arbiter of correct social arrangements. It would be only a guess to conclude that the authors of the message, taking advantage of the uncertainties confronting the new political leaders, decided to indicate that the church was going to be the hardest of bargainers.

The Epiphany (6 January) sermon of the Primate (unlike the restrained and conciliatory Christmas Eve address) reiterated the hard line posture. The Cardinal delivered what sounded like an *ex cathedra* admonition to the government to respect the workers' rights and never to resort to force to keep them in line. In another vein, in his next (15 January) sermon he appealed for the return of the Catholic church to the areas of "apostolic work which had been denied to it since the war, namely those of the press, charitable organizations and cultural associations."[19] The pronouncement clearly suggested that minor concessions on the part of the government would not satisfy the ecclesiarchs.

---

[17] Referring specifically to the disturbances on the coast and their suppression, the Cardinal pleaded "We beg of you, do not accuse. Show understanding, feel compassion. . . . We bishops and priests in our free fatherland for whose independence and prosperity we work — struggling on the sector assigned to us of spiritual renovation of the nation — we feel co-responsible and we beg the families of those who were beaten to accept our confession and our plea for forgiveness." *Radio Free Europe*, Polish Situation Report, 28 December 1970.

[18] *R.F.E.*, Polish Situation Report, 5 January 1971.

[19] *R.F.E.*, Polish Situation Report, 20 January 1971.

On 25 January Radio Warsaw and then the Polish Press Agency reported that the government "has authorized the appropriate agencies to prepare the necessary legal documents for the transfer to the Catholic church of property titles to churches and other ecclesiastical buildings in the western and northern territories." Here was a sign of governmental good will for all to see at home and abroad. Was this an important concession? Certainly not in economic terms; the government was not losing much in rents. The psychological impact of the decision, on the other hand, could have been great. Although it would be too much to expect for either the government or the Episcopate to say so, this move signified a sort of recognition of the permanent nature of organized religion in Poland — no mean admission for the Marxist regime.[20]

It was time at last for the Episcopate to respond directly. Meeting in a two-day conference, the bishops issued a communique "accepting with satisfaction the Premier's December normalization declaration" and viewing his 25 January property transfer decision as "indicative of further acts seeking to establish normal relations between the church and the state." In addition, the communique (in a show of good will and responding perhaps to the widespread rumours of new strikes on the coast) came down strongly on the side of law and order and decreed that 14 February would be "a day of universal prayer for the fatherland." At the same time, the conference designated Bishop Dąbrowski as the Episcopate's representative for the forthcoming talks with the government, even though his terms of reference were narrowed to discussion of the property transfer legislation.[21]

The communique, however, included a complaint. It stated that "in some bishoprics the attitude of education authorities to religious instruction has not only remained unchanged but has even in many cases in a certain respect become worse." This cryptic allegation may have referred to the government's efforts to enforce the 1961 regulations relating to catechetic centres. If so, the government may have been testing its good will in the new situation with the previously recalcitrant parishes, rather than deliberately stirring up trouble.

About the time the bishops were meeting, the auxiliary bishop of Warsaw, Jerzy Modzelewski, became a member of the Committee for the Reconstruction of the Royal Castle in Warsaw. It was seemingly

---

[20] *Słowo Powszechne*, 25 January 1971.
[21] U.P.A., 29 January 1971.

unprecedented in the annals of socialist Poland for a church prelate to hobnob with the Party and state dignitaries. This fact assumes even more significance if one remembers that for decades the government stubbornly kept refusing to rebuild this historical structure in the face of much popular clamour, and the new leaders' reversal of this posture was widely viewed as a sign of a new political era of responsiveness to the wishes of the people.

About the middle of February, a prominent Catholic lay intellectual and director of the Znak Publishing Institute, Dr. Jacek Woźniakowski, granted an interview to the *Christian Science Monitor* in which he stated that "if there is now a chance of getting on talking terms with the government we should take it. Even if the talks prove fruitless . . . what other position can there be if you want a dialogue?" More importantly, he stressed that the church should make no undue demands on the government: "What it should seek is more openness from the government, more equal treatment of citizens according to merit and not organization. But it would be indecent for the church to ask for special rights outside the general framework of life in Poland." Woźniakowski then speculated that this view might be shared by a large number of believers and younger clergy.[22]

On 3 March the Premier and the Primate met for several hours and, in the words of the Polish Press Agency, "they discussed problems . . . connected with the normalization of relations between the state and the church." Was this truly a summit parley, preceded by much spadework and preliminary lower-level discussion to pave the way for some sort of agreement? The complete lack of information about what transpired during the conference and the subsequent developments suggest no such meeting of minds. Perhaps the Premier, after explaining in no uncertain terms what was not negotiable, delineated the scope of acceptable dialogue. After this narrowing of the terms of reference, he may have alluded to the specific concessions the government was prepared to make and even to the price that the church was expected to pay in return. The Cardinal, it is fairly safe to guess, remained intransigent. This scenario may, of course, err in not allowing that the government may have been genuinely hopeful that (some of the utterances of the Episcopate notwithstanding) it had already established a modicum of good will with the church and that a few private promises of future conces-

---

[22] *Christian Science Monitor*, 17 February 1971.

sions related by the Premier were likely to assuage the hard-bargaining Cardinal. The fact remains, however, that whatever was said at the meeting, no agreement was reached.

After the March meeting it became clear that no dramatic changes in state-church relations were in the offing and that if the "normalization" policy were to continue, it was going to be a very slow process indeed. Not that the government has ever retracted its intention to "normalize." Quite the contrary, the policy to "appeal to believers as well as non-believers" has been repeatedly asserted in the *Sejm* and even at the Party Congress.[23] And the words were followed in the last year or so by a few deeds. These steps, though hardly spectacular, did appear to reflect with considerable consistency the government's stated intentions. But the new strategy and tactics were different, as "normalization" of state-church relations had become a long range rather than proximate objective.

*   *   *

The specific acts of government directed at the Catholic church since March 1971 can be conveniently discussed under three categories: (1) concessions to the church; (2) initiatives toward the Vatican; and (3) efforts to mobilize support among the believers for the government's terms of "normalization." The list of governmental fiats that were *bona fide* beneficial to the church is far from impressive both in size and substance. Yet, while these actions fall short of the expectations of many believers and are considered utterly inconsequential by the church hierarchy, they must be viewed by others as a token of good will. A good case in point is the new policy toward church building. Toward the end of Gomułka's regime hardly any permits had been issued for this purpose. In the first quarter of 1971, seventeen new churches were authorized. By July the number was almost doubled.[24] These figures contrast sharply with the church's needs as perceived by the Episcopate. The Primate reiterated on a number of occasions that one thousand new churches were needed to cope with the population shifts, fifty in Warsaw alone. On the other hand, if the annual rate of fifty were to be maintained this would constitute a tenfold increase over past practice. Moreover, one cannot dismiss the continuing acute housing shortage in the

[23] *Nowe Drogi* (January 1972), p. 166.
[24] Adam Bromke, "Poland Under Gierek: A New Political Style," *Problems of Communism* (September-October 1972), p. 13.

context of a growing population whose appetite for comfort is constantly on the increase. The question of priorities, always looming large in human pursuits, has in this case a peculiarly polarizing import as between the purveyors of earthly and heavenly perfection. Fifty churches a year, in these circumstances, would be quite a prize![25]

On 22 February 1972 the church inventory regulations were abolished. In addition, this fiscal decree freed from taxation all parish income from the sale of agricultural produce. The authorities were not giving up much in monetary terms, since this income of the church was verging on the infinitesimal.[26] Abolition of the requirement for maintaining detailed inventories may even have been beneficial to the state through eliminating the need for inspections and minimizing opportunities for local functionaries to indulge in arbitrary decisions. At the same time, the new measure was bound to be received well, or at least with a considerable sigh of relief, by the clergy, especially at the crucial parish level.

There were a few other gestures of good will facilitating the pilgrimage of several thousand Catholics to Rome to attend the beatification rites of Father Maksymilian Kolbe in October 1971; that is, speeding approval of passports and organizing air and rail transportation. A few foreign church and lay dignitaries were allowed to visit the Polish church leaders,[27] and permission was granted for some Catholic institutions to engage in publishing activities.

After Vatican II, persistent rumours circulated in Poland that Gomułka intended to sign a comprehensive treaty with the Holy See. Gossip also had it that several indirect and informal probes were attempted in order to explore the attitude of the Vatican authorities toward

---

[25] This writer feels that even the Episcopate would be satisfied with a firm assurance that, say, five hundred churches would be completed within the next decade; not that this admission is likely to be forthcoming in what is akin to a bargaining situation.

[26] The law limits church landholdings to a maximum of 125 acres in the case of the parishes and to 12.5 acres in the case of the monasteries and convents. The average holding, however, is only about ten acres and all the church land amounts to about 82,000 acres. Markiewicz, p. 48.

[27] Most interesting of these was a visit in October 1972 of Cardinals Krol and Wright of the United States and Bartoli of Italy to participate in the religious ceremonies marking the first anniversary of the beatification of Father Maksymilian Kolbe. It should be noted that Cardinal Krol, the Archbishop of Philadelphia and the President of the National Conference of the Catholic Bishops, is of Polish extraction and speaks Polish. *The New York Times*, 12, 16, 17 October 1972.

such an action. The Catholic grapevine reported that Gomułka's crude gambit of playing the Pope off against the Primate was at once seen through in Rome and dismissed out of hand.[28]

It was only after Gierek's coming to power that the first official meeting between the representatives of the government of the Polish People's Republic and those of the Roman Curia took place. The talks were held on 27-30 April 1971 in Rome and conducted at the deputy minister level. The communique issued on 3 May referred to an "exchange of views on questions that interest the two sides" and to the fact that "the two delegations agreed to resume talks at a date to be agreed upon." Some additional light on the meeting was shed by the Deputy Foreign Minister, Józef Czyrek, who, appearing on Polish Television on 17 September, stated that "normalizing" relations between the state and the church in Poland on the one hand, and the Vatican's favourable posture on the nuclear non-proliferation treaty and on the Budapest proposal for a European conference for security and cooperation on the other, were the main topics under discussion. In addition, one other unavoidable topic must have been on the agenda: that long-standing source of bitter resentment, the Vatican's persistent refusal to recognize Polish ecclesiastic administration in the western and northern territories.[29] The second round of the discussions took place in Warsaw on 12-18 November 1971. The official communique was no more enlightening than the one after the first meeting. For months afterwards, rumours circulating in Warsaw and Rome were decidedly optimistic. Indeed, in June 1972, soon after the Warsaw Treaty was ratified in Bonn, the Vatican recognition of Polish ecclesiastic administration in the formerly German held territories was granted. For all that, the negotiations were never resumed.[30]

The Catholic church paved the way for cooperation of the believers with the Communists in the Second Vatican Council. "While rejecting

---

[28] See Hansjakob Stehle, "Vatican Policy Towards Eastern Europe," *Survey* (January 1968), p. 115.

[29] Following a long established usage, the Roman Curia has refused, ever since 1945, to install as fullfledged bishops in these territories the Polish nominees, on the grounds that these territorial changes have not been finally recognized in a binding international treaty. What added insult to injury was the fact that the surviving German ex-holders of the sees in question continued to be listed in some Vatican publications with their old titles.

[30] This writer is inclined to speculate that perhaps one factor in the Polish Government's decision not to resume the negotiations was a hint to that effect from Moscow.

atheism, root and branch, the church sincerely professes that all men, believers and unbelievers alike, ought to work for the rightful betterment of this world in which all alike live."[31] But what was the Polish *raison d'état* for a concordat, or even a lesser agreement with the Vatican? In the first place there was the favourable climate of détente between the Communist and capitalist giants. There were also precedents to follow. Hungary and Yugoslavia had signed minor agreements with the Holy See in 1964 and 1966, respectively. The advantages for the Polish government of a comprehensive treaty would hinge, of course, on the specific terms that could be agreed upon. But even the very fact of the concordat would be viewed by the masses of the believers, if not by the more sophisticated among them, as lending the government an aura of respectability which until then it had been peculiarly lacking.

At the same time, if the government could deal directly with Rome, the image and prestige of the Polish church hierarchy and especially of its militant leader was likely to suffer considerably. The concordat might also serve as a convenient catalyst for the disaffected groups within the church, lay and clerical, to voice publicly their long-nourished disagreements with the Primate's pristine prescription. That the Curia was aware of these ramifications can be readily assumed. Apparently it was also wholeheartedly on the Polish Primate's side. Under these circumstances the chances for successful negotiations were slim. Iron-clad guarantees not to cut the Cardinal down to size, that may have been hinted at by the Vatican negotiators, would, in the eyes of the Polish government, defeat the very purpose of the whole undertaking or, at least, eliminate the major pay-off.

Parallel to these developments were the government's efforts to influence Catholic public opinion. These suasions were clearly directed at winning the support of the believers for the government's own plan for "normalization"; or at least at engendering resentment against the official church policy. It would be misleading not to offer a word of caution at this point. There has been no massive campaign to put the government's point of view across. All that has occurred has been some airing of the issue in the mass media. But the significance of these few articles and official utterances would hardly be lost on the native observers

---

[31] Walter M. Abbott, S.J., ed., *The Documents of Vatican II* (New York, 1966), p. 219.

accustomed to paying special attention to the slightest change in the form as well as the substance of governmental pronouncements.

The main tenor of these communications was unmistakable. The government was now quite explicit about the *quid pro quo* of its "normalization" program. The Episcopate was to acknowledge for all time to come, by deeds as well as by words, its good will toward the socialist authorities. In the words of the Director of the Office for Religious Affairs, Aleksander Skarżyński, "the Church authorities must consistently recognize the socialist system in our country, the political orientation of People's Poland, as firmly existing reality and patriotically a point of supreme importance." This particular message, part of a policy paper entitled "The Principles for the Normalization of State-Church Relations," was delivered at the celebration of the twenty-fifth anniversary of the Pax Society, the organization of Catholic laymen that never wavered in its enthusiastic support of the governmental program. The authorities' choice of the Pax pulpit for this important policy statement speaks for itself.[32] Premier Jaroszewicz himself, adressing the first session of the new *Sejm* on 28 March 1972, confirmed the subordination of the "normalization" policy to the Polish *raison d'état* when he stated he was hopeful that "guarantees will be obtained that religious activity of the Roman Catholic church will remain within the framework defined by our national interest and by the law." Official declarations were accompanied by a few articles authored by unofficial government spokesmen; even the representatives of the other two Catholic organizations, "Znak" and the Christian Social Association, were given an opportunity to state their positions in print.[33]

*   *   *

So much for the recent developments in state-church relations. Perhaps some speculation is now in order. It should be pointed out that no compelling conclusions are intended, merely a few tentative observations. It would appear that the government has indeed found it necessary in the wake of the December events to make some concessions to the Catholic church. From the official point of view, the state-church détente

---

[32] *Słowo Powszechne*, 4 October 1971.
[33] J. Makowski, "Against Religious Criteria — On Both Sides," *Polityka*, 14 August 1971; A. Micewski, "What Kind of Democratization?" *Polityka*, 18 September 1971, English translation in Radio Free Europe, *Polish Press Survey* Nos. 2323 and 2339.

was the price that had to be paid for broadening the support for social-ism among the Catholics. At the same time the government was not likely to go out of its way to sustain a hydra. A friendly, or at least, a non-antagonistic and "non-political" attitude of the Episcopate seemed not too much to ask in view of the presumed benefits to religion. Yet the prelates remained intractable. Under these circumstances a new strategy appears to have been adopted. It is a long range master plan of gradual softening of the Episcopal hard line. Incentives are as much a part of this undertaking as deterrents, except that the latter must be indirect so as not to give the impression that the government has aban-doned its normalization policy and is persecuting the church. (The March 1972 police raid at Zbrosza Duża was clearly an embarrassment to the government and must have occurred without the sanction of the higher authorities.)[34] Furthermore, the mainstay of this policy is to grant special favours to any and all Catholic groups and even individuals, lay and clerical, who are likely to dissent from the Episcopate's guide-lines.

Is this policy likely to succeed in the long run in changing the present attitude of the Episcopate toward the socialist state? Time alone will tell. At this juncture it is clear, however, that the most the government could claim in the way of success is the coming into the open of some muffled and still minor expressions of factionalism. Perhaps, after all, the Primate is right. It may well be that the real strength of the Catholic church in Poland can only be maintained by the policy of non-yielding to any of the government's crucial demands. Thus, by not rendering unto Caesar his (subjectively perceived) due — by, indeed, sustaining a modicum of state-church friction, can it be that the Episcopate may be contributing to the maximization of benefits for the church?

---

[34] Reuter, 1 April 1972.

The Catholics and Politics in Poland

LUDWIK DEMBIŃSKI

In order to analyze the political attitudes of Polish Catholics, it is necessary to keep in mind a number of factors which give the Catholic religion in Poland its unique position.

The most important is probably the strong identification of the Catholic church with Polish nationalism. From the tenth century, when Prince Mieszko I was baptized, Poland was the eastern outpost of Western Christianity. Defending itself against the incursions of the Tartars and the Turks, it defended at the same time the whole of Christian Western Europe.

This traditional identification of the Poles with Catholicism was enhanced after the partitions of Poland at the end of the eighteenth century, especially in the territories taken over by Orthodox Russia and Protestant Prussia. The nineteenth century in Poland's history was a period of uprisings and struggles to uphold the national identity, which the occupying powers tried to suppress. In these struggles, the Catholic church played an important role, either by direct participation, or at least by serving as a national rallying point. Along with the entire Polish population it suffered repressions by the occupying powers, such as the expulsion of certain religious orders and the confiscation of church property.

In the inter-war period the national minorities (Jews, Ukrainians, Belorussians and Germans), who constituted a high percentage of the inhabitants of Poland, were also religious minorities. This again contributed to the strengthening of the link existing in the mind of the average Pole, between national and religious identity.

During the last war and the German occupation, the church and its hierarchy, practically without exception, took an active part in the national resistance movement. They suffered heavy losses, with thousands of priests imprisoned and more than 2,000 of them killed. For these reasons, when at the end of the war the Communist Party and its allies took over power in the country, they could not blame the church for any past anti-national activities.

Another factor which has to be mentioned is the national and religious homogeneity of present-day Poland. The loss of former eastern Polish territories populated mainly by Ukrainian and Belorussian national and religious minorities, and the massive transfer of its Polish inhabitants to the newly acquired western territories, from which the original German population had been removed, enormously strengthened the social basis of the Church. At that stage more than 90 per cent of the Poles could be considered Catholics.

The last important factor is economic. As has already been mentioned, most of the church property and especially its big latifundia were confiscated in the nineteenth century. Since then it could not have been considered as a big landowner. The relative poverty of the Catholic church had another important, practical consequence. One of its main sources of income were small-sized parochial farms which seldom exceeded fifty acres of land. The land reform of 1944 decreed the confiscation and distribution among the peasant population of all land property exceeding one hundred acres. The parochial farms were not confiscated and the main economic base of the church was preserved.

The political role of the Catholic church in Poland after World War II has been shaped by the elements of its history. Traditionally, the Polish church and its hierarchy were not inclined to participate directly in the exercise of power. They learned from history about the instability of political regimes. They understood that institutions deeply rooted in the society, in its feelings and traditions, are in fact better fitted to survive. Instead of fighting for political power, the church concentrated its efforts on strengthening itself institutionally.

The political Catholic groups or organizations which emerged after World War II thus are fully independent from the hierarchy. Nevertheless, their programmes and activities have been strongly influenced by the attitudes of the church and its relations with the state.

In the first post-war years an attempt was made to establish in Poland a Christian Democratic Party, called the Labour Party. It was a short-lived experience, however, and came to an end in 1947 when it became clear that in the new political environment the traditional multiparty system was not to be maintained.

A different approach to politics was adopted by the Christian Association, "Pax," which was established in the late 1940's by Bolesław Piasecki. It had its roots in the tradition of the Christian and nationalist extreme right, of which Piasecki in pre-war years had been one of the young leaders. "Pax," with a great deal of realism and a lack of prejudice against the dictatorial regime, chose to participate actively in the political life of the country. It did not, however, constitute itself as a political party. Contrary to the Christian Democrats, it did not put forward a political programme, opposed to, or even different from, the programme of the ruling Communist Party. Instead, the Pax Association fashioned itself as a loyal partner of the Communist Party, accepting *in toto* its political programme, but for moral reasons presenting it as derived from the Catholic doctrine. In exchange, it hoped to be permitted eventually to participate in the government.

In its relations with the church hierarchy and in its actions directed at the Catholic population at large, the Pax Association tried to convince them that the principles of a socialist system, as they were developed in Poland, were not opposed to the Catholic doctrine or to the social teaching of the church. This way "Pax" hoped to secure for the church a certain freedom of worship, religious publications and education.

By acting simultaneously in these two directions "Pax" tried to achieve the strategic position of a unique and indispensable intermediary between the Catholic church and the state. This objective, however, was not really attained, even though "Pax" was able to create for itself an impressive social and economic base. The reason for its failure was the fact that both parties felt themselves strong enough to deal directly with one another, without having recourse to an intermediary. Instead of achieving a real partnership in the exercise of power, "Pax" became a political tool of the state in its dealings with the church. This was particularly true during the Stalinist period.

* * *

A third possible option evolved which could be called "apolitical," but which nevertheless had certain political importance. This attitude was adopted by the group of Catholics gathered around the weekly *Tygodnik Powszechny*, and the monthly *Znak*, published in Cracow. With the addition of other groups and individuals, and after the establishment of the publications, they became known, although rather imprecisely, as the "Znak Group."

"Znak" began as a group of writers, journalists, and professors, former members of the prewar intellectual and student movement known as "Odrodzenie" (The Renewal). The founders of the two publications aimed primarily at the renewal of the Polish church, inspired in this endeavour mainly by the French theologians and philosophers. They also aimed at creating a current of free and independent Christian thought. They did not attempt to present their own, independent and alternative political programme or to undertake any sort of political activity, but instead strove to present a critical, but free of prejudice, view of the political, social, and cultural evolution of the country. In spite of the limitations imposed on the circulation of their publications, their intellectual and even political influence and position remained strong with the church, with the Polish population in general, and especially with the intelligentsia.

The first period of the "Znak" activities came to an end after they refused to publish on the front page of *Tygodnik Powszechny* an obituary of Stalin. The authorities ordered the closing down of both publications and transferred them to the Pax Association, which (without advising the readers about the change of ownership) continued their publication for a couple of years.

When in 1956 Gomułka came to power he immediately allowed the former editors to resume publication of *Tygodnik Powszechny* and *Znak*. The group was also allowed to organize, in five major cities, Clubs of Catholic Intelligentsia and to present five candidates for the coming parliamentary elections on the list of the Front of National Unity. Since then, the *Sejm* has included five "Znak" deputies, who form a separate parliamentary circle.

Although various restrictions were placed on its activities and publications, the group has expanded considerably since 1956. It has a very loose structure and has no central bodies with executive power over its various constituent members. These by now are five Clubs of Catholic Intelligentsia, two publishing houses, four newspapers and journals, a study centre, and the parliamentary circle. Coordination of activities among them is achieved through more or less informal consultations, personal ties, and the overlapping membership in their different governing bodies. It may not be the most efficient form of organization but it helps to preserve a variety of tendencies and attitudes, and as such is a good example of a truly functioning pluralism.

In spite of its political representation in the *Sejm*, the group maintains that it is not a political movement. According to one of its leaders, the late Jerzy Zawieyski, the only aim of this parliamentary representation is "to bear witness" and "to be present" in the political life of the country, without having any sort of political ambitions of its own. The ambiguity of this formula is obvious and at times it creates discussion and even friction in the movement itself. In the existing circumstances, however, this attitude is not as contradictory as it may appear. In a non-pluralist political system, bearing witness publicly to a doctrine and a faith, totally independent of the system, has in itself a certain influence upon the political life of the country.

Apart from this symbolic function, the "Znak" group also uses its political position to promote an evolution of the political and social system according to the principles of Christian personalism. This aim is pursued in the regular parliamentary work, in the various publications of the movement, and by study sessions.

At various critical moments the group has taken upon itself the role of defending the interests of the church. This happened, for example, in the case of the nationalization of church property in the Polish western territories in 1964, and in the case of the 1965 letter, much criticized by the Communist government, sent by the Polish Catholic hierarchy offering reconciliation to the German bishops.

Due to its independence, as well as its lack of political ambitions, the "Znak" group has gained a strategic position which the Pax Association has never achieved. Without ever becoming the sole intermediary between the Catholic church and the government, the members of the group have always been considered by both as serious partners, who could render valuable services, especially at a time of crisis.

Finally, mention has to be made of an important and often difficult function performed by the "Znak" group, as well as by the Pax Movement; namely, defending the Catholics, priests and laymen alike, against any form of discrimination on the part of the state.

*　　*　　*

In a non-pluralist political system of the Marxist type the various ideological options are never clear-cut or explicit. It is then rather difficult to analyze them properly. In past years the official ideology has undergone serious transformation amounting to (what is publicly never admitted, but is evident nevertheless) a growing gap between the official political and socio-economic policy and the philosophical doctrines of Marxism-Leninism. This provides the basis for a certain philosophical pluralism, which admits the existence of various motivations for the acceptance of the socialist society, although the goal of socialism itself cannot be questioned.

The concept of a nation plays a fundamental role here, and raises delicate problems in the ideological field. Catholicism and communism are both international and universalistic ideologies. But in Poland, because of historical tradition, any accepted system of ideas has to be national in character. This gives rise to opposing claims: for the church

Poland is Catholic; for the Communist Party Poland is socialist. From the political point of view, of course, these two positions are mutually exclusive. The nation is an indivisible notion; both conflicting ideologies pretend to be indivisible too. Who, then, has the right to speak in the name of the nation, to express its deepest aspirations and to defend its interests? Is it the Cardinal Primate or the First Secretary? This is not a purely theoretical question, for in 1966 it in fact led to a serious conflict between the church and the state. The occasion was furnished by the celebrations of the one thousand years of the Polish state, the founding of which coincides with the baptism of Mieszko I. The church and the state organized, throughout the country, separate and even conflicting celebrations to commemorate this anniversary. The conflict came to a head in Poznań, Poland's first capital, when at the same time as Cardinal Wyszyński was preaching to throngs of the faithful assembled around the Cathedral, Gomułka was addressing an officially organized mass meeting in front of the University. In the new political climate prevailing since December 1970 such incidents are unlikely to happen again, but the problem remains.

The Catholic groups cannot stay completely aloof from this controversy. For the Pax Movement, coming from the nationalist tradition of the political right, the only problem is to make a choice between the two conflicting, non-pluralist theses. Having a Hegelian vision of the nation and seeing no real opposition between Catholicism and socialism, "Pax" takes the side of the Communist Party.

The position of the "Znak" group is different. Because of the pluralism which its members profess, they cannot accept the validity of the controversy which exists between the church and the state. For them the nation is not a mystical entity, which could as such take up a creed or an ideology. The "Znak" followers, then, try to transfer the debate to the level of individual choices and social institutions, which could give it a meaningful political expression.

The attitude toward socialism is a different problem. As has been indicated above, the Polish Catholic church right from the beginning has accepted the establishment of the Communist political system. This was accepted as a new *de facto* situation which neither needed to be approved morally nor opposed openly. By the same token the church accepted the major post-war socio-economic reforms, such as the nationalization of industry and the banks, the land reform, etc., without voicing any moral objections. Nor did it enter into a doctrinal dispute with the

Marxists. It has to be stressed that the Polish Episcopate did not enforce the decree of Pope Pius XII, excommunicating the members of Communist parties. It can be seen from all this, that the church accepted the socialist reality as imposed on the country, but at the same time tried to ignore its doctrinal and philosophical basis.

The Pax Movement, on the other hand, accepted the socialist system not simply as a *de facto* situation, but precisely as a matter of principle. Because of this attitude it has been often considered abroad as a progressive Catholic group. Its dominant characteristic, however, especially in the early stages of its existence, was the acceptance of the Stalinist structure of power with all its consequences. As far as state-church relations were concerned it clearly favoured the submission of the church to the secular power; it also adhered to the official ideology, leaving a very narrow margin for different motivations.

For the "Znak" group the socialist system also constitutes a reality, but a reality capable of evolution. For its members it was not a question of accepting socialism as a *de facto* historical situation, or as a matter of principle but rather of accepting it as a reality, the evolution of which should be directed towards a more just, more humane and pluralistic society. With this in mind the "Znak" members have tried to keep open all possibilities for a true dialogue, philosophical as well as political, with the Marxists.

*   *   *

Since 1970 Poland has entered a new phase of its political, economic and social development. The changes which have been taking place are bound to affect, and have already positively affected, the relations between the church and the state. These changes are influencing the positions of both the "Pax" and "Znak" movements.

First of all, it appears that in the near future there are no possibilities, nor in fact any need, for either group to play the role of intermediary between the church and the state. Thus, both groups have to look for new roles for themselves. At a certain stage "Pax" tried to transform itself into a political party, but this proposal was rejected by the Communists. This could have been easily foreseen because in a people's democracy there is no prospect of expanding the existing party system, and also because the idea of creating in the 1970's a Catholic party in Poland appears utterly anachronistic.

The "Znak" group is somewhat less affected by the new situation. Even when serving, in a crisis situation, as an intermediary between the church hierarchy and the political authorities, it has never confined itself to this particular function. Its main concern has always been to promote a pluralistic and humanist evolution of the system, and to make a positive contribution to it by the committed Catholics. In a period of dynamic development and change this contribution could be especially important. To play this role in today's Poland there is no need, nor in fact the possibility, to form a new political party — a fact which is accepted by all the members of the "Znak" group. What is needed is a strong commitment to higher human and spiritual values and a sense of responsibility for the future of the country. This, I believe, the "Znak" group already provides.

Polish Foreign Policy: Historical Perspectives

ANDRZEJ MICEWSKI

Western ideas about Poles and Polish policy are often mistaken. During the period of over one hundred years (1795-1918), in which the Polish nation was deprived of its independence and took up arms time and again against the occupying powers, a certain stereotype of Polish conduct in international affairs emerged in the West. This stereotype presents the Poles as a nation of unrepentant romantics, rebels, and fighters, whose outlook has been rarely determined by concrete political realities.

Another deeply entrenched idea is that, as a result of Poland's geopolitical position, the same policy patterns have persistently repeated themselves throughout history. The German historian, Professor Golo Mann, writing in the journal *Survey*, observed that Poland's position between Germany and Russia "allows for only a few, ever-repeating variants."[1]

Is this really the case? Can it be said that Polish foreign policy still follows the patterns which have persisted throughout history? To answer this question it is necessary to examine briefly the main Polish international perspectives, past as well as present.

* * *

The dominant current in the distant, and still not so distant past, has been one of reliance on the West. In the period following the partitions, Poles counted either on assistance from the Western governments or on the popular revolutionary turmoil in Western Europe which would help them to regain their independence.[2] These hopes, however, turned out to be unrealistic. In the nineteenth century the revolutionary movements in the West did not succeed in overthrowing European imperialisms. At the same time the Western governments did little to assist Poland in any significant way. Indeed, in the era of the Holy Alliance, Poland seemed to have been buried forever.

---

[1] Golo Mann, "Rapallo: The Vanishing Dream," *Survey* (October 1962), p. 74.
[2] Marian Kukiel, *Dzieje Polski Porozbiorowe 1795-1921* (London, 1961).

During World War I, the Entente, including even France which traditionally had been most disposed towards us, did not declare themselves in favour of Polish independence until 1917. Only after the March Revolution in Russia and the passing of the resolutions in favour of Polish independence by the Soviet of Workers' and Soldiers' Delegates on 14-27 March 1917 and by the Provisional Government 17-30 March 1917, did France, England and Italy (in a joint telegram of 14 April 1917) announce their solidarity in recognizing Polish independence.[3]

At the peace conference France loyally supported the Polish objectives but England, guided by a misconceived concept of the European balance of power, supported a defeated Germany against France and Poland. President Wilson, even though he was generally sympathetic to Poland, lacked a good grasp of intricate Eastern European affairs, and often followed the British position. The overall result was that many of the provisions of the Versailles Treaty were unfavourable to Poland.[4]

In the inter-war period France, despite the Franco-Polish alliance of 1921, was at times less than loyal to us. At Locarno in 1925 France obtained guarantees of its own frontier with Germany, but left open the question of Germany's eastern boundaries. From that time on Germany, which had never reconciled itself to the settlement of the Versailles Treaty, presumed that its territorial claims in the east would not be opposed by the Western nations.[5] Only once, in Barthou's proposal of 1934, did the French come out with a serious initiative to conclude a collective security pact with the participation of both France and the Soviet Union. Yet, German and indeed Polish, opposition prevented the adoption of this otherwise very complicated plan. After that neither France nor any other Western European nation showed any serious concern about Poland's security. The British guarantee of 1939 turned out to be of little value. Poland fought alone in September without any effective military help.[6] During and after the Second World War, Eastern Europe was not of great interest to the Western nations — a fact which was best demonstrated by their attitude at the Yalta conference.

---

[3] Tadeusz Piszczkowski, *Odbudowanie Polski 1914-1921, Historia i polityka* (London, 1961).

[4] Roman Dmowski, *Polityka polska i odbudowanie państwa* (Warsaw, 1925).

[5] Władysław Pobóg-Malinowski, *Najnowsza historia polityczna Polski,* 2nd vol.: *1914-1939,* 2nd ed. (London, 1967).

[6] Hanna i Tadeusz Jędruszczak, *Ostatnie lata II Rzeczypospolitej 1935-1939* (Warsaw, 1970).

The experience of history, then, points out to the ineffectuality of relying on the West in Polish foreign policy. Western European nations attach only a secondary importance to this region,[7] being guided exclusively by their own interests. Only Germany and the Soviet Union have vital interests in the developments in Eastern Europe. France too has interest in this region but only indirectly, because of its relationship to Germany.

*　　*　　*

In the inter-war period and even during World War II some Polish politicians of the right and the centre favoured the idea of forming a political bloc of the Central and Eastern European states located between Germany and Russia. It was most often described as the "isthmus" concept, since its objective was to bridge together the states lying between the Baltic and the Black Sea.[8] There were many widely differing opinions on how to carry out this plan in practice, from Piłsudski's concept in 1920 of a federation of Poland with the Ukraine, Belorussia and Lithuania, to General Sikorski's design during World War II to form a Polish-Czechoslovak confederation as a foundation for a broader association with other Central and Eastern European states. In all cases, this idea was aimed against not only Germany, but also the U.S.S.R., and as such it was bound to meet with firm Soviet opposition. Although it was never precisely formulated, this was probably the main concept underlying the foreign policy of the *Sanacja* regime in the 1930's. But Poland's conflict with Lithuania and Czechoslovakia, which persisted throughout the entire inter-war period, posed serious obstacles to its realization. It was precisely in order to overcome them that Foreign Minister Beck strove for cooperation with Hungary and Rumania. Yet, it all proved to be an illusion. It did not stop the expansion of Germany in the region, or prevent Hitler's invasion of Poland.[9]

The "isthmus" concept was not only one of the greatest delusions of Polish foreign policy, it was also dangerous and damaging for Poland. It did not prevent German aggression, it cut us off from the Soviet Union, and tied Polish security to lost causes. A federation of states situated between Germany and Russia could not be created without a leader.

---

[7] Andrzej Micewski, "Wschód, Zachód i polityka polska," *Tygodnik Powszechny,* 16 January 1972.

[8] Marian Kukiel, *Generał Sikorski* (London, 1970).

[9] Andrzej Micewski, *W cieniu marszałka Piłsudskiego* (Warsaw, 1968).

Yet, Poland was too small a nation to play this role. The country was weak economically, and technologically backward. Moreover, there were serious differences in social development among the various nations in that region and the conflicts of interests separating them were too great. Even assuming that such a federation had been established, a change of policy by one of its members would have probably resulted in its disintegration.

The idea of a federation, or "isthmus," arose in Poland from an exaggerated estimate of our own strength and possibilities. It was the nostalgic throwback to an imperial role, which stemmed from reminiscences of the Jagiellonian era. Yet it had no relation to the real possibilities of a medium-sized nation, backward in culture and socioeconomic structure.[10] Some of the advocates of the federalist schemes held the view that the bloc of Central-Eastern European states should assume the role similar to that played by the Austro-Hungarian Empire. They were forgetting, however, that in the final stages of its existence the Habsburg Empire had fallen under the sway of Germany, and that this was largely responsible for its ultimate collapse at the end of World War I.

* * *

The idea of linking Polish policy to one of our powerful neighbours had already made an appearance in the post-partition era, although at that time it did not have majority support. It was presented most persuasively by the leader of the National Democracy, Roman Dmowski, in his book published in 1908, *Germany, Russia and the Polish Question.* The crux of Dmowski's argument was that Poland's position in the international sphere is a function of German-Russian relations. The logical consequence of this analysis was the necessity of Poland's alignment with one of its powerful neighbours.[11]

The possibility of looking to Germany for support has not been popular in Poland. It really appeared only during World War I. Piłsudski made use of it occasionally, but merely for tactical purposes. Some other people took it more seriously, but without any significant response either in Germany or Poland. The reason for that was that an alignment with Germany would have meant permanent acceptance of

---

[10] Józef Lewandowski, *Imperializm słabości* (Warsaw, 1967).
[11] Roman Dmowski, *Niemcy, Rosja i kwestia polska,* 2nd ed. (Częstochowa, 1938).

the loss of the German-occupied Polish western territories. Moreover, the Germans were only interested in establishing a caricature of a Polish state — a *Nebenstaat*, a little country subordinate to Germany.

In the inter-war years the pro-German policy was advocated only by a few isolated individuals, such as Władysław Studnicki[12] and Stanisław Mackiewicz.[13] They formed what was known as the "Wilno school" of Polish foreign policy which was characterized, above all, by an intense antipathy towards the Soviet Union. It ended in a complete fiasco. During the war Studnicki's pleas for better treatment of the Polish population by the Germans led to his internment in Berlin. Mackiewicz realized even before the war what the true objectives of Germany were and changed his line of thought. Yet his pro-German leanings came to the fore once again in 1940, at the time when Petain's France was suing for peace. Mackiewicz then urged the President of the Polish Government-in-Exile, Władysław Raczkiewicz, to follow Petain's example. The result would have been not only political disaster but also dishonour for Poland.

Whatever the personal motives of the Polish Germanophiles, they represented not only the least popular, but also the most futile concept of Polish foreign policy. It was motivated by a profound animosity towards our eastern neighbour and stemmed from very specific historical, psychological, and social traditions. Politically, it was completely erroneous.

* * *

Of a very different standing was the idea of cooperation with Russia. Although most of the Polish uprisings in the post-partition era were directed against the Tsars, all the great realists of the period strove to link Poland's interests with Russia.[14] The pro-Russian orientation of Roman Dmowski and of the National Democracy led by him, was aimed to bring the Polish question into the European forum at a time when World War I was looming on the horizon. After the occupation by Germany and Austria of the central Polish provinces in 1915, it played an important role in preventing the Poles from cooperating with the Central Powers and as such had an influence on the course of the war. Even then, however, the Tsar refused to regard Poland as a serious

---

[12] Władysław Studnicki, *System polityczny Europy a Polska* (Warsaw, 1934).

[13] Stanisław Mackiewicz, *Zielone oczy* (Warsaw, 1959).

[14] Andrzej Micewski, *Z geografii politycznej II Rzeczypospolitej* (Warsaw, 1964).

partner. Dmowski and the other right-wing Polish politicians, for all practical intents and purposes, abandoned their concept of cooperation with Russia after the Revolution of October 1917. Their ideological perceptions and social considerations affected their attitude towards the Soviet government.[15]

In the inter-war period a rapprochment between Poland and the Soviet Union was extremely difficult. A complex interplay of circumstances influenced by both class attitudes of the forces dominating the inter-war Polish political scene and the psychological barriers on the part of Polish public opinion stemming from a long history of conflict stood in its way. This contributed to the difficulties in organizing a general security system which alone could have saved Europe from war, and also deprived Poland of Soviet support at the time of German aggression in 1939.

The pre-war political imponderables also prevented the Polish wartime émigré government in London from reorienting Polish foreign policy from a reliance on the Western powers towards the recognition of the USSR as Poland's main ally.[16] Such a reorientation of foreign policy came only when the revolutionary camp took power in the country and Poland entered the bloc of socialist states.

The new political situation assured the security of Poland's western frontier along the Oder and the Neisse. The idea of alliance with the Soviet Union, despite the entire historical legacy, also began gradually to gain ground among the Polish people. The events of 1956 represented a psychological breakthrough creating firm foundations for an alliance with the USSR. This alliance, in contrast to earlier attempts at Polish-Russian cooperation, has not only geopolitical but also social aspects. It is founded on principles of political realism as well as on the community of interests between the two nations in overcoming their recent economic and social backwardness. The Poles appreciate its political as well as economic importance and look forward to an expanded cooperation with the USSR and other socialist states within the framework of CEMA.

*   *   *

Moreover, after World War II, in place of the old alternative between Germany or Russia, there arose a new choice — between West and

---

[15] Andrzej Micewski, *Roman Dmowski* (Warsaw, 1971).
[16] Jan M. Ciechanowski, *Powstanie Warszawskie* (London, 1971).

East. A totally new situation has emerged whose essence is that world politics, including Poland's place in it, has undergone a process of universalization. Poland's position is no longer, as Dmowski perceived it, only a function of German-Russian relations. It is now determined by relations between the two world nuclear powers. The concept of "Germany" has become immensely complicated because there now exist the two German states — a situation likely to persist at least for some time to come. The world described by Professor Golo Mann, then, where Polish policy is condemned to a few, ever-repeating variations simply no longer exists.

Poland's association with the USSR and the Eastern bloc need not make our country forever anti-German. On the contrary, it is this very association which paved the way for the signing of a treaty normalizing relations between Poland and the FRG. As Chancellor Brandt put his signature to this document, many people in Poland felt that the sacrifice of six million dead in the last war had not been in vain. At the same time, however, everyone must have realized that the treaty with the FRG would not have been possible had it not been for Poland's ties with the Eastern bloc in general, and with the USSR in particular.

The FRG ratified the Warsaw-Bonn accord with the abstention of a majority of the parliamentary CDU/CSU opposition. Chancellor Brandt was not deterred by the opposition and forced the ratification of the eastern treaties through the *Bundestag* because he realized that their rejection would have been extremely costly for the FRG. It would have cut West Germany off from the process of East-West détente and made it immensely unpopular around the world. In contrast the ratification of the eastern accords created a favourable atmosphere for the development of a security system in Europe, and for the consolidation of peaceful coexistence between East and West.

The signing of the treaty between Poland and the FRG almost coincided with the visit to Warsaw of the French Prime Minister, Chaban-Delmas. The steady improvement of relations between Poland and France expresses their joint desire for European security and peaceful coexistence between East and West. A revival of traditional ties between Poland and the Western European nations also took place within the context of the universalization of Poland's and the world's politics. Both President de Gaulle and the present French leaders have been interested in Poland not just for Poland's sake, but also because it is an important member of the Eastern bloc. Their visits to Poland have been an integral element of world-wide politics. Poland's alliance with the Soviet Union and its participation in the Eastern bloc have given impetus to the Polish-German reconciliation and to the revival of the traditional friendships with the Western countries, particularly with France.

We are thus dealing with an entirely new situation in which the Russian variant of Polish policy is no longer incompatible with the expansion of other international ties. In the past, historical circumstances have been such, that this course had almost inevitably excluded all others. At present, the Polish-Russian alliance, and the ties with the other socialist states, are conducive to the expansion of other international relations. Naturally, this will be possible only if European security is developed and East and West coexist peacefully.

Polish foreign policy has great possibilities when based on firm ties with the Soviet Union and the socialist commonwealth. At the same time, because of Poland's cultural links with Western Europe, the USSR has in Poland a valuable ally in promoting collective security on our continent. It is precisely for these reasons that there is a widespread conviction in Poland that, regardless of our considerable internal problems, we should actively continue our present course of foreign policy and exploit the opportunities ahead of us in the international sphere.

Polish Foreign Policy in the 1970's *

ADAM BROMKE

Foreign policy was somewhat of an exception to the gloom surrounding the twilight of the Gomułka era. While in the domestic sphere, on the government side there was deepening stagnation and widespread popular dissatisfaction which culminated in the explosion of December 1970, in external relations, especially from the spring of 1969, there was an upsurge of activity.[1] Taking its cue from the appeal for all-European cooperation issued by the meeting of Communist leaders in Budapest in March 1969, Polish diplomacy increased its contacts with various Western European capitals. The attempts to reduce tensions in Europe were linked to earlier Polish proposals, especially the Rapacki and the Gomułka plans, and Poland soon emerged as a major proponent of a European conference.

On 17 May 1969 Gomułka offered to undertake negotiations aimed at normalization of relations between Poland and West Germany. His speech maintained that the FRG must accept the Polish western boundary, but otherwise was surprisingly moderate in its tone. In the fall, after Brandt's coming to power, Bonn responded favourably to Warsaw's overture, and by February 1970 Polish-German talks were underway. The negotiations, in which the Poles displayed a good deal of flexibility, went on until late that year. By November the treaty providing for acceptance by the FRG of the Polish western boundary and the establishment of diplomatic relations between the two countries was agreed upon. It was signed during Chancellor Brandt's visit to Warsaw on 7 December 1970.[2] Two weeks later, after the workers' rebellion in

---

* The author is grateful to the editors of *Problems of Communism* for their kind permission to use the material contained in his article, "Poland Under Gierek: A New Political Style," XXI (September-October 1972), pp. 1-19, on which this chapter is largely based.

[1] For a more detailed account of Polish foreign policy in the late stages of the Gomułka period see Adam Bromke, "Beyond the Gomułka Era," *Foreign Affairs* (April 1971); also A. Ross Johnson, "Polish Perspectives: Past and Present," *Problems of Communism* (July-August 1971).

[2] For a comprehensive review of Polish-German relations in the 1960's see Adam Bromke and Harald von Riekhoff, "Poland and Germany: A Belated Détente?" *Canadian Slavonic Papers* (Summer 1970); also by the same authors, "The West German-Polish Treaty," *The World Today* (March 1971).

the coastal cities, Gomułka resigned as First Secretary and was replaced in that post by Edward Gierek.

Despite their preoccupation with the domestic crisis the new Polish leaders did not neglect foreign relations. Immediately after coming to power both Gierek and Jaroszewicz emphasized continuity in Poland's foreign policy. In fact, its momentum has not only been maintained but has been greatly accelerated. As one Polish commentator noted: "Since December [1970] many earlier initiatives have acquired new dynamism."[3] In the 1970's Polish diplomacy has been at the height of its activity in the post-war period.

* * *

The fundamental tenet of Poland's foreign policy, of course, is unchanged — an alliance and friendship with the Soviet Union. In his first address to the nation on 20 December 1970, Gierek praised "brotherly and cordial cooperation" with the U.S.S.R. and promised to consolidate it even further in the future.[4] He has reiterated this theme, in terms no less exuberant than those which had been used by Gomułka, in virtually all his major pronouncements. Polish Foreign Minister Stefan Olszowski reported late in 1972 that the system of consultations with the Soviet Union on the principal international problems has been expanded.[5] Premier Piotr Jaroszewicz emphasized that Polish activities on the international scene are "part and parcel of the common policy of peace conducted by the U.S.S.R., together with the other socialist countries."[6]

Economic ties with the U.S.S.R., both bilateral and within the CEMA, also have been strengthened. In the current five year plan joint production of automobiles and computers has been undertaken. An agreement was signed to build a large metallurgical combine in Poland, with Soviet assistance. Polish-Soviet scientific and technical cooperation has also been developed. At present, in this sphere, regular contacts are maintained between eighteen Polish and thirty-three Soviet ministries and between 130 Polish and 180 Soviet scientific research institutes.[7]

---

[3] Władysław Machejek, "Czy Polska sie wychyliła?" *Życie Literackie,* 9 July 1972.
[4] *Trybuna Ludu,* 21 December 1973.
[5] Stefan Olszowski, "Main Trends of Polish Foreign Policy," *International Affairs* (Moscow, October 1972), p. 3.
[6] Piotr Jaroszewicz, "Obecne problemy polityki zagranicznej i zadania w dziedzinie handlu zaganicznego," *Nowe Drogi* (July 1972).
[7] "USSR-Poland: Broad Cooperation," *International Affairs* (Moscow, July 1972), p. 3.

Poland also has had good relations with the other Communist countries in Eastern Europe. Immediately after their takeover, top members of the Gierek team were despatched to the various Eastern European capitals to establish contact with the local Communist leaders. Polish-East German relations which had been seriously strained in the latter years of Gomułka and Ulbricht because of Poland's conciliatory attitude toward West Germany, have visibly improved. Evidently, with Hoenecker falling into line with the rest of the Communist countries on the issue of European détente, the main obstacle in relations between Warsaw and Pankow has been removed. In January 1972 a step unprecedented in the Communist orbit was taken — the boundary between Poland and GDR was opened to tourist traffic.

Contacts between the Polish and the Czech, as well as the Hungarian, leaders have been frequent. Poland's relations with Rumania and Yugoslavia have also undergone marked improvement; President Tito was accorded a warm welcome during his visit to Warsaw in June 1972. Only Poland's relations with China have remained cool. In evident solidarity with the Soviet position, the Polish leaders, including Gierek himself, have harshly denounced the Chinese for splitting the international Communist movement.

New elements in Polish-Soviet relations, however, have also been emphasized. Commenting on Gierek's visit to Moscow in January 1971, a writer in *Polityka* rebuked those who in looking at the substance of Poland's alliance with the Soviet Union "stubbornly cling to yesterday's patterns while ignoring the passage of time and the changes which come with it."[8] And a well known commentator on international affairs, Ryszard Wojna, in an article in *Życie Warszawy,* struck an even more assertive tone: "Our contribution to the Warsaw Treaty," he wrote, "is by no means unimportant. Taking into account our demographic, economic and military potential we are the second — next to the Soviet Union — strongest power in the socialist bloc."[9]

There are, in fact, reasons to believe that the new Polish leaders are in a better position than their predecessors to put their relations with the Russians on a more equal footing. Gierek's team appears to be more attuned to the present Soviet leadership than the Gomułka group ever was. While Gomułka had a good rapport with Khrushchev, Gierek,

---

[8] S. K., "Zawsze bliżej," *Polityka,* 16 January 1971.
[9] Ryszard Wojna, "Nasze funkcje europejskie," *Życie Warszawy,* 17 January 1971.

even though he speaks Russian poorly, probably finds it easier to get along with Brezhnev. The two men belong to the same post-revolutionary Communist generation; they both talk the language of practical administrators rather than that of doctrinaire ideologists. Indeed, their partnership seems to work well. In February 1971 the U.S.S.R. extended to Poland badly needed credits, and in the spring of the same year Moscow threw its support behind Gierek in the intra-Party struggle for power. In December Brezhnev personally appeared at the VI Polish Party Congress to give approval to Gierek's course.

* * *

The new Polish leaders have stressed from the very outset that they plan to continue along the course started by Gomułka in 1969, aimed at a reconciliation with West Germany and a détente in Europe. They apparently believe that in the present international situation their continued alliance with the U.S.S.R. and their efforts at improving relations with the Western powers are not only compatible, but indeed, complementary. "The effectiveness of our policy in the West," wrote a commentator on foreign affairs, Ignacy Krasicki, "depends upon our position in the socialist system. . . . In the present constellation of forces in Europe our country is the first ally of the strongest European power — one of the two world superpowers — the Soviet Union."[10]

Since 1970 Polish diplomatic activity has been greatly intensified. Poland has continued its conciliatory policy toward the German Federal Republic. During the bitter debate in Bonn over the ratification of the West German treaties with Poland and the USSR, the Poles acted with considerable restraint. The Polish press did not conceal its apprehension, but its tone was moderate. Extensive contacts between the two countries were maintained; in 1971 not only supporters of Chancellor Brandt, but also several ranking members of the CDU, notably Barzel, visited Warsaw. When in mid-May 1972 the treaties were eventually ratified by Bonn, Warsaw reacted promptly. On 26 May the treaty with the FRG was ratified by Poland and on 5 June Polish Deputy Foreign Minister Józef Czyrek went to Bonn to exchange ratification documents with his West German counterpart.[11]

---

[10] Ignacy Krasicki, "Nasze miejsce w sojuszu," *Zycie Warszawy*, 26 January 1971.

[11] A significant difference between the Polish and the Soviet stand appeared on that occasion. While the U.S.S.R. implicitly accepted the *Bundestag* resolution which held that the treaties do not prejudice the ultimate settlement of German

In mid-September 1972 Stefan Olszowski, in making the first visit of a Polish Foreign Minister to the FRG, went to Bonn. He was received by Chancellor Brandt, and in talks held with Foreign Minister Scheel explored a broad range of possibilities for expanding cooperation between the two countries. In November ambassadors from Poland and West Germany were exchanged. The breakthrough in relations between Poland and the FRG was hailed by Karol Małcużynski in the Party daily, *Trybuna Ludu*, as a step "opening new perspectives, and even a new chapter in the post-war history of Europe." This success, he added, not only confirmed the correctness of Poland's course, but, above all, its close alliance with the U.S.S.R.[12]

Meanwhile, Poland continued to develop broad contacts — aimed both at expanding bilateral relations, especially in the economic sphere, and at preparing for a European conference — with several other Western European countries. Polish-French relations, after the chill in the late 1960's, warmed up once again. Early in October 1972 Gierek, reciprocating President de Gaulle's visit to Poland in 1967, paid a five-day visit to France.[13] During his stay in Paris Gierek had three meetings with President Pompidou, while at the same time Minister Olszowski and the head of the Foreign Affairs Department of the Party, Ryszard Frelek, held talks with the French Foreign Minister, Maurice Schumann. The communique issued at the end of the visit stressed the common objectives of the two governments to promote all-European cooperation and undertook to continue regular consultations. Special attention was given to the expansion of human contacts, especially among the youth. On the same occasion a new economic agreement was signed and Poland

---

boundaries at a peace conference, Poland made it clear that it regards the territorial settlement as final. Indeed, at the joint session of the Foreign Affairs and Legislative Committees of the *Sejm*, Foreign Minister Olszowski explicitly stated that "all of the reservations of the unilateral resolution of the *Bundestag* have no validity in international law." *Krajowa Agencja Informacyjna*, 31 May 1972.

[12] Karol Małcużyński, "Sukces i egzamin dojrzałości," *Trybuna Ludu*, 21 May 1972.

[13] It was one of those unexpected twists of history that in the case of both national leaders it was not their first visit to the other country. De Gaulle had been in Poland in 1920 as a military advisor to the Polish army fighting the Russians, while Gierek had worked in France as a miner in his youth and had been expelled from that country in 1933 for his activities in the Communist movement. For a discussion of Polish-French relations in the 1960's see Adam Bromke, "Poland and France: The Sentimental Friendship," *East Europe* (February 1966).

was granted French credits amounting to some eleven billion francs.[14] Prospects of further cooperation in joint industrial ventures, along the lines of an agreement in co-production of buses which had been concluded a few months earlier, were anticipated by the Poles.

Poland's relations with the other Western European countries have also been expanded. In October of 1971 an agreement was made for the mass production of small Fiat cars in Poland, and in November a protocol guaranteeing Poland long-term Italian credits was signed. Despite Britain's reserved attitude toward a European conference, economic cooperation between the two countries continued to progress. In the winter of 1971 an agreement for a Polish-British venture in co-production of machine tools was concluded, followed in the summer by a contract with the British Petroleum Company for joint construction of an oil refinery at Gdańsk. In mid-June Foreign Minister Olszowski visited Austria. A month later an agreement to abolish visas between the two countries was signed.

Especially good relations have been developed with the Scandinavian countries. At the end of June 1972 Foreign Minister Olszowski went to Oslo and in October of the same year Premier Jaroszewicz visited Stockholm. Tourism between Poland and Sweden is to be facilitated and the Swedes are to build a luxury hotel in Warsaw. The Finns have been in close consultation with the Poles on preparations for a conference on European Security and Cooperation. Early in 1972 a senior Polish diplomat, Adam Willman, obviously with the prospect of a conference being held there, was appointed Ambassador in Helsinki. At the same time informal contacts aimed at promoting a European conference were intensified. Foreign diplomats, scholars and journalists were invited to discussions by the Polish Institute of International Affairs, roundtables were organized, and Western views on European problems were published in the Polish press.[15]

Even Poland's relations with the Vatican have undergone a marked improvement. Early in 1971, side by side with the efforts at a reconciliation with the Catholic hierarchy at home, negotiations between the Polish government and the Vatican were begun. In April 1971 Alek-

---

[14] *Na antenie* (London, December 1972), p. 30.
[15] For instance, articles by the editor of *The Economist*, Alastair Burnet in *Polityka*, 19 June 1971; Adam Bromke, "Europa, ale jaka?" *Tygodnik powszechny*, 12 December 1971; and Andrew Gyorgy, "USA: Konferencja europejska," *Polityka*, 1 July 1972.

sander Skarżynski, the Deputy Minister in charge of religious affairs, visited Rome to confer with the Secretary of the Council for Public Affairs, Archbishop Agostino Casaroli, and in November of the same year they held a second meeting in Warsaw. In October 1971 during the beatification of the Polish martyr from Auschwitz, Father Maksymilian Kolbe, the Polish authorities were extremely cooperative. An air lift was arranged to take some 1,500 Polish Catholics to Rome, and Skarżynski formally represented the Polish government at all of the religious ceremonies. Soon after the ratification of the Polish-West German treaty terminating the territorial dispute between the two countries, the Vatican proceeded to appoint Polish bishops in the six western dioceses, thereby acknowledging the ecclesiastical control of the Polish church over these areas and implicitly recognizing them as part of Poland.

* * *

The most dramatic change, however, has taken place in Polish-American relations. After Gierek's ascent to power the distinctly cold climate which prevailed in the latter Gomułka years gave way, first to businesslike contacts and then to mutual efforts at cooperation not devoid of some cordiality. In the spring of 1971 two high level Polish missions, headed by the Minister of Chemical Industry and the Chairman of the Committee of Science and Technology respectively, visited the United States. In June Gierek and Jaroszewicz visited the American pavilion at the Poznań trade fair and in a chat with Ambassador Walter Stoessel, expressed interest in increasing trade and in obtaining technological information from the United States.

Washington's response to Warsaw's overtures was both positive and swift. In August 1971, reversing the decision which had been made shortly before Gomułka's ouster, the United States agreed to grant Poland an export licence for the purchase of a catalytic cracking plant. In October a small credit to finance the purchase of American agricultural produce by Poland was offered. In November U.S. Secretary of Transportation, John Volpe, visited Warsaw to sign an agreement for cooperation in research on transportation problems; he was followed in December by the Secretary of Commerce, Maurice Stans, who explored the prospects for expanding trade between the two countries.

By early 1972 the road was clear for even more dramatic steps, which were soon taken. In an address in the *Sejm* on 28 March Premier Jaroszewicz noted "the interest of the United States in expanding economic, scientific and technical relations with Poland" and stressed a positive attitude on the part of the Polish government.[16] President Nixon, in turn, in a congratulatory message to the newly elected Chairman of the State Council, Henryk Jabłoński, noted the betterment in relations between the two countries which had taken place in 1971 and voiced the hope that this trend would continue in the future.[17] On 17 April at a meeting which was described as "elaborate and warm," Ambassador Trąmpczyński extended to Mr. Nixon an invitation to visit Poland.[18]

President Nixon stopped over in Warsaw on his way back from Moscow on 31 May and 1 June. The official reception accorded to him was in every respect proper, but not demonstrative. He was compensated for that, however, by a tumultuous welcome from the crowds which gathered for a wreath-laying ceremony at the Tomb of the Unknown Soldier in Victory Square. Immediately afterward the American President held the first of his two meetings with the Polish leaders.[19] The talks were described in an official communique as "frank, businesslike and constructive."[20] Differences, especially over the war in Vietnam, were acknowledged, but at the same time various accords were reached. In bilateral relations it was agreed to hold regular consultations to develop trade and to expand scientific cooperation. Increased personal contacts were envisaged; air and sea connections between the two countries are soon to be developed; and a consular agreement clarifying the status of Polish-Americans was signed. Nixon also extended an invitation to Gierek, Jaroszewicz, and Jabłoński to visit the United States.

In a broader area of European politics an accord was also reached on various points. The Americans expressed satisfaction at the conclusion of the treaty between Poland and West Germany, specifically including its border provisions. They also subscribed to the Polish view that multilateral consultations to prepare for a conference on European security and cooperation should begin soon. In his speech at the state dinner in the Radziwił Palace, President Nixon stressed that he expected

---

[16] *Trybuna Ludu*, 29 March 1972.

[17] *Krajowa Agencja Informacyjna*, 12 April 1972.

[18] *The New York Times*, 20 April 1972.

[19] For an extensive personal account of Mr. Nixon's visit to Warsaw by a Polish-Canadian journalist, see Benedykt Heydenkorn, *Związkowiec* (Toronto, 13, 20, and 27 June 1972).

[20] *The New York Times*, 2 June 1972.

Poland to play an important role in the forthcoming negotiations on Europe.[21]

The Poles had every reason to be pleased with the results of the President's visit. There is no doubt that it enhanced the prestige of Gierek both at home and abroad. The tone of satisfaction was evident in the Polish press. Ryszard Wojna in *Życie Warszawy* described the visit as the beginning of "a new chapter in relations between Poland and the United States," but he hastened to add that the way had been "paved by the historic results of the Moscow accord."[22] Another well-known writer on international affairs, Janusz Stefanowicz, in an article significantly entitled "An Important and Fruitful Visit," in *Słowo Powszechne,* made a more general observation. In his opinion Nixon's visit to Warsaw demonstrated that "the role of the middle powers . . . increases proportionately to the progress of détente in East-West relations."[23]

Following the visit of President Nixon to Warsaw the momentum in expanding Polish-American relations has been maintained. In July the Presidential Scientific Advisor, Dr. Edward David, paid a visit to Poland; he was followed in August by Secretary of Commerce Peter Peterson. On the latter occasion a Polish-U.S. Commission on Trade was set up. In the meantime, Poland concluded agreements with Universal Oil Products of Des Plaines for the acquisition of technical drawings of a fluid catalytic cracking process for a petrochemical plant to be built in Płock, and with Standard Oil of Indiana for a new refinery at Gdańsk.

In mid-September Polish Foreign Minister Olszowski visited Washington where he had talks with Secretary of State William Rogers and was also received by President Nixon. A month later the controversial issue of payments for the Polish bonds owned by Americans, dating back to the 1920's, was settled. At the end of October 1971 a five-year agreement providing for broad cooperation in science and technology was concluded. Early in November, during the visit to Washington of the Polish Minister of Foreign Trade, Tadeusz Olechowski, a number of accords to develop trade between the two countries were signed. Poland was granted access to credits from the Import-Export Bank, and the expansion of industrial cooperation was envisaged.

The political significance of all these exchanges and agreements is

---

[21] *Krajowa Agencja Informacyjna,* 7 June 1972.

[22] Ryszard Wojna, "W kierunku wytyczonym prozumieniem moskiewskim," *Życie Warszawy*, 3 June 1972.

[23] Janusz Stefanowicz, "Wizyta ważna i owocna," *Słowo Powszechne,* 3 June 1972.

clear. In the overall climate of East-West détente, Poland no longer feels restrained from expanding substantially its bilateral relations with the leader of the Western alliance. Relations between Poland and the United States in the early 1970's have been better than ever before in the post-war period.

* * *

Yet, satisfaction at the expansion of Poland's relations with the West has not been universal. There have also been some voices expressing caution and even apprehension. Concern has been expressed that closer contacts with the Western countries, and the United States in particular, may lead to the erosion of Communist ideology. In mid-1972, *Trybuna Ludu* reminded its readers that a climate of détente in East-West relations does not imply the abandonment of the ideological struggle between them. Indeed, peaceful coexistence was characterized by the Party daily as "a form of ideological warfare [in a] world-wide confrontation between socialism and imperialism."[24]

In an article published in an army monthly, *Wojsko Ludowe,* Colonel Julian Sokół was even more explicit in pointing out the dangers of a détente for the Communists. He warned that the new international climate may well be exploited by the West to penetrate the socialist countries with its own ideological concepts. "It is obvious," he wrote "that imperialism taking advantage of the struggle for détente and peaceful coexistence will intensify its attempts at ideological subversion."[25]

Sokół admitted that the West has at its disposal better technical facilities for psychological warfare and greater skill in propaganda. He was particularly apprehensive about the Western proposals to expand the exchanges of people and ideas between the two blocs. Tourism, he asserted, could be used to demonstrate to the visitors from Poland "the outward and frequently attractive aspects of capitalism," while cultural exchanges would be exploited as a "channel for smuggling ideas." He was even distrustful of economic exchanges: "A definite ideological and propaganda role," he observed, "will be played by the mere fact that Western goods and Western technology will become much more widespread in our country."

---

[24] Bolesław Wójcicki, "Pokojowe współistnienie," *Trybuna Ludu*, 27 June 1972.
[25] J. Sokół, "Pokojowa koegzystencja i ideologiczna dywersja," *Wojsko Ludowe* (May 1972).

In short, Sokół felt that the new pattern of international relations may affect the political climate in the country. "It may lead us to lower our guard [and to fall into] the temptation of extending compromise from politics to ideology." To prevent this from happening Sokół advocated continued ideological vigilance. Barriers to prevent Western infiltration should be maintained and Communist propaganda should be intensified, "ceaselessly making use of the ideological achievements of the Party."

Still, not all the opinions about the expansion of contacts with the West have been as conservative as those of Colonel Sokół. Mieczysław Rakowski, in an article significantly entitled "The Chances of a Great Peace," published in the Party theoretical monthly *Nowe Drogi*, admitted that broader contacts pose certain risks for the socialist countries, but on the whole he sounded much more optimistic. He stressed that economic exchanges with the West are advantageous, and indeed necessary to Poland. He also observed that the extensive flow of Western tourists into Hungary, Bulgaria and especially Yugoslavia, had not changed the nature of the political systems in those countries. Finally Rakowski emphasized that the impact of personal contacts may work both ways and that several aspects of socialism may also appeal to the visitors from the West.

A particularly interesting aspect of Rakowski's article was his acceptance of the fact that in the new international situation an internal evolution is inevitable. He bluntly challenged the view of some of the Western analysts who claim that the Communist objective in promoting a détente in Eastern Europe is to uphold the existing *status quo*. He acknowledged that inasmuch as the maintenance of peace is concerned, this is true. As to social change, however, Rakowski ridiculed this Western view. "Looking at the *status quo* from a historio-philosophic perspective," he observed, "it must be remembered that the existing state of affairs is ever changing. Had this not been the case we still would be living in trees!"[26]

* * *

There seems to be little doubt that the great majority of the Poles do not share the apprehension voiced by some Party conservatives, but on the contrary welcome the present thrust of Polish foreign policy in

---

[26] Mieczysław F. Rakowski, "Szanse na wielki pokój," *Nowe Drogi* (November 1972), p. 64.

the direction of rapprochement with the West and a détente in Europe. Despite acceptance by the FRG of the Polish western boundary the Poles still regard their alliance with the USSR to be in their interest. They noted the strong opposition to the ratification of the treaty with Poland in the *Bundestag* — in fact, it was even stronger than that against the ratification of the West German treaty with the Soviet Union. The Poles thus continue to view Russia's support against Germany as essential to them. At the same time they welcome the revival of their traditionally close bonds with the various Western countries, such as France or the United States.

Poland's present foreign policy represents a synthesis of the two main traditional currents in its external relations: the pro-Russian and pro-Western tendencies.[27] In an entirely different social context it resembles somewhat the policy followed early in the century by the National Democrats led by Roman Dmowski. Dmowski's objective was not only to gain influence in St. Petersburg, but also to capitalize on it in the different Western capitals, particularly in Paris. His policy paid off handsomely when at the end of World War I, with French support, he managed to win substantial concessions for Poland at the expense of Germany.[28]

Continuation of the present course of external policy, paradoxically, also offers Poland the best chance of eventual reconciliation with Germany. Soviet support was of crucial importance to Poland to extract from West Germany the acceptance of the present Polish boundary and the normalization of relations between the two countries. The Poles, no doubt, noted that the treaty between Bonn and Warsaw had been preceded by the one between Bonn and Moscow in which the territorial *status quo* in Central Europe was for the first time acknowledged.

Foreign policy of the Polish People's Republic in the 1970's in some respects runs parallel to that of the Federal Republic of Germany under Chancellor Brandt. The West German *Ostpolitik* has been aimed at improving relations between that country and its eastern neighbors, but not at the expense of reducing the FRG's ties with its Western allies. It is not a *Schaukelpolitik* of trying to enhance Germany's position by balancing between the West and the East. On the contrary, continued

---

[27] For a fuller discussion of this subject see Adam Bromke, *Poland's Politics, Idealism vs. Realism* (Cambridge, Mass., 1967), especially Chapter 13, "Political Idealism and Political Realism: The Synthesis."

[28] Roman Dmowski, *Polityka polska i odbudowanie państwa* (Hanover, 1947).

close cooperation with its Western partners is regarded by Bonn as a foundation for the success of the eastern policy. In this way West Germany has made an important contribution to the progress of European détente and at the same time has greatly enhanced its international status.

Warsaw's external policy to a large extent is that of Bonn *au rebours*. The expansion of cooperation with the West is firmly anchored in Poland's alliance with the USSR and the other Communist states. It is entirely different from Beck's attempts to steer an independent course between Germany and Russia. This has enabled Poland to play a significant role in the improvement of the international climate in Europe. Yet, the progress of a détente in Europe, of course, also works in reverse. The expansion of Poland's contacts with the different Western countries has enhanced Poland's position *vis-à-vis* the Soviet Union. The greater Warsaw's influence is in Paris, Bonn, or Washington, the stronger is its voice in Moscow. The Poles, then, can play a greater role in the formulation of the common policy of the Communist bloc.

The coincidence in foreign policies between Warsaw and Bonn may be of a profound importance for the future of Europe. The location of these two countries in the very heart of the continent makes their respective contributions to the European détente essential.[29] The maintenance of their present alliances side by side with the expansion of their contacts with the countries across the ideological barrier may well be the most effective way to gradually overcome the division of Europe. Superimposing new bonds of cooperation on the existing ones may eventually pave the way for the disappearance of the two blocs and the emergence of an all-European system of cooperation.

---

[29] For the importance of Poland and Germany to the resolution of the European problem, and the peculiar interdependence between their policies, seen in the context of the debate on the proposals for "disengagement" in the late 1950's, see Adam Bromke, "Disengagement in Eastern Europe," *International Journal* (Summer 1959), especially pp. 173-174.

Poland and European Security

STANISŁAW TREPCZYŃSKI

Poland is a country which feels very deeply involved in matters of European security. Her involvement has been well evidenced by the numerous initiatives we have taken over the past few years, and by our constant activity in this field. But do these initiatives and activities imply that Poland feels endangered or insecure in the Europe of today?

By no means. In fact, quite to the contrary; never throughout its chequered history has Poland felt as safe as she does at present. In the first place we are linked by a well proven alliance and by relations of friendship with our powerful neighbour, the Soviet Union. We also have friendly relations with our other neighbours; we have established sound economic cooperation within the Council for Economic Mutual Assistance; we are protected by our joint defensive treaty; and we have lively political and economic relations with many other countries of the world.

Yet, we gained our independence and established Poland's present political position at the cost of painstaking sacrifices and efforts, far greater than those which any of the other European nations had to make.

Ours was a continuous struggle for freedom and independence, because for over one hundred years Poland was partitioned and ruled by foreign powers. We had not yet recovered from the time of subjugation and the destructions of World War I when, completely isolated, we again had to face the Nazi aggression of 1939. Despite her weakness, Poland was the first state to have the courage to fight, not to surrender to the enemy, but to keep resisting the Nazi occupant. Poland was also one of the few countries which did not accept any form of collaboration with the enemy. Poles fought in their own occupied country and on all fronts during World War II. Although Poland had been occupied by the Nazi enemy, on the European front our military effort placed us second in strength among the armies of the great anti-Nazi coalition, next only to the Soviet Union.

During the last world war, Poland suffered comparatively the heaviest losses. Six million Polish citizens — nearly one fifth of the population — lost their lives. As much as 40 per cent of the national economy and most Polish cities were ruined. Poland's capital, Warsaw, was methodically and deliberately destroyed by the occupant. After the liberation by Soviet and Polish troops, the people of Poland made an unprecedented effort to rebuild the country after the war's destruction, to organize the Polish state within its new frontiers, and to settle and fully integrate the Polish population in the old Polish territories recovered in the north and west.

Today the Polish People's Republic constitutes a uniform and compact state organism with a rapidly developing economy, a leading role in science and technology, and a flourishing culture. Though not yet able to solve all her problems, Poland is in every respect an equal partner of other European countries and an active participant in international cooperation.

Yet, the people of Poland well remember that in the not too distant past they had to pay a high price for their right to freedom and development under conditions of peace. This is why the basic objective of Poland's foreign policy is to ensure her people — now and in the future — economic stability and a secure position in a peaceful Europe.

* * *

The multilateral preparatory talks for the European Conference on Security and Cooperation which began recently in Helsinki, indicate that in all probability, all interested European states, together with the United States and Canada, will meet next year at a joint conference table. Indeed, we attach great importance to this conference and we strongly believe that it will succeed in fulfilling its goals of initiating a new era in the history of our region, one of consolidation, of collective security and development, and of peaceful cooperation.

Our optimism may sometimes seem surprising: seen from the perspective of the United Nations — from an international political forum — the world is moving forward too slowly towards fuller international security, and too many conflicts still await solution. Nor is the historical experience of Europe very encouraging: the various attempts to organize regional security in Europe before World War II have all failed. The early post-war period in Europe was characterized by a constant growth of tension and very dangerous confrontation. Why therefore should we not be facing yet another failure?

It is not the intention here to go into an assessment of all the reasons why European states failed to coexist in peace in the past. Analyzing only modern times, one should, above all, realize that thirty years will have soon elapsed since the end of the Second World War, and that a profound evolution has taken place during this period, both in the world and in Europe. The new relationships that have evolved create prospects for a lasting peace — provided, however, that we succeed in taking full advantage of the enormous opportunity before us.

The United States and the Soviet Union are fully aware today that on a world scale they have reached a parity of forces based on the respective potential of each, and that this parity of powers is, in fact, now so developed that it calls for new forms of mutual relations. The results of President Nixon's talks in Moscow and the course of the SALT negotiations indicate that the era of confrontation from a position of strength is nearing the end.

Can one hence conclude — and we know that there exists such a school of political thinking — that matters of world security have been monopolized by the two biggest powers of the world? Does this mean that smaller states have no important role to play in this respect, since — as some say — they have been practically deprived of their right to speak, or — as others say — because the only constructive approach they could take would be not to stand in the way of agreements between big powers?

It would seem that both these interpretations of relationships between big and smaller powers are grossly mistaken, as they are based on the erroneous assumption that states like the Soviet Union or the United States are operating in some kind of a political vacuum. In fact, reality is entirely different. Big powers naturally have problems to solve which are commensurate with their size, but in their policies they cannot lose sight of the role and the significance of other states of the world, be they allied with them or not, neutral or non-aligned, small, medium, or large. For as the United Nations practice has shown on many occasions, it is the activity of these states in the world forum which is of paramount importance to international developments. Were it not for their actions for peace, world security would always be both unstable and uncertain. This is particularly applicable in the case of Europe, and is particularly important now, when we are entering a period in which, despite differences of interests and ideologies, and in spite of evident contradictions between capitalism and socialism, any further competition for the future of mankind between these diverging ideologies and systems will take place only in conditions of peaceful co-existence. This implies in turn that both sides will have to make sincere efforts to prevent competition from turning into conflict involving the use of force.

The present evolution of international relations is of great importance for the future of Europe, for Europe is a region of the world where the two systems, socialism and capitalism, have become firmly rooted and where acute and dangerous confrontations have taken place among competing systems in the not too distant past. The present atmosphere of international détente measurably increases the stability of European relations. One may safely say that at last the political map of this region is firmly defined and that there is no intention to upset the existing equilibrium.

The sound evolution of relations in Europe is all the more important because its roots can be traced to the relationship of forces established in Europe following World War II. For many decades, Eastern Europe had been a constant source of tension and conflict. It was an economically backward region where more powerful and more expansionistic states competed with one another. Internal conflicts, problems of national minorities and the incompetence of governments were the main causes of conflict and wars. The emergence of socialist states, their dynamic internal development, and their solidarity have helped to bring about a situation which has made the whole European continent more stable and safer. What we need now is for partners from Eastern and Western Europe to cooperate with one another in maintaining peace, and this is one of the tasks of the forthcoming Conference on Security and Cooperation in Europe.

*   *   *

Peace and security, first and foremost, call for a realistic vision of Europe. Any attempts at imposing a concept contrary to reality are doomed to failure since they are deprived of durable foundations. All attempts made so far on the basis of narrow-minded and selfish interests of a single group of states have ended in a fiasco. In general terms, selfishness of this kind boiled down exclusively to sacrificing the interests of smaller and weaker states; it never led to peace and it frequently provoked conflicts.

Therefore, only cooperation between all European states, based on a true recognition of the existing realities, can provide appropriate conditions upon which to build a system of lasting security in Europe and to ensure peace in that region. At the same time, we all realize the importance of the consolidation of peace in Europe for the rest of the world. The developing dialogue on problems of European security has for some time now been stimulating valuable initiatives on the part of many European states, such as the activities developed by Finland, and proposals advanced by Austria, Belgium, and the Balkan States. In addition, mention should also be made of the fact that Polish disarmament initiatives have been accompanied by a number of other similar actions, like the Swedish Unden plan and the Belgian Harmel plan. Nor should one forget the significance of the breaking of the Cold War political ice when the state treaty with Austria was signed in 1955.

Thus, whereas the period of tension and deepening divisions into blocs limited the role and effectiveness of initiatives put forward by medium-sized and small countries, the time of emerging détente and dialogue creates favourab!? conditions for action by these states.

Similarly, it would be impossible to build a lasting system of security in Europe were it not for the present elements of the American-Soviet agreement and the parallel French-Soviet rapprochement, because the position of those big powers in Europe is part and parcel of the realities of which one should not lose sight. Yet, they are by no means contradictory with the active role of the small and medium-size states in Europe.

It is the concept of the European Conference on Security and Cooperation to ensure a realistic, efficient and lasting system of peaceful coexistence among European states. Such a conference will provide a platform for action on an equal footing by all states of the region, irrespective of their political system, whether they be small, medium, or large. The conference is expected to outline a system of obligations to ensure full security and favourable conditions of cooperation for all.

One of Europe's recent achievements is the universal recognition that all of its state frontiers are final and inviolable. The Federal Republic of Germany assumed an obligation to this end in relation to Poland's western frontier on the Oder and Neisse. Likewise, the state frontier between the Federal Republic of Germany and the German Democratic Republic has been officially recognized in the treaty initialled recently by the governments of the two German states. The three successive treaties concluded by the Federal Republic of Germany with the Soviet Union, Poland and the GDR constitute an extremely important bond, strengthening peaceful order and ensuring good-neighbour relations in a region for many years affected by grave tensions. In addition, the results of recent elections in the FRD testify to the fact that political forces which used to preach revisionist slogans and stir the yet unextinguished feelings of chauvinism have lost an audience among the majority of the West German population. This is a fact of great significance for Europe although it would be too optimistic to forget that the influence of revisionist forces continues to be very substantial in the Federal Republic and that the efforts to overcome a nationalistic political mentality must be continued.

As a result of the last world war and of post-war developments, two separate and different states were established on what had been German territory. This fact has not only influenced the new European situation, but it has also been instrumental in consolidating trends toward peace in Germany. Today each of the two German states has its own ties with its allies and each of the two German communities has evolved within the framework of its own political system. Under such circumstances one should not be prophetic about the future development of relations between the two German states which are so vastly different. Chancellor Brandt was right when he said recently that "we must leave such a broad development to historical process." It would seem that the durability of the socialist German state has already become an inseparable element of this process. It is also an established fact that European security will always be an inseparable element of the historical process. The rights acquired by the four powers *vis-à-vis* Germany as a result of the post-war settlement are one of the guarantees of the durability of European security. All signs seem to indicate that now, contrary to the situation following World War I, a legal and political structure has been established which will eliminate the threat of any new armed conflict on German territory. It may also be added here that as reflected by the feelings prevailing at the last session of the General Assembly all political conditions are now ripe for the admission of the two German states to the United Nations.

Another extremely important factor of the present European situation is that socialist countries have, in all respects, become attractive economic partners for capitalist countries. New possibilities of broad and mutually advantageous contacts between them have been opened. Given the proper development of mutual relations, the two different, yet very active and lastingly integrated groupings may help to bring about an equitable division of labour and ensure advantages to all sides.

We think, however, that the incipient trends within the Common

Market toward setting up a closed and discriminatory organism pose a danger both to relations in Europe and in the world as a whole. For in the long run it is hardly conceivable to pursue a policy of détente and cooperation, while at the same time to set up economic organizations which provoke tension and jeopardize such cooperation. This is why we consider it so indispensable that problems of economic, scientific and technological cooperation be discussed at a European conference attended by members of the Common Market and the Council for Economic Mutual Assistance, as well as by nations which are not members of these economic groupings, such as the United States and Canada.

Last but not least, détente in Europe and the future of peaceful relations in this part of the world require that conditions be achieved which will permit agreement for the reduction of armaments and armed forces now concentrated in this comparatively small part of the world. Such agreements should be the logical consequence of progressing détente, of better mutual understanding, and of the new forms of collective security now being established.

Armed peace is not the correct formula for international relations and there is no justification for it in Europe. Poland, on numerous occasions in the past, has advanced initiatives on these matters. The unquestionable successes reached as a result of SALT negotiations, and prospects that the nuclear non-proliferation treaty may soon be ratified by states affiliated with the Euratom, provide a good atmosphere in which to seek regional disarmament solutions, most especially in the centre of Europe, the key area of the continent.

* * *

There now exist realistic conditions in Europe to transform that continent, once the seedbed of wars, into an area of lasting peace. The fact that we have succeeded in overcoming many difficult problems gives rise to our justified satisfaction. Politics, however, knows no stagnation. Should we fail to continue the work already started, the retrograde forces — still existing in Europe — will again provoke tensions and conflicts. Such forces may threaten not only European order, but also seriously affect the constructive development of relations between the United States and the Soviet Union; and practice has already shown that the political situation within Europe seriously affects Soviet-American relations.

Favourable development of relations on the European continent will also promote the further growth of détente all over the world and will constitute important support for the activity of the United Nations. The achievements reached in Europe pave the way for bringing into universal practice the principle of the non-use of force in international relations — as set forth in the United Nations Charter — and for commencing efforts to hasten international disarmament and to strengthen security in other regions of the world.

APPENDIX

The Workers Speak

Statements of the workers from the Adolf Warski Shipyard in Szczenin, made during the meeting with Gierek on 24 January 1971:*

Delegate K-4

Work in our division is harmful to one's health. At present every second worker who works on the slips is blind, deaf, rheumatic or suffers from some form of lung disease, and all for so little money. . . . An assistant makes 1,800-2,000 złotys [a month]. Let's look at his expenditures for a family of five: For breakfast each has a roll with water — cost, 2 złotys; for supper the same, a total of of 4 złotys. The least expensive lunch is 12 złotys per person, i.e., 60 złotys — a total of 64 złotys a day. In a month this amounts to 1,800-1,900 złotys — for mere subsistence. . . . And in the shipyard work is hard — a man must eat well. Otherwise, after fifteen years he is ready for the coffin. That's the way it is.

Delegate W-6

In our division the average wage is 2,000 złotys. . . . This is really very little. Very little! After paying rent, electricity, gas, etc., a worker is left with 1,600 złotys. No family can survive on it. So, to make more money we work overtime. . . . I know many people who regularly do 150 or even 200 hours overtime a month. This means that they are virtually visitors in their own homes.

Delegate ZWG

. . . there have emerged men who live off the efforts of manual workers, but who sit behind their desks and decide our wages. Is this democracy? (Pounding his fist on the table) No! (Applause).

A member of the strike committee

If we emphasize the change and we talk openly, I would like to know what the income is of a director. I do not know whether this is just

---

* Ewa Wacowska, ed., *Rewolta szczecińska i jej znaczenie* (Paryż: Instytut Literacki, 1971).

gossip or a lie, but I have heard that Director Skrobot makes 18,000 złotys a month. If so, this has to be changed, for some live in luxury and others have barely enough for bread. . . .

Delegate SCW1

Here we had a Comrade Skrzydłowski. During eleven months, it is said that he was paid over 170,000 złotys. Not as basic salary, of course, but from all sorts of bonuses.

But all the evil is not at the bottom! Our manager is like an estate overseer in the inter-war period. . . . People frequently blame the Party and the system for all of this. . . .

Delegate W-4

The average income in our division is 2,600 złotys for eight hours a day. . . . 2,600 or even 3,000 złotys at the current prices, amounts to very little, especially if one has three or four persons to support. . . . This should be taken into account by those comrades from the Central Committee who are here today. It is necessary to understand the position of the people who earn so little — for what can they do? We have a saying: "When a Pole is hungry he is angry"; hence the present upheaval. (Strong applause). It stems directly from our dissatisfaction. (Applause).

Delegate K-2

Many young people were killed — they were shot in the back. There is evidence of that. So many people were killed, so many people. . . .

People who were killed were put in nylon bags and buried like animals. This is true! Nothing can change this. . . .

Delegate K-1

We are not going to count bodies, for it is difficult to count exactly how many fell on the streets. We were given the figure of seventeen for Szczecin. . . . Well, I am not going to contradict this, but I know there were more — for sure! For where bullets fly, people die. But it is sad that our hard-earned money paid for these very bullets which were used against us. . . . How is it possible for the working class to turn against the working class?

Delegate W-2

I ask for a frank answer from the First Secretary of the Central Committee of the PUWP. Is it necessary to shed blood to change the Central

Committee and the government? Is it not possible to consider a fixed term of office in order to avoid a repetition of 1956 and 1970?

Delegate MAMOR

. . . we demand that the guilty ones — both those who actually did the shooting and those who gave the orders to shoot the workers — be punished. (Applause). Regardless of who they are or what positions they occupy. . . .

Delegate K-3

We must give Comrade Gierek a chance. . . . We must have confidence in him, as we had confidence in Gomułka. Except that the latter failed us. . . .

Delegate W-4

The situation in our division is that everybody wants to continue the strike. Comrade Gierek, Comrade Jaroszewicz, your arguments did not convince the people from our division. Yet, after long and stormy discussion, we came to the conclusion that alone we cannot continue to strike. We are ending the strike not because we think we should, but because all the others are doing it. That's all.

Delegate MKP

We have to give the government a chance for a year or two. . . . We must do it! If in a year or two there is no improvement then we will say: Comrades, we were deceived.

Chairman of the Strike Committee

The strike is over, the strike is over! As of tomorrow the shipyard is back at work.

Unidentified Voice

Sorry, I would like to say something about those who will not report for work tomorrow. I would like to ask everybody to pay a tribute to their memory by observing a minute of silence. . . . (37 seconds of silence).

The Party Leaders Speak

Statements made by the members of the Central Committee of the Polish United Workers' Party at a special session held on 6-7 February 1971:*

Wincenty Kraśko (Head, Cultural Division, Central Committee)

The tragedy of the December days is behind us, but the drama is not yet over. It goes on in the form of intense discussions in each factory, each village, in each Polish family. These are discussions full of pain and bitterness not only because of the confidence that was abused but, above all, because of the missed opportunities for quicker development of our country, of the losses which could have been avoided and of the moral damage which Poland has suffered.

The [December] events signalled that our country is threatened with a serious disease. The brain of the Party suffered from serious disorders. . . . There was a sharp contradiction between the intellectual and educational achievements of the people, and the anachronistic (not to use a stronger expression) working style of the leaders. . . . Their work was characterized by subjectivity, dilettantism, lack of systematic information, and insufficient preparation before making decisions.

Andrzej Werblan (Head, Division of Science and Education, Central Committee)

We were faced with the situation in the Party where the top political leaders remained too long — until their intellectual potentialities were totally exhausted; they were unable to deal with new problems, and were more and more inclined to make irrational decisions.

Jerzy Łukasiewicz (Secretary, Warsaw City Committee)

The leaders did not want to talk to the Party activists or to listen to their critical observations and suggestions. . . . The members of the inner leadership lived in their own imaginary world and their reac-

---

* "VIII Plenum KC PZPR (6-7 luty 1971 R.)," *Nowe Drogi*, Special Issue (May 1971).

tion to the views and opinions reflecting the reality was simplistic: if there were signs of dissatisfaction anywhere this was entirely due to the weak, ineffectual work of the local Party organization.

Jan Ossowski (Member of the Central Planning Commission)
The comrades from the former leadership cut themselves off from reality. They denied it. They did not understand the daily affairs of the working man. They did not know about his living conditions, the difficulties in getting to work, the lines at the shops, the shortages of goods, etc.

Henryk Szafrański (Secretary, Warsaw Provincial Committee)
For a long time one could sense that there was something terribly wrong with the Party. . . . Doubts were repressed by using the authority of the Politbureau and especially that of Comrade Gomułka. . . . We got entangled in the mechanism of power which we ourselves had created. Authority became transformed into autocracy.

Józef Kępma (First Secretary, Warsaw City Committee)
Comrade Gomułka did not respect the principle of collectivity and made his decisions in an autocratic fashion. Comrade Gomułka's characteristics: his intolerance of opinions different from his own, his suspiciousness toward many people . . . to a very large extent were responsible for the negative phenomena in the Party.

Józef Cyrankiewicz (Politbureau Member: Chairman of the State Council; former Premier)
In the leadership of the Party . . . there was almost a complete decline of the principle of collectivity. . . . It was not possible to present one's views . . . at the meetings of the Politbureau for it only aroused the egotistic sensitivity of Comrade Gomułka, and assailed his sense of authority. . . . It produced brawls and intensified personal rivalries. The only thing there that could be done was to mitigate harmful decisions in private talks. . . . In the last few years, however, even this was hardly possible. . . . By then Gomułka was losing his temper almost daily.

Mieczysław Moczar (Politbureau Member; Secretary, Central Committee)
Comrade Wiesław [Gomułka] . . . was an autocrat. He could not stand independent people around him. This he would not tolerate. . . . In such a situation, as usual, some "helpful" people emerged and they

did "help" Wiesław. . . . They confirmed him in his conviction that everything he did was wonderful.

As a result Wiesław simply shut himself up in his office and avoided contact with the people. He became less and less accessible and, in turn, people avoided him in order not to be exposed to his rude behaviour. And his closest collaborators presented him with all sorts of statistics and tables, arguing that these were the truths which only his enemies could contradict.

Piotr Jaroszewicz (Premier)

It is generally known and well documented that the former Economic Secretary of the Central Committee, by exploiting the authority of the First Secretary and by referring to the opinions and decisions which had been influenced by himself, interfered in all the activities of the government. . . . In the last few years the interference with the administration became monstrous and intensely harmful.

Antoni Radliński (Vice-Chairman, Supreme Chamber of the State Control)

In the industry we were well aware that Comrade Wiesław and the Politbureau were cut off by the Economic Secretary from receiving information from below, and that Comrade Jaszczuk was the sole source of communication, the only liaison between the Party leaders and the workers.

Wiesław Bek (Head, Press Division, Central Committee)

Any critical remarks in the newspapers, even the most innocuous, if they contradicted the views of the people who had been responsible for the economic decisions, immediately aroused their nervousness. This was illustrated by the government decision made in mid-October 1970, to stop supplying [the press] with essential information. This, in effect, reduced the task of the journalists to the mere reiteration of the ideas . . . of the former leaders.

Władysław Kruczek (Politbureau Member; Chairman, Central Council of the Trade Unions)

With the complete abandonment of the principles of socialist democracy within the Party and the state, the trade unions played little part in the decisions affecting vital problems of the working people. . . . In the trade unions a style and atmosphere of work developed which . . . were divorced from everyday human problems, from the needs of the workers.

Bolesław Rumiński (Member, State Council)

The divorce between the leadership and the masses was frightening. It was evident not only in the Party and in the trade unions, but also in other social organizations.

Kazimierz Rusinek (Vice Minister of Culture)

We witnessed the spread of conceit and irresponsibility. . . . People who dared to critically appraise the existing situation were removed from positions of influence.

Władysław Kozdra (First Secretary, Lublin Provincial Committee)

Among the many problems . . . which the political crisis revealed to the Party and the nation, one is foremost in our minds: how to avoid tragic upheavals in the future? How to achieve an effective way to formulate and implement the best methods of development; how to create the conditions in which the Party and the society, in a natural, simple and obvious way, without pain, riots and upheavals, can select new leaders; how to ensure that the rights of the ruling class, the working class, are secure; and how to make certain that the constitutional rights of all citizens of People's Poland are observed? What sort of checks are needed to prevent the inherent tendencies of some individuals restricting the process of collective decision-making and abusing democracy both within and without the Party?

Selected and translated by Adam Bromke

ABOUT THE CONTRIBUTORS

BROMKE, Adam   Professor of Political Science, Carleton University, Ottawa

CHRYPIŃSKI, VINCENT V.   Professor of Political Science, University of Windsor

DEMBIŃSKI, LUDWIK   Associate Professor of History, Catholic University of Lublin; former Secretary General, "Pax Romana"

FALLENBUCHL, ZBIGNIEW M.   Professor of Economics, University of Windsor

HEYDENKORN, BENEDYKT   Editor-in-Chief, *Związkowiec*, Toronto

LIPSKI, WITOLD   Editor-in-Chief, *Wieś współczesna,"* *Sejm* Deputy, Warsaw

LOTARSKI, SUSANNE S.   Junior Fellow, Institute of Communist Studies, Columbia University, New York

MATEJKO, ALEXANDER   Associate Professor of Sociology, University of Alberta, Edmonton

MICEWSKI, ANDRZEJ   Publicist and historian, Warsaw

MOND, GEORGES H.   Lecturer at the University of Paris; Member of the National Centre of Scientific Research in Paris

PEŁCZYNSKI, ZBIGNIEW A.   Fellow, Pembroke College, Oxford University

RAKOWSKI, MIECZYSŁAW F.   Editor-in-Chief, *Polityka, Sejm* Deputy, Warsaw

STAROŃ, STANISŁAW   Professor of Political Science, University of Vermont, Burlington

STRONG, JOHN W.   Associate Professor of History, Carleton University, Ottawa

SZCZEPAŃSKI, JAN   Vice-President, Polish Academy of Sciences; Chairman of the committee of experts on the reform of the education system in Poland; *Sejm* Deputy, Warsaw

TREPCZYŃSKI, STANISŁAW   Deputy Minister, Polish Ministry of Foreign Affairs; former President of the Twenty-Seventh Session of the General Assembly of the United Nations Organization, Warsaw

TRZECIAKOWSKI, WITOLD   Director of Research, Polish Ministry of Foreign Trade, Warsaw

TUROWICZ, JERZY   Editor-in-Chief, *Tygodnik Powszechny,* Cracow

THE CARLETON SERIES IN SOVIET
AND EAST EUROPEAN STUDIES

East-West Trade, Ed. Philip E. Uren. Intro. Hon. Mitchell W. Sharp. Toronto: The Canadian Institute of International Affairs, 1966.

The Communist States and the West, Ed. Adam Bromke and Philip E. Uren. New York: Frederick A. Praeger, Publishers, 1967; London: Pall Mall Press, 1967.

The Soviet Union under Brezhnev and Kosygin: The Transition Years, 1965-1968, Ed. John W. Strong. New York: Van Nostrand Reinhold, 1971.

The Communist States in Disarray, 1965-1971, Ed. Adam Bromke and Teresa Rakowska-Harmstone. Mineapolis: University of Minnesota Press, 1972; London: Oxford University Press, 1972.

Religion and Atheism in the USSR and Eastern Europe, Ed. Bohdan R. Bociurkiw and John W. Strong. London: Macmillan & Co.; Toronto: University of Toronto Press, Fall, 1973.

RELATED TITLES
Published by Praeger Special Studies

OPINION-MAKING ELITES IN YUGOSLAVIA
                              Barton/Denitch/Kadushin

THE SOVIET ECONOMY IN REGIONAL PERSPEC-
TIVE
                              Bandera/Melnyk

THE PATTERN OF REFORM IN HUNGARY: A
Political, Economic and Cultural Analysis
                              Dimitrijevic/Macesich

EAST GERMAN CIVIL-MILITARY RELATIONS:
The Impact of Technology, 1949-72
                              Herspring

GOVERNING SOVIET CITIES: Bureaucratic Politics
and Urban Development in the USSR
                              Taubman